Etyma graeca : an etymological lexicon of classical Greek

Edward Ross Wharton

ETYMA GRAECA

BY THE SAME AUTHOR

Crown 8vo. 7s. 6d.

ETYMA LATINA

AN ETYMOLOGICAL LEXICON OF CLASSICAL LATIN

PERCIVAL AND CO.

KING STREET, COVENT GARDEN, LONDON

ETYMA GRAECA

AN ETYMOLOGICAL LEXICON OF
CLASSICAL GREEK

BY

EDWARD ROSS WHARTON, M.A.

LECTURER AND LATE FELLOW OF JESUS COLLEGE, OXFORD

PERCIVAL AND CO.
KING STREET, COVENT GARDEN, LONDON

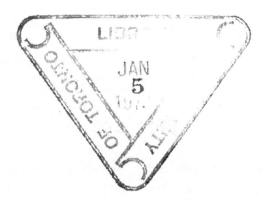

Preface

OF the 41,000 words used by Greek authors down to 300 B.C. about seven-eighths are derivatives or compounds, and their formation is sufficiently explained in Liddell and Scott's Lexicon : the remaining 5000 form the subject of the present work. In Part I. they are arranged alphabetically, in Part II. according to the etymological processes involved in them.

Proper names are here excluded, unless such as disguise their real character, ἀχάτης ἀχερωΐς ἕρμαιον ἰασιώνη καρχήσιον καυνός κιμμερικόν κρησφύγετον πιττάκιον σάρδα τηλέφιον and perhaps βατύλη βρίκελος λιβνός φορμύνιος. The words are mostly given in their older forms : many of the Homeric forms however are probably only due to the metre, not genuine archaisms. Dialectic forms—Laconian ἄικλον ἀποπυδαρίζω δωμός λισσάνιος πλαδδιάω ῥυάχετος σιώκολλος χάιος, Sicilian ἀμφίας βατάνη κύβιτον λίτρα μοῖτος νούμμος ὀγκία, Aeolic ἄμπελος ἀπέρωπος ἄσπαλος βράκος πέπλος σαβακός, from other dialects ἀμάμαξυς ἀρβύλη ἄτερπνος βύσταξ γνάφαλος δεῖνος καπάνη κοσκυλμάτια μνοία μοκλός μύκλος περώτια σατίνη σαυσαρισμός τιθαιβώσσω τραύξανα ὕφεαρ—are marked as such in Part I., and their peculiarities belong properly to the province of Greek Grammar. For convenience' sake the alphabetical order is sometimes slightly broken, and a word will be found a few lines *above* its just place.

The articles on loan-words are put in brackets (and so with loan-words throughout). Of these words 161 are by-forms, 480 root-words; and of 134 of the latter the originals can be given. The Persian equivalents I owe to Mr. Redhouse, the Hebrew and Aramaic to Dr. M. Friedländer: the Coptic is from Peyron.

Of the native-Greek words :—

(1) about 520 are of doubtful or unknown origin, many of them indeed possibly foreign. Of some, ἀνωόμενος κάτωρ πήκασμα χάλανδρος, not even the meaning is known :

(2) about 2180 are derivatives compounds or by-forms of the words mentioned in the next paragraph, and after each of them are given the words with which it is connected. Some forms are due to false readings, θυλάγροικος περιχαμπτά; some to false division of words, αἶα εἴβω ἠβαιός νηγατέος νήδυμος ὀκρυόεις; some to false analogy, ἀγαυρός ἕκαστος–ἑκατόν–ἕτερος ἐνίπτω B. ἐπήβολος ἴτηλος κέαρ μελάγχιμος ὄχα περιώσιος; some to false etymology, ἀμφίσβαινα ἀνδράποδον βοσκάς δύσκηλος κηκίβαλος μεγακήτης μεταχρόνιος νέποδες τανηλεγής ψάκαλα :

(3) the remaining 1580 words have cognates in other Indo-celtic languages. Where possible these are given from Latin, Irish, Gothic, Lithuanian, and Sanskrit; the Armenian and Zend forms being mentioned only when they have any independent value. The following list of languages quoted gives in each case the authority in which the word has been verified. These authorities are accessible at the British Museum :

> Latin (Lewis and Short): Oscan and Sabine (Mommsen): Umbrian (Bréal).
>
> Old Irish (Rhys, Stokes, Windisch): Irish (O'Reilly and O'Donovan, Rhys): Welsh (Pughe, Rhys).

Gothic (Heyne) : Anglosaxon (Leo) : English (Skeat) :
Old Norse (Vigfusson).—Old High German (Graff),
Middle High German (Lexer), New High German
(Weigand).

Prussian (Pierson) : Lithuanian (Nesselmann) : Lettish
(Ulmann).—Bohemian (Rank) : Old Slavonic (Mik-
losich).

Armenian (Bedrossian).

Zend (Justi).

Sanskrit (Böhtlingk and Roth).

After a Gothic form the English is given in preference to
the Anglosaxon if they differ but little ; and so the New
High German in preference to Old or Middle.

The cognate forms are given in italics. As a rule the
Nominative of Nouns is given, the Article being omitted
(the indefinite Article usually denotes that the particular
species of the thing referred to is unknown) ; but in Sanskrit
the stem, when ending in a liquid, *e.g. pitar–* (Nominative *pitā*).
Of Greek and Latin Verbs the Present Indicative is given,
of Zend and Sanskrit Verbs the root, of Verbs in other
languages the Infinitive : the sign *I* to be supplied in the
first case, the sign *to* in the others (*e.g.* "Lat. *sero* sow, Got.
saian"=Latin *sero* I sow, Gothic *saian* to sow). Enclitics
are marked by a dash preceding (or in Greek by the grave
accent, except ἐ), words found only in composition by a dash
following.

Ordinary Latin words are left untranslated ; in the case of
other words (except sometimes where two similar forms con-
cur) the translation, if none is given, is the same as that of
the next-preceding *translated* word ; the sign *I* or *to* in the
case of Verbs to be supplied according to the language denoted.

The abbreviation *Eng.* followed by a comma denotes that the English cognate will be found in the preceding part of the article. For convenience' sake the translation is sometimes given in Latin.

Many exceptions to Grimm's Law will be noticed besides those in onomatopoeic words. Some are due to an *s* preceding or once preceding the mute; some to the dislike to bi-aspirate forms; some to accent originally falling *after* the root-syllable; but most to the existence in the *Ursprache* of roots of the same meaning differing slightly in form, *e.g. mek, meg, megh,* "strong", originally perhaps belonging to different dialects.—Sanskrit sometimes loses *r* or *l* before a Dental, which then becomes Cerebral; see under βραδύς κύρτη μεῖραξ νάρθηξ πόρνη κυλίνδω πλατύς **B**.

Some of the derivations given are original; the rest are from Fick, Johannes Schmidt, Curtius, Hehn, and the writers in Kuhn's *Zeitschrift* and Bezzenberger's *Beiträge*. For several notes on Celtic words I am indebted to Professor Rhys, and on German words to Mr. A. A. Macdonell. Many invaluable suggestions I owe to Professor Sayce.

The punctuation often shows that our information about a word is incomplete: in many cases the root has yet to be discovered. Unscientific derivations and comparisons are as far as possible excluded, but many of those given must be regarded as suggestions rather than as certainties. An asterisk denotes that the form is merely presumed to have existed.

Terminations and inflexional elements belong to another branch of inquiry; but it is often difficult to decide how much of a word is root and how much termination. A simpler root seems sometimes to have been formed out of two or three longer ones by dropping the final consonants; in such cases the sign *cf.* (compare) is here prefixt to the simpler root. The *Ursprache* had probably more vowel-sounds than the Greek alphabet could represent. It distinguished *kv, gv, ghv* (Lithuanian *k, g, g,* Sanskrit *k* or *c, g* or *j, gh*) from *k, g, gh* (Lithuanian *sz, ż, ż,* Slavonic *s, z, z,* Zend *ç, z, z,* Sanskrit *ç, j, h*): Greek properly represents the former by π, β, ϕ, but sometimes instead by κ, γ, χ, which in other cases stand for original *k, g, gh.*

The general principles of Greek etymology are fairly given in Gustav Meyer's *Griechische Grammatik.* The vowels ϵ and o are used to distinguish different forms of the same root; a neighbouring liquid often reduces either to *a*; in the weaker forms of the root the vowel disappears entirely. The vowel *a* often also represents original ϵ or o+a liquid, as in English *wonderful* is pronounced *wondaful.* Initial ρ, unless due to metathesis, has always lost a preceding *s* or *v.* Initial *s* before a vowel represents original *sv* (or sometimes *sj*): original initial *sv* becomes sometimes *s* *e.g.* σέλας, sometimes ϝ *e.g.* ϝέξ (ἔξ), the sibilant in the latter case having been perhaps originally *sh.* The original full-consonant *j* (as in French *jeu*) is represented in Greek by initial ζ, the original semi-vowel *y* (as in English *yew*) by the rough breathing.—The *regium praeceptum Scaligeri* seems not to apply to some early Verbs: ἀδαχέω ἀτέμβω contain the copulative ἀ- (=*σεμ-), as ὀκέλλω the copulative ὀ- (=Sanskrit *sa-*), and ἀμπλακεῖν ἀτίζω the negative ἀ- (=*ἐν-). In many words it is difficult to distinguish such elements from prosthetic vowels.

The references after each article are to the sections of Part II. The absence of a reference on any particular point denotes either that it is too simple to need remark, or that it is too obscure to be satisfactorily disposed of.

Appendix **A.** is a list of the 92 onomatopoeic words found in classical Greek. From the nature of the case no derivation can be sought for these, though many may be paralleled in other languages.

In Appendix **B.** the 641 loan-words in classical Greek are arranged as far as possible according to the languages from which they were taken. Most of them are Substantives, and denote material objects.

I hope shortly to bring out an *Etyma Latina* on a similar plan.

E. R. WHARTON.

OXFORD, *August* 1882.

ABBREVIATIONS

al.	. .	aliter.
copul.	. .	copulative.
neg.	. .	negative.
praeced.	.	vocabulum praecedens.
prob.	. .	probably.
sq.	. .	vocabulum sequens.

Ags.	. .	Anglosaxon.
E M.	. .	Etymologicum Magnum.
Heb.	. .	Hebrew.
Hesych.	. .	Hesychius.
MHG.	. .	Middle High German.
NHG.	. .	New High German.
O. .	. .	Old, *e.g. OHG.* Old High German, *OIr.* Old Irish, *ONor.* Old Norse.
Sk.	. .	Sanskrit.
Zd.	. .	Zend.

The abbreviations for other languages may be gathered from the list in the Preface.

PRONUNCIATION

In Greek words j = Eng. *y* in *yet*, and so in other European languages:
F = Eng. *w* in *wet*, and so *v* in other languages.

Got. *gg* = Eng. *ng*: *q* = Eng. *qu*.

Ags. and ONor. *đ* = Eng. *th* in *then*.

Lit. and Slav. *ą* and *ę* = a nasalised vowel, *i.e.* followed by a sound like French final *n*. So Sk. *ą*.

Lit. *ė* = *ē* as in German *see*.

    ě (also written *ie*) = a diphthongal *e*.

    ù = Eng. *oa* in *roar* (and so in Lettish).

    y = *ī*.

    w = German *w*, nearly Eng. *w* (and so in Lettish).

    z = Eng. *s* in *rose* (and so in Slav.).

    ž = French *j*, Eng. *s* in *measure* (and so in Slav.).

    cz = Eng. *ch* in *cheat*.

    sz = Eng. *sh*.

Slav. *ě* = *ē*, nearly like Eng. *yea*.

    ĭ and *ŭ* = a scarcely audible *i* and *u*.

    c (26th letter) = Eng. *ts*.

    č (27th letter) = Eng. *ch* in *cheat*.

    š = Eng. *sh*.

    ch = Germ. *ch* in *noch*.

In Irish, Old Norse, Prussian, Lithuanian, Lettish, and Bohemian the long vowel is marked by an acute accent. In Ags. *ae oe* denote the long diphthongs, *ä ö* the short.

Armenian *wou* (also written *oo* or *ū*) = Eng. *oo* in *boot*.

Zend and Sanskrit *c* = Eng. *ch* in *cheat*: *j* = Eng. *j* in *jet*: *ç* = Eng. *sh*.

Sanskrit r=Eng. *ri* in *merrily.* The cerebrals t d n may be pronounced like ordinary t d n. (These letters are in this book printed in Roman type.)

In Hebrew

    ' before a Vowel = Aleph.

    ° = Ayin.

    ' before a Consonant = *Shevā* (ἀνάπτυξις).

CORRIGENDA

ἀπο-σκολύπτω strip off : Lat. *glūbo*.   2. 19.
γλάφω＝γλύφω.   19. 11.
γλύφω carve : *σκλύφω, ἀπο-σκολύπτω.   19.

Contents

PAGE

PART I.—WORDS 17

PART II.—FORMS :

  A. GROWTH :

    I. Vocalic :

      (1) πρόσθεσις 137

      (2) ἀνάπτυξις 138

      (3) Lengthening 139

    II. Consonantal :

      (4) Initial Aspiration 139

      (5) Reduplication 139

      (6) Affrication 140

  B. CHANGE :

    I. Vocalic :

      (7) Interchange of *o* and *e* 141

      (8) Interchange of *o* and *a* 142

      (9) *a* from *e* or *o* before a close vowel . . . 143

      (10) *a* from Sonant Liquid 144

      (11) *a* (*ι*, *υ*) through neighbouring Liquid . . 144

      (12) *ι* or *υ* from radical open vowel . . . 146

      (13) *ι* before double consonant . . . 146

      (14) *υ* (*a*) between two consonants . . . 146

      (15) Assimilation of Vowel 146

      (16) Dissimilation of Vowel 146

      (17) Compensatory Lengthening . . . 147

II. Consonantal :   PAGE
    (18) Rough Breathing from Initial Spirant .   .   .   148
    (19) Assimilation of Consonant   149
    (20) Dissimilation of Consonant   150
    (21) Aspiration through Sibilant or Liquid .   .   151
    (22) Assibilation   151
    (23) Vocalisation of *F*   151
    (24) Metathesis   152
    (25) Labdacism   153
    (26) Dentalism   154
    (27) Labialism   154
    (28) Weakening at end of root .   .   .   155
    (29) Aspiration at end of root .   .   .   155

C. LOSS :

  I. Vocalic :
    (30) Vowel-shortening   155
    (31) Compression of root   156

  II. Consonantal :
    (32) Loss of one of two consonants .   .   .   156
    (33) Loss of initial spirant   157
    (34) Loss of medial spirant   158
    (35) Loss through Dissimilation .   .   .   159

APPENDIX A.—ONOMATOPOEIC WORDS .   .   .   160
APPENDIX B.—LOAN-WORDS   161

ETYMA GRAECA.

PART I.

WORDS.

ἀ- negative : Lat. *in-*, Pruss. *en-*, Sk. *an-*, cf. ἀν-, νη-. 10.

ἀ- copulative, ἁ- : *σεμ-, ἅμα. 33. 10.

ἄ ᾶ Interj. : Lat. OHG. Lit. Sk. *ā*.

ἀάζω breathe out : *ἀϜάδ-jω, MHG. *wazen*, cf. ἄημι. 1.

ἄανθα ear-ring : *ἄϜ-ανθα (cf. ἄκ-ανθα), Hesych. ἄτα ὦτα, οὖς. 34.

ἄαπτος inviolable : *ἀ-japτος, ἰάπτω. 34.

ἀάω mislead : *ἀϜά-jω, αὐάτα. 34. 17.

(ἄβαξ board : Egyptian ?)

ἄβδης whip : ἰάπτω. 33. 19.

ἀ-βέλτερος stupid : 'inferior', βέλτερος.

ἀβληχρός = βληχρός. 1.

(ἄβρα ἅβρα bonne : Heb. *chabrāh* socia.)

ἀβρός delicate : νεβρός. 4. 10.

ἀβροτάζω miss : ἀμαρτάνω. 19. 24.

(ἀβρότονον southernwood : Sk. *mrātanam* cyperus rotundus.)

(ἀβυρτάκη a sauce : Persian.)

ἀγαθίς clue : ἀ- copul., Lat. *nōdus*, Ags. *cnotta* knot Eng., Sk. *gandas*, cf. χανδάνω. 10. 29.

ἀγαθός good : *ἀχϜαθός, Got. *gods* Eng., χατέω, 'desirable'. 1. 32. 20.

ἀγαλλίς iris, ἀγάλλω glorify, ἄγαμαι am surprised at, ἄγαν much : μέγας. So ἀγανός gentle, 'admirable', ἀγαπάω love. 10.

ἀγα-νακτέω am distressed : μέγας + ἐνεγκεῖν (cf. χαλεπῶς φέρω). 10.

ἀγαυρός = γαῦρος, ἀ- on analogy of ἀγανός (ἄγαμαι).

(ἄγγαρος courier, ἄγγελος messenger : Persian, Sk. *angiras* demigod.)

ἄγγος vessel : 'smeared, moulded', Lat. *ungo*, OHG. *anco* butter, Sk. *anj* anoint, ἐγγυθήκη. 11.

ἀγείρω collect, ἀγέλη herd : ἀ- copul., Lat. *grex*, O Ir. *ad-gaur* convenio, Ags. *cirran* turn Eng. *char-woman*, Lit. *gratas* close together, Sk. *jar* approach. 25.

B

ἀγ-έρωχος proud : μέγας + ἐρωή A. (cf. ἤσυχος).   10.

ἀγ-ήνωρ manful : μέγας + ἀνήρ.   10.

ἀγής pure : 'clear', cf. εὐαγής, ἄγος.   33.

ἀγής cursed : ἄγος.   4.

ἀγκάλη ἀγκών arm, ἄγκος glen, ἄγκυρα anchor : Lat. *ancus uncus*, O Ir. *aécath* hook, Ags. *angil* Eng. *to angle,* Sk. *ankas* hook, ὄγκος.   11.

ἀγλαός bright : γλαυ-κός.   1. 34.

ἀ-γλευκής sour : γλυκύς.   31.

ἀγλῖθες garlic : ἀ- copul., γελγίς.   24.

ἄγνος willow :

ἄγνυμι break : Lat. *vagus*, Ir. *fann* weak, Ags. *vancol* vacillating Eng. *wince winch wink lap-wing*, Lit. *winge* curve.   33.

ἄγος pollution : Sk. *āgas* offence.   30.

ἄγος expiation : Sk. *yaj* to sacrifice.   18.

ἀγοστός hand : ἀ- copul., Got. *kas* vessel, Lit. *pa-žastis* armpit, Sk. *jasus* ambush, 'hiding'.

ἄγουρος Od. vii. 64 young : Sk. *agrus* unmarried.   2.

ἄγρα chace : Zd. *azra*, ἄγω.

ἀγρός field : Lit. *ager*, Got. *akrs* Eng. *acre*, Sk. *ajras* : ἄγω, 'place to move in'.

ἀγρ-υπνος sleepless : ἐγείρω + ὕπνος.   1.

ἀγχι near : Lat. *angustus*, O Ir. *occus*, Got. *aggvus* narrow, Lit. *anksztas* : ἄγχω.

(ἄγχουσα ἔγχουσα, alkanet : ὀνοχειλές ὀνοκίχλη, foreign.)

ἄγχω choke : Lat. *ango angor anxius*, O Nor. *angr* sorrow Eng. *anger*, Sk. *ghas* alarm, ἄχος.

ἄγω lead : Lat. *ago*, O Ir. *agaim* I drive, O Nor. *aka* to drive, Sk. *aj*.   30.   Hence ἀγωγός guide.   5.

ἀδαχέω scratch : ἀ- copul., δάκνω.   29.

(ἄδδιξ gallon : Persian ?)

ἀδελφός brother : ἀ- copul., δελφύς.

ἀ-δευκής unseemly : δοκέω.   12. 31.

ἀδέω am sated, ἀδο-λέσχης gossip, ἄδος satiety, ἀδινός thronging : οἰδέω.   30.   So—

     ἀδημονέω am distressed, ἀδήμων (cf. Ags. *säd* 'sated' Eng. *sad*).

     ἀδήν ἀδήν gland : O Slav. *jędra* testicles, Sk. *andam* testicle.   4.

     ἀδρός thick : Sk *sāndras*, ἀ- + οἰδέω.

(ἀδράχνη = ἀνδράχνη.)

ἄεθλος contest : ἀ- copul., Lat. *vas* surety, Got. *vadi* pledge Eng. *wed*, Lit. *wadóti* redeem.   34.

ἀείδω sing : *ἀϜένδω, O Ir. *fáed* cry, OHG. *far-wāzan* refuse, Lit. *wadinti* call, Sk. *vad* speak, αὐδή.   1. 17.

ἀείρω raise : ἀ- copul., Lit. *swerti* weigh, αἰώρα σάλος.   32. 33.

ἄελλα storm, ἀελλής eddying : ἀολλής.   7.

ἀέξω foster : O Ir. *fásaim* I grow, Got. *vahsjan* grow Eng. *to wax*, Sk. *vaksh*, αὔξω ὑγιής. 1.

ἄεσα passed the night : Sk. *sas* slumber. 33. 16. 34.

ἀεσί-φρων silly : ἄημι, 'ventosus'. 30.

ἄζα mould, ἄζω parch :

ἀζηχής excessive : ἀ- copul., Sk. *yahvas* restless.

ἀηδών nightingale : ἀείδω. 17.

ἄημι blow : Got. *vaian*, Lit. *wëjas* wind, Sk. *vā* blow, ἀυτμή. 1. Hence ἀήρ air (cf. αἰθ-ήρ). 17.

ἀήσυλος wicked : ἀάω.

ἀήσυρος light : Sk. *vātulas* windy, ἄημι. 22.

ἄητος = αἴητος. 34.

(ἀθάρη porridge : Egyptian.)

ἀθέλγω strain off : *ἀστλέγγω, στράγξ, cf. στελγίς = στλεγγίς. 1. 32. 24. 25.

ἀ-θερίζω slight : Sk. *dhar* support, θρῆνυς.

ἀθερίνη smelt : sq.?

ἀθήρ spike : ἀνθέριξ. 32.

(ἀθραγένη = ἀνδράχνη.)

ἀθρέω look : ἀ-copul., Lat. *firmus*, Sk. *dhar* hold (cf. Eng. behold). So ἀθρόος ἀθρόος together, 'holding together'.

ἀθύρω play :

αἰ = εἰ. 9.

αἴ Interj. : NHG. *ei*, Lit. Sk. *ai*.

αἶα land : from πατρίδα γαῖαν, quasi πατρίδα γ' αἶαν, cf. εἴβω. (Sayce.)

αἰανής dismal : αἴητος.

αἰγανέη spear, αἴγειρος poplar : 'shaken, shaking', Sk. *inj* move, ἐπείγω. So αἰγιαλός beach, Hesych. αἶγες waves. 9.

(αἰγίθαλλος titmouse, αἴγιθος αἰγίοθος hedgesparrow : foreign.)

αἰγίλιψ steep :

αἰγίλωψ oats : 'white-looking', αἴγις B. *αἴγιλος (cf. αἱμάλωψ θυμάλωψ νυκτάλωψ πηνέλοψ, ἀκαλανθίς ἀμιχθαλόεις βροαλίκτης ὀνοπαλίζω) + ὦπα.

αἰγίς A. shield of Zeus : αἰγανέη 'brandished'.

αἰγίς B. αἰγίας white speck :

αἴγλη brightness : ἀκτίς. 17.

αἰγυπιός vulture : ὄις + γύψ. 9.

(αἰγώλιος αἰτώλιος owl : foreign.)

αἰδώς shame : *αἰσδώς αἰσθάνομαι (cf. ἀλδαίνω ἀλθαίνω, κορδύλη κορθύω, λοίδορος λάσθη, νεοαρδής ῥαθάμιγξ, ὀρόδαμνος ὀρθός, σκινδάριον σκινθός, σκόρδαξ σπυρθίζω, σπιδής σπιθαμή, τένδω τένθης, ψευδής ψύθος), 'observation.' 32.

(αἰέλουρος αἴλουρος cat : Egyptian ?)

αἰεί always : Got. *aiv* ever Eng. *aye* Ags. *aefre* always Eng. *ever*, αἰών.

αἰετός eagle : οἰωνός. 9.

ἀ-ίζηλος hidden : ἰδεῖν. 6.

αἰζηός youth :

αἴητος mighty :

αἰθήρ sky, αἰθόλιξ pustule, αἴθουσα corridor : 'bright, hot, sunny', αἴθω.

αἴθυια gull :

αἰθύσσω shake :

αἴθω kindle : O Ir. *aed* fire, Ags. *ād* Eng. *oast-house*, Sk. *idh* kindle. 9.

αἰκάλλω wheedle : ἀκά. 17.

ἄικλον supper (Spartan) :

(αἴλινος = λίνος.)

(αἴλουρος = αἰέλουρος.)

αἷμα blood, αἱμάλ-ωψ weal (cf. αἰγίλωψ) : Welsh *hufen* cream, NHG. *seim* thick fluid : 18.

αἱμασιά stone wall :

αἱμός thicket :

αἱμύλος wily, αἵμων skilful :

αἶνος story, praise : ἠμί.

αἰνός terrible : αἴητος.

αἴνυμαι take : Lat. *oitor ūtor.* 9.

αἴνω sift : ἠθέω. 18.

αἴξ goat : Welsh *ewig* gazelle, Lit. *ožys* goat, Sk. *ajas* : ἄγω, 'agile'. 17.

αἰόλος nimble :

αἰονάω foment :

αἰπόλος herdsman : δις + κέλλω. 9. 27.

αἰπύς steep : ἰάπτω. 33. 17.

αἶρα darnel : Sk. *ērakā* a grass.

αἱρέω take : Got. *vilvan*, Sk. *var* cover, hold, εἰλέω ἐλεῖν εὐρύς ὀράω. 18. 9.

αἱρό-πινον sieve : αἶρα + πίνω.

αἶσα portion : Osc. *aeteis* of a part, O Nor. *ítr* glorious, οἶτος. 9.

αἰσάλων merlin : foreign ?

αἰσθάνομαι perceive : Lat. *aestimo*, Got. *aistan* observe.

ἀίσθω breathe out : *ἀϜέτ-θω, ἀυτμή. 1. 13. 20.

ἀίσσω rush : *ἀ-jίκ-jω, ἀ- copul., ἰάπτω. 34. 12. 32. 19.

αἰσυητήρ Il. xxiv. 347 :

αἴσυλος wicked : αἰνός.

αἰσυ-μνήτης umpire : αἶσα + μνήμη. 11.

αἶσχος shame : αἰδώς.

αἰτέω beg : αἴνυμαι. Hence αἴτιος originating, 'demanding, giving occasion for'.

ἀίτης beloved : ἀίω B., ἐνηής.

αἰφνίδιος sudden, αἶψα quickly, αἰχμή spear-point : αἰπύς. 21.

ἀίω A. breathe out : ἄημι. 12.

ἀίω B. perceive : Lat. *aveo*, O Ir. *conn-ói* qui servat, O Slav. *u-mŭ* mind, Sk. *av* observe. 34.

αἰών time : Lat. *aevum aetas*, O Ir. *áis*, Got. *aivs*, Sk. *ēvas* course, ἰέναι. 9. 34.

αἰώρα oscillation : ἀείρω. 7.

ἀκᾶ gently, ἀκάκητα gracious : ἦκα. 30. 5.

ἀκαλανθίς goldfinch : ἀκίς *ἄκαλος (cf. αἰγίλωψ), cf. ἄκανθα.

ἀκαλήφη nettle : *ἀσκλήφη, σκαριφισμός. 1. 32. 2. 25.

ἄκανθα thorn, spine : ἀκίς.

ἄκαρι mite : foreign ?

ἄκαρνα ἄκορνα thistle : *ἄσκαρνα, σκάλλω. 1. 32.

ἄκασκα gently : ἀκᾶ.

ἄκατος boat : foreign ?

ἀκαχμένος sharp : ἀκίς, Perf.

ἀκέων ἀκήν silent : ἀκᾶ.

ἀκιδνότερος inferior, ἀκιρός weak : ἀ- neg., κίω.

(ἀκῑνάκης κῑνάκη knife : Persian.)

ἀκίς point, ἀκμή edge : Lat. *acus acuo*, Welsh *awch*, Ags. *ecg* Eng., Lit. *asztrus* sharp, Sk. *aç* reach, ἵππος ὠκύς. 30.

ἄκμηνος fasting : Hesych. ἄκμα νηστεία :

ἄκμων anvil : Lit. *aszmŭ* edge, Sk. *açman-* stone : 'sharp stone', ἀκίς.

ἄκνηστις spine : ἄκανθα.

ἄκολος morsel : Sk. *aç* eat ?

ἀκόνη whetstone : Sk. *açnas* stone, ἄκμων. 2.

ἄκος cure : Welsh *iach* sound. 33.

ἀκοστή barley : Lat. *acus* chaff, Lit. *akótas*.

ἀκούω hear : *ἀσκούω, Welsh *ysgyfarn* ear, θυο-σκόος. 1. 32. 23.

ἀκρ-αίφνης uninjured : ἄκρος + ἰάπτω, 'very lively', cf. αἰφνίδιος.

ἀκρῑβής exact : Got. *and-hruskan* enquire. 1. 11. 17. 27.

ἀκρίς locust : ἄκρος, 'walking on tiptoe', ἀκροβατοῦσα.

ἀκροάομαι listen : ἄκρος *ἄκροϜος (Hesych. ἀκροβᾶσθαι) + οὖς, cf. ἄανθα. 34. 17.

ἄκροπις disabled :

ἄκρος extreme : ἀκμή.

(ἀκταία robe : Persian.)

ἀκταίνω move : ὠκύς.

ἀκτή A. headland : ἀκίς. So ἀκτῆ eldertree, 'with pointed leaves'.

ἀκτή B. corn : ἀκοστή.

ἀκτίς ray : Lat. *ignis*, Ir. *án* fire, Got. *uhtvo* morning, Lit. *ugnis* fire, Sk. *agnis*. 19.

ἄκυλος acorn : Lit. *ilex* (= *eclex), NHG. *eichel* : 2.

ἀκωκή point, ἄκων javelin : ἀκίς. 5.

(ἀλάβαστος ἀλάβαστρος salve-box (made of alabaster) : foreign, ἀλφός.)

ἀλαλαί Interj. : Ags. *lā* lo Eng., Sk. *ararē*, ἐλελεῦ.

ἄλαλκε he warded off : ἀλκή.

ἀλαός blind : ἠλεός. 30.

ἀλαπάζω = λαπάζω. 1.

ἀλάστωρ avenger, accursed : ἄλη *ἀλάζω, 'making or made to wander'.

ἄλγος pain : ἀλεγεινός. 24.

ἀλδαίνω nourish : Lat. *arduus*, ἀλθαίνω (cf. αἰδώς). 25.

ἀλεγεινός grievous, ἀλέγω heed : Lat. *dīligo negligo religio*, Ags. *rēcan* reck of Eng. 2.

ἀλέη warmth : εἴλη. 33. 11.

ἄλεισον cup : Lat. *lino dē-leo*, Got. *leithus* wine, Lit. *lēti* pour, Sk. *ri* let go?

ἀλείφω anoint : *ἀσλέμφω, Got. *salbon* anoint Eng. *salve*, λέμφος. 1. 35. 17.

ἀλέξω ward off : Sk. *raksh* protect, cf. ἀλκή. So ἀλέκτωρ cock, 'guardian'. 1.

ἀλεύομαι avoid : λύω, 'separate from myself'. 1.

ἀλέω grind : μύλη. 10.

ἄλη wandering : ἔρχομαι. 11. 25.

ἀλής crowded : εἰλέω. 18. 11.

ἀλθαίνω heal, ἀλθαία marsh-mallow (used in healing), ἄλθεξις healing (ἕξις) : Lat. *arbos*, O Nor. *örðugr* erect, O Slav. *rasti* grow, Sk. *ardh* thrive, cf. ἄναλτος. 25.

ἀλίβας dead : foreign?

ἀλίγκιος like : ἀ- copul., Got. *ain-lif* eleven Eng., O Slav. *lice* countenance.

ἀλινδέω roll : εἰλύω. 11.

ἄλιος fruitless : ἠλεός. 4.

ἅλις enough : εἰλέω. 18. 11.

ἁλίσκομαι am caught : ἐλεῖν. 18. 11.

ἀλιταίνω offend : *ἀσλιταίνω, Got. *sleitha* harm. 1. 35.

ἀλκή strength : ἀρκέω. 25.

ἀλκύων kingfisher : Lat. *alcēdo*, OHG. *alacra* merganser.

ἀλλά but : Got. *alja*, Bohem. *ale*, ἄλλος.

(ἀλλᾶς = ὀρύα.)

ἀλλο-δαπός foreign : *δογκ-Fός δοκέω. 10. 27.

ἀλλό-κοτος monstrous : κότος 'temper' (cf. ὀργή).

ἅλλομαι leap : Lat. *salio*, Lit. *selěti* creep, Sk. *sar* go. 18. 19.

ἄλλος other : Lat. *alius aliquis*, O Ir. *all*, Got. *aljis* Eng. *else*. 19.

ἀλλο-φάσσω rave : φημί, cf. παιφάσσω.

ἀλοιάω smite : ἀλέω.

ἄλοξ furrow : ἕλκω. 33. 11. 2.

ἄλπνιστος sweetest : Zd. *rap* rejoice. 24. 25.

ἅλς ἡ sea : Ir. *sal*, Sk. *saram* pond *sar* flow, ὁρός. Hence ἅλς ὁ salt :
 Lat. *sal*, Ir. *salann*, Got. *salt* Eng., O Slav. *solĭ*, Sk. *saras* saline.
 18.

ἀλσίνη a plant :

ἄλσος grove : ἄναλτος.

ἅλυσις chain : ἐλεῖν. 18. 11.

ἀλύσκω = ἀλεύομαι. 31.

ἀλύω am distraught : Lat. *ālūcinor*, O Nor. *ölr* drunk, ἄλη.

(ἄλφα A : Heb. *aleph*.)

ἀλφάνω bring in : Lit. *alga* price, Sk. *arghas*. 27.

ἀλφηστής (cf. ὀρχηστής) busy : Lat. *labor*, Got. *arbaiths* work, Lit. *loba*,
 Sk. *rabh* seize, λάβρος. 24.

ἄλφιτον barley (cf. Eng. wheat white), ἀλφός white leprosy : Lat. *albus*,
 Ags. *elfet* swan, O Slav. *lebedĭ*, Sk. *rabhasas* glaring. 24.

ἀλωή ἅλως threshing-floor : ἀλέω. 4.

ἀλώπηξ fox : *ἀϜλώπηξ, Lat. *volpes*, Lit. *lápe*. 1. 35.

ἅμα together : Lat. *simul similis simplex*, Ir. *samail* like, Got. *sama*
 same Eng., O Slav. *samŭ* ipse, Sk. *samam* alike, ὁμός. 18. 11.

ἄμαθος = ψάμαθος. 32. 33.

ἀμαιμάκετος fierce :

(ἄμαλα navem : Egyptian ?)

ἀμαλάπτω see ἡμαλάψαι.

ἀμαλδύνω destroy : Got. *ga-malteins* dissolution Eng. *melt*, O Slav.
 mladŭ soft, Sk. *mard* rub, cf. sq. 1. Hence ἀμάνδαλος unseen,
 *ἀμάλδαλος. 20.

ἀμαλός weak : Ags. *mearo* soft Eng. *mellow*, μύλη. 1.

ἀμ-άμαξυς vine on poles : ἄμα + ἀμάκιον board (Laconian), ἄβαξ (cf.
 ἀρβύλη βάρμιτον βύσταξ κυμερνήτης τιθαιβώσσω). 33.

ἄμαξα ἅμαξα wagon : ἄμα + ἄξων. 33.

(ἀμάρακος marjoram (Eng.) : foreign.)

ἀμάρη trench : O Slav. *jama* pit, ἀμάω.

ἁμαρτάνω miss : ἀ- neg. + μέρος ?

ἀμαρύσσω twinkle : *ἀμρύχ-jω, Ir. *márach* morning, Got. *maurgins*
 Eng. *morrow morning*, Lit. *mirgěti* glitter, cf. μαρμαίρω. 1. 2. 24. 19.

ἀμαυρός dim : μαυρόω. 1.

ἀμάω collect : Lat. *emo*, O Ir. *fo-emat* sumunt, Lit. *imti* take. 11.

ἀμβλίσκω cause miscarriage ; μύλη B. 1. 6. 31.

ἀμβλύς dull : ἀμαλός. 6. 31.

ἄμβων projection : Lat. *umbo*, ὀμφαλός. 11. 19.

ἀμείβω exchange : Lat. *migro*, O Slav. *miglivŭ* mobile. 1. 27.

ἀμείνων better : O Lat. *mānus* good. 1.

ἀμέλγω milk : Lat. *lac* (= *mlact), Ir. *melg* milk, Got. *miluks* Eng.,
 Lit. *milszti* to milk, sq. 1. 25.

ἀμέργω pluck : Lat. *mergae* pitchfork *merges* sheaf, Sk. *marj* rub off, ὁμόργνυμι. 1.

ἀμέρδω deprive, blind : ἀμαλδύνω. 25.

ἀμεύομαι surpass : ἀμύνω. 31.

ἄμη mattock : ἀμάω. So ἄμης ἄμιθα milk-cake, ἀμάομαι collect milk in baskets Od. ix. 247.

ἀμία tunny :

ἀμιθρός = ἀριθμός. 24.

ἄμιλλα contest : Lat. *simultas*, ἅμα.

ἀμίς pot : Lat. *ama*, Sk. *amatram* vessel, ἀμάω.

ἀμιχθαλόεις inaccessible : ἄ-μικτος, μίγνυμι (cf. αἰγίλωψ). 29.

ἄμμες we : Sk. *a-smē*, *νό-σμες, νῶι. 10. 19.

ἄμμος = ἄμαθος.

ἀμνίον bowl : Hesych. νάνιον, Sk. *nimnam* depression *nam* bend. 10.

ἀμνός lamb : *ἀβνός = *ἀγϜνός, Lat. *agnus*, Ir. *uan*, O Slav. *jagnę* : 19. 27.

ἀμόθεν ἀμόθεν from some source : Got. *sums* some one Eng., ἅμα. 33.

ἀμολγῷ darkness, ἀμοργή oil-lees ; Ags. *meorc* murky Eng. 1. 25.

ἀμορβέω follow : ἀ- copul., Sk. *mrgas* beast of chace, μολοβρός. 27.

ἀμοργίς flax : ἀμέργω.

ἀμός our : ἄμμες. 17.

ἄμοτον confusedly : ἀ- copul., μάτη.

ἀμουργός sheltered : *ἄμος wind μεταμώνιος + εἴργω.

ἄμπελος vine : ἀμφί Aeol. ἀμπί + ἑλίσσω, 'clasping' the elm. 33.

ἀμπλακεῖν miss : ἤμβλακον.

ἄμπυξ head-band : ἄντυξ. 27.

(ἀμυγδάλη almond (Eng.) : Phrygian.)

ἄμυδις = ἅμα. 33.

ἀμυδρός obscure : Got. *bismeitan* anoint Eng. *smut smudge*, O Slav. *modrŭ* black, Sk. *mid* become fat. 1. 35.

ἀμύμων noble : ἀ- neg., μῶμος.

ἀμύνω ward off : μύνη. 1.

ἀμύσσω tear : μάχη. 1. 11.

ἀ-μυχνός undefiled : μύσος. 32.

ἀμφί about : Lat. *ambi-*, O Ir. *imb-*, Ags. *ymbe*, Sk. *abhi* : cf. Got. *bi* by Eng.

ἀμφίας ἄμφης a wine (Sicilian) :

ἀμφί-γυος double-pointed : γυῖον. 34.

ἀμφί-δυμος double : δί-δυμος.

ἀμφι-λαφής abundant ; λαμβάνω. 32.

ἀμφι-λύκη twilight : λυκάβας.

ἀμφίσ-βαινα a snake : βαίνω, popular etymology, Hesych. ἀμφίσμαινα E M. ἀμφίσθμαινα from ἰσθμός, 'double-necked '. 32.

ἀμφι-σβητέω doubt : 'fasten on both sides ', σάγη. 31. 27.

ἄμφω both : Lat. *ambo*, Lit. *abbu*, Sk. *ubhau*, ἀμφί : cf. Got. *bai bajoths* Eng.

(ἄμωμον a spice-plant : Semitic, cf. κιννάμωμον.)

ἄν in that case : Lat. *an*, Got. *an* num : ἀνά, 'up there'. So ἀν- negative : Osc. Ir. *an-*, Got. Eng. *un-*, 'away there'.

ἀνά up : Ir. *an-* intensive, Got. *ana* on Eng., Lit. *nů* from, Zd. *ana* up, ἐνί. 15.

ἀνα-βλύω boil over : Hesych. ἀναβλύες πηγαί, βάλλω. 24.

ἀνα-γαργαρίζω gargle : γαργαρεών.

ἀνάγκη constraint : Lat. *necesse*, O Ir. *écen* need, Got. *ga-nohs* enough Eng., ἐνεγκεῖν. 1. 11.

(ἀνάγυρος a plant : ὀνόγυρος, foreign.)

ἀναίνομαι refuse : ἀνά + ἀπ-ηνής, 'turn the face away '.

ἀνα-κογχύζω keep still : κωχεύω, 'hold in '.

ἀνακῶς carefully : ἄναξ (cf. γλάγος νύχιος ἔνεροι) ?

ἀν-ᾱλόω spend : ἀνά + ὄλλυμι. 11.

ἀν-αλτος insatiate : Lat. *alo adolesco*, O Ir. *alim* I nurse, Got. *alan* grow *altheis* old Eng., ἔρνος. 11.

(ἄναξ lord : Lat. *Venus venia vindex*, Sk. *van* love, desire, acquire, ἐριούνιος, Phrygian.)

(ἀνα-ξυρίδες trowsers : Persian *chāh-chŭr*.)

(ἀνᾱρίτης = νηρείτης.)

ἀνα-ρρύω draw back : ἐρύω. 19.

ἀνα-σταλύζω weep : σταλάσσω.

ἀνδάνω please : Lat. *suādeo*, Sk. *svad* relish, ἡδύς.

ἀνδράποδον slave : *ἀνδρ-όπαδον ὀπᾱδός, as if from ἀποδόσθαι.

(ἀνδράφαξις ἀτράφαξις orach : foreign.)

(ἀνδράχνη purslane, arbute : foreign, ἀδράχνη ἀθραγένη.)

ἄνεμος wind : Lat. *anima animus*, Ir. *anim* breath, Got. *us-anan* expire OHG. *unst* storm, O Slav. *achati* to smell, Sk. *an* breathe, ἀπηνής. 30.

ἄνευ without : *ἄσνευ, Lat. *sine*, ἄτερ. 1. 35.

ἀνεψιός cousin : ἀ- copul., νέποδες. 22.

ἄνεω silent : ἐνεός. 11.

(ἄνηθον ἄνητον ἄνῑσον dill : ' strong-smelling ', Lat. *alum allium*, ἄνεμος.)

ἀν-ήνοθε rose up : ἀνά + ἄνθος, cf. κεάνωθος. 2

ἀνήρ man : Sabine *nero* brave, O Ir. *nert* strength, Lit. *nóras* will, Sk. *naras* man. 1.

ἀνθέριξ ear of corn, stalk : Lit. *adata* needle, Sk. *atharis* spear-point. So ἀνθερεών chin, 'pointed'.

ἄνθος τό blossom : Sk. *andhas* herb. Hence ἄνθος ὁ wagtail, 'like a flower' ?

ἄνθραξ charcoal : νάθραξ νάρθηξ tinder-plant. 24.

(ἀνθρήνη hornet : τενθρηδών, cf. ἤγανον ἴφυον.)

(ἄνθρυσκον ἔνθρυσκον a plant : foreign.)

ἄνθρωπος human being : Bohem. *mudrák* wise : Hesych. μενθήρη thought, Welsh *medr* skill, Got. *mundrei* aim NHG. *munter* lively, Lit. *mandrus*, μανθάνω. 10.

ἀνία grief : Aeol. ὀνία, Lat. *onus*. 11.

(ἀνιακκάς a tune : foreign.)

(ἀνόπαια Od. i. 320 sea-eagle : foreign, al. πανόπαια.)

(ἀντακαῖος sturgeon : Lat. *acipenser*.)

ἀντί opposite, ἄντα before, ἄντομαι meet : Lat. *ante*, O Ir. *étan* forehead, Got. *and* towards Ags. *and-svare* answer Eng., Lit. *ant* on, Sk. *anti* opposite.

ἀντῖ-κρύ opposite, ἄντι-κρυς straight on : κυρέω. 24.

ἄντλος hold of a ship : O Lat. *anclo* draw wine, Sk. *up-anc* draw water. 26.

ἄντρον cave : ἄνεμος (cf. σπέος).

ἄντυξ rim : ἀγκών. 26.

ἀνύω accomplish : Sk. *san* win, ἔναρα. 33. 11.

ἄνωγα command :

ἀνωόμενος Hom. Hymn. Apoll. 209 :

ἀξίνη axe : Lat. *ascia*, Got. *aqizi* Ags. *eax* Eng., ὀξύς. 8.

ἄξιος worth : ἄγω weigh.

ἄξων axle : Lat. *axis*, Welsh *echel*, Ags. *eax* Eng., Lit. *aszis*, Sk. *akshas*, *aksh* reach, ὀξύς. 8.

ἄοζος servant : ἀ- copul., ὁδός (cf. Lat. *com-es*). 19.

ἀολλής collected : ἀ- copul., εἰλέω. 7.

ἄορ sword : ἀείρω αἰώρα, 'swung'. 7.

ἀοσσητήρ helper : ἀοσσέω help, *ἀ-σοκϜ-jέω, ἀ- copul. + ἕπομαι. 34. 32. 19.

ἀπάδις wits :

ἀπαλός soft :

ἅπαξ once : ἀ-, πήγνυμι.

(ἀπάπη dandelion : foreign, al. ἀφάκη.)

ἀπατούρια a feast : ἀ- copul., *πάτωρ πατήρ, 'assembly of fathers'.

ἀπ-αυράω take away : εὑρίσκω. 33. 9.

ἀπαφίσκω cheat : ἅπτομαι. 35. 5. 20.

ἀπ-ειλή promise, threat :

ἀπέλλητος antagonist :

ἀπ-εράω pour off : *ἐράσω, Lat. *rōs* dew, Lit. *rasa*, Sk. *rasas* sap, ἄρσην. 1. 34.

ἀπέρωπος shameless : ἀ- neg- + περί (Aeol. περ-) + ὦπα, 'not circumspect'.

ἀ-πέσκης uncovered : πέσκος skin, σκέπας, = ἀσκεπής. 24.

ἀπ-ηλεγέως outright : ἀλέγω, 'without care'. 3.

(ἀπήνη = λαμπήνη.)

ἀπ-ηνής harsh : Sk. *ānanam* mouth, face (cf. Lat. *ōs*), ἄνεμος.

ἄπιον pear : sq., 'foreign.'

ἄπιος beyond sea : Lit. *uppë* river, Sk. *ap* water, ὀπός. 10.

ἀ-πλετος immense : πλεῖος, 'not to be filled'.

ἀπλόος simple : ἀ-, πλεῖος, cf. διπλόος. 7.

ἀπό from : Lat. *ab*, Got. *af* from Eng. *of off*, *aftra* back Eng. *after*, Sk. *apa* from, ἐπί.

ἀπο-διδράσκω escape : δραπέτης.

ἀπό-ερσε it swept away : ἐρύω.

ἀπό-θεστος despised : θέσσασθαι (cf. Lat. abominatus).

ἄποινα ransom : ἀ- copul., ποινή.

ἀπο-καπύω breathe forth : Lit. *kwápas* breath, καπνός. 32.

ἀπο-κίκω remove : κίω. 5.

ἀπο-λαύω enjoy : Lat. *Laverna lucrum*, Got. *laun* reward, O Slav. *loviti* seize, λεία. 23.

ἀπο-μύττω blow the nose : Lat. *mūcus ē-mungo*, Ir. *muc* pig, Lit. *maukti* to strip, Sk. *muc* let free, σμύξων. 32.

ἀπο-πῡδαρίζω dance : πυγή (Laconian, cf. γέφυρα).

ἀπο-πῡτίζω spit out : *σπῡτίζω πτύω. 32.

ἄπος Eur. Phoen. 851 weariness :

ἀπο-σκολύπτω strip off : σκορπίζω. 25. 2.

ἀπο-σμιλαίνω open : σμίλη, 'am cut open'.

ἀπο-στυπάζω beat off : Lat. *stuprum*, OHG. *stumbalon* mutilate NHG. *stummel* stump, Sk. *pra-stumpati* trudit.

ἀπο-υράς taking away : ἀπαυράω. 31. 23.

ἀπο-φώλιος vain : φηλόω. 8.

ἀππαπαῖ = παπαί.

ἀπρίξ tightly : ἀ- copul., πρίω grind the teeth.

ἀπτο-επής throwing words about : ἐάφθη + ἔπος. 18.

ἅπτω fasten : *ἄφ-τω : 19.

ἀπφάριον darling : onomatopoeic, Sk. *ambā* mother.

ἄρα therefore, ἆρα num (= ἦ ἄρα, Lit. *ar*):

ἄραβος gnashing : Sk. *rambh* roar. 1. 10. 28.

ἄραδος rumbling : Hesych. ἀράδει θορυβήσει, O Nor. *erta* to taunt.

ἀραιός thin : Lat. *rārus*, Lit. *irti* to separate *rétas* thin, Sk. *rta* without, ἀρόω. 1. 24.

(ἄρακος vetch : Sk. *arakas* a plant.)

ἀραρίσκω join : Lat. *armus artus* Subst. Adj., Got. *arms* arm Eng., Lit. *arti* near, Sk. *ar* fasten. 5.

ἀράσσω strike : ῥάσσω. 1.

ἀράχιδνα = ἄρακος.)

ἀράχνη ἄραχνος spider (Lat. *arānea*): ἄρκυς. 2. 21.

ἀρβύλη boot : Hesych. ἄρμυλα boots (Cyprian), ἁρμός (cf. ἁμάμαξυς).

ἀργαλέος painful : Ags. *veorcsum* irksome Eng., εἴργω.   11.

ἀργέλοφοι feet of a sheepskin :

ἀργῆς snake : ἀργός, 'swift'.

(ἄργῖλα cave : Italian, ῥόγος.)

ἀργιλιπής white : ἀργός + ?

ἄργιλλος potter's earth (Lat. *argilla*), ἀργός bright : Lat. *arguo*, Welsh
 eira snow, Lit. *regěti* see, Sk. *arjunas* light-coloured.   So
   ἄργυρος silver : Lat. *argentum*, O Ir. *argat*, Sk. *rajatam*.
   ἀργύφεος white : φάος.

ἄρδα dirt : 'sprinkling', ἄρδω.

ἄρδις point : Lat. *rādo*, Ir. *altan* razor, Sk. *rad* scratch.   24.

ἄρδω water : Sk. *ārdras* wet, *ard* be scattered.

ἀρείων better, ἀρετή valour : ἀνήρ.   10.

ἀρέσκω please : ἀραρίσκω.   1. 24.

ἀρή prayer : Umbr. *arsir ἀραῖς*, Sk. *ār* praise.

ἀρήγω help : ἀλέγω.   1.

ἀρημένος distressed : ὄλλυμι.   11. 25.

ἀρθμός friendship, ἄρθρον joint : ἀραρίσκω.

ἀρι- well- : ἀραρίσκω.   1. 24.

ἀρία holm-oak :

ἀρί-ζηλος = δῆλος.   6.

ἀριθμός number : Lat. *ratio reor ritus*, O Ir. *rīmim* I count, Got. *garath-
 jan* count Ags. *rīm* number Eng. rhyme, νήριτος ἀραρίσκω.   1. 24.

ἀρίς auger :

ἀριστερός left : *νερτ-τερός, Umbr. *nertru* sinistro, Ags. *norð* north Eng.
 (cf. Sk. *dakshinas* 'right, south', O Ir. *dess*) : νέρτερος, 'lower' (cf.
 Eng. lar-board Dutch *laager* 'lower').   10. 2. 20.

ἄριστον breakfast : ἦρι.

ἄριστος best : ἀρείων.

ἄρκευθος juniper :

ἀρκέω ward off : Lat. *arceo arx arca*, O Ir. *tess-urc* servo, Got. *arhvazna*
 arrow Eng., Sk. *sam-arc* fix.

ἄρκτος bear : Lat. *ursus*, Welsh *arth*, Sk. *rkshas*, ὀλέκω.   11.

ἄρκυς net :

ἄρμα car : Sk. *rathas*, ἀραρίσκω.   So ἁρμός fastening.   4.

ἀρμαλίη food :

ἄρνα ram : Sk. *uranas*, εἶρος.   11.

ἀρνέομαι deny :

ἀρνευτήρ diver : Lit. *nerti* dive.   10.

ἄρνυμαι gain : Sk. *ar* reach.

ἄρον cuckoo-pint :

ἀρόω plough : Lat. *aro*, Ir. *ar* ploughing, Got. *arjan* to plough Eng. *to
 ear*, Lit. *árti : ἀραιός*.   Hence ἄρουρα field.   5.

ἁρπάζω seize, ἁρπαλέος attractive : Lat. *rapio*, λύπη. So ἅρπη A. kite.
4. 24.

ἁρπεδόνη rope :

ἅρπη B. sickle : O Lat. *sarpo* prune, OHG. *sarf* sharp, O Slav. *srŭpŭ*
sickle. 18.

(ἀρραβών pledge : Heb. °*ērābōn*.)

ἄρρατος steady :

ἀρριχάομαι climb :

(ἄρριχος basket : ῥίσκος σύριχος ὑρισός, Ir. *rusg* bark, cover.)

ἀρρωδέω = ὀρρωδέω. 11.

ἄρσην male : O Ir. *eirr* champion, Zd. *arshan* man : Sk. *arsh* flow,
'generator'. 11.

(ἀρτάβη a measure : Persian.)

ἄρταμος butcher : μερίζω μέρος. 10.

ἀρτάω hang : ἀραρίσκω.

ἀρτεμής sound, ἀρτέομαι ἀρτύω prepare, ἄρτι just now, ἄρτιος complete :
ἀραρίσκω.

ἄρτος loaf : ἀρτύω, 'preparation'? Hence ἀρτο-κόπος baker, πέσσω.
32.

ἀρύω draw water : ἄρνυμαι.

ἀρχός ānus : *ἀρσ-χός, ὄρρος. 11. 32.

ἄρχω am first : Ir. *arg* champion, Got. *raginon* to rule, Sk. *arh* be
worth.

(ἄρωμα spice : Indian ?)

ἆσαι to satiate : Lat. *aveo*, Sk. *av* satisfy, ἀίω B. 17.

ἀσάμινθος bath : σομφός ?

ἄσβολος soot : ψόλος. 1. 19.

ἀσελγής wanton : *ἀσλεγγής (cf. ἀθέλγω), λέγος. 1. 24.

ἆσθμα panting : ἀτμός. 20.

ἄσιλλα Simonides 163 yoke : foreign ?

ἄσις mud : Lat. *sentina*. 33. 10. 22.

ἀσκαλαβώτης lizard : κωλώτης, *σκαλαϜώτης (see ἀκροάομαι) : 1.

ἀσκάλαφος owl :

(ἀσκαλώπας = σκολόπαξ.)

ἀσκάντης bed : foreign ?

ἀσκαρίζω = σκαρίζω. 1.

ἀσκαρίς worm : σκαίρω. 1.

ἀσκέρα fur shoe, ἀσκός hide : Lit. *ůda* skin, Sk. *atkas* garment. Hence
ἀσκέω work, 'dress skins, mould into shape'. 19.

ἀ-σκηθής unhurt : κτείνω.

ἄσμενος gladly : ἀνδάνω. 33. 19.

ἀσπάζομαι welcome :

ἀσπαίρω = σπαίρω. 1.

ἀσπάλαθος a prickly plant : σφάλαξ buckthorn, Lit. *spilka* clasp, σκάλλω.
  1. 27.

ἀσπάλαξ = σπάλαξ. 1.

ἀσπαλιευτής angler : ἄσπαλος fish (Athamanian) :

(ἀσπάραγος asparagus : Pers. *ispargām* basil, σπαργάω.)

ἀσπερχές hastily : ἀ- copul., σπέρχω.

ἄ-σπετος immense : ἀ- neg., ἐνι-σπεῖν.

ἀσπίς A. shield : Lit. *skyda*, σκῦτος. 1. 27.

ἀσπίς B. asp : ἄφθαι.

(ἄσπρις oak : ὀστρύα.)

ἀστακός = ὄστακος. 8.

ἀσταφίς = σταφίς. 1.

ἄσταχυς = στάχυς. 1.

ἀ-στεμφής unmoved : ἀ- neg., στέμβω.

ἀστεροπή = στεροπή, ἀστράπτω = στράπτω. 1.

ἀστήρ star : Lat. *stella*, Welsh *seren*, Got. *stairno* Eng., Sk. *star* :
  στορέννυμι, 'strewn about the sky '. 1.

ἀστράβη saddle : ἀστραβής straight, ἀ- neg. + στρεβλός.

ἀστράγαλος vertebra : στραγγαλίς. 1. 10.

ἄστριχος vertebra : ὄστρειον. 1.

ἄστυ city : O Ir. *fosaimm* I stay, Got. *visan* to stay Eng. *was*, Sk. *vāstu*
  house *vas* dwell. 33.

ἀσύφηλος vile : ἀ- neg., NHG. *sauber* clean, O Slav. *chubavŭ* fair.

(ἄσφαλτος bitumen : Persian ?)

ἀσφόδελος lily (Eng. *daffodil*) : σφαδάζω, 'quivering '. 1.

ἀσχαλάω am distressed : ἀ- neg. + ἔχω, cf. ἄσχετος intolerable.   31.

(ἀσχέδωρος boar : Italian.)

(ἄσχιον truffle : ἰξός, foreign.)

ἀτάλλω foster, ἀταλός tender : Ags. *ädol* noble :

ἀτάρ but : ἄτερ, NHG. *sondern*. 11.

ἀταρπός = ἀτραπός. 24.

ἀ-ταρτ-ηρός restless : ἀ- neg., τείρω. 11.

ἀτάσθαλος reckless : *ἀ-ταθ-ίαλος (cf. φέρεσθαι Sk. bharadhyāi), ἀ-
  copul. + τωθάζω. 8.

ἀτέμβω perplex : ἀ- copul., O Nor. *dapr* sad, Sk. *dabh* injure. 20. 19.

ἀτενής tense : ἀ- copul., τείνω.

ἄτερ without : Got. *sundro* apart Eng. *sunder*, Sk. *sanutar* away, ἄνευ.
  33. 10.

ἄτερπνος sleepless (Rhegine) : ἄγρυπνος.

ἄτη = αὐάτα. 34.

ἀτιτάλλω = ἀτάλλω. 5. 16.

ἀτμός vapour : Ags. *aedm* breath, Sk. *ātman*.

ἄτρακτος spindle : ἀ- copul., Sk. *tarkus*, τρέπω. 11.

ἀτραπός path : ἀ- copul., τραπέω.

ἀ-τρεκής true : ἀ- neg., τρέπω.

ἀ-τρύγετος restless : ἀ- neg., τρύω (νε = υϝε = υγϝε = υγε, cf. τηλύγετος).

ἄττα father : onomatopoeic, Lat. Got. *atta*, Sk. *attā* mother.

(ἀτταγᾶς godwit : Lydian ?)

(ἀττανίτης pancake : ἄττανον = ἤγανον.)

ἀτταταῖ ἀτταταιάξ Interj. : Lat. *attat*, ὀτοτοῖ.

(ἀττέλαβος locust : Libyan ?)

ἄττομαι weave :

ἀτύζομαι am dismayed : Lat. *metus*. 10.

αὖ again : Lat. *au-fero aut autem*, Sk. *ava* away, ἠέ οὐ οὖν. 9.

αὖ dog's bark : Eng. *bow-wow*.

αὐάτā infatuation : *ἀϝέντā, οὐτάω. 1. 23. 10.

αὐγή light : ἀκτίς. 17.

αὐδή voice : ἀείδω. 24.

αὐερύω draw back : ἀ- copul., ἐρύω. 23.

αὐθέντης murderer : αὐτός + ἀνύω, Lat. *sons*, Ags. *syn* sin Eng., Zd. *han* deserve. 18.

αὖλαξ furrow : εὐλάκα. 9.

αὐλή court, αὐλών hollow way : ἄημι, ' open to the air ' (cf. θύρα). 24.

αὔληρα = εὔληρα. 9.

αὐλός flute : Sk. *vānas*, ἄημι. 24.

αὔξω increase : ἀέξω. 24.

αὖος αὐστηρός dry, αὐχμός drought : *αὖος cf. ἀφαύω, εὕω. 9. 32.

αὔρα breeze : οὖρος A. 9.

αὐρι-βάτης swift : αὖρι swiftly, O Ir. *aururas* running, Ags. *earu* quick *ärende* errand Eng., Zd. *aurva* swiftly, ὄρνυμι.

αὔριον tomorrow : ἠέριος, ἠώς Aeol. αὔως.

αὔσιος vain : ἄημι, cf. ἀεσίφρων. 24.

αὐτάρ but : αὐτός + ἄρ, ἄρα.

ἀυτμή breath : O Ir. *feth* air, Ags. *veder* weather Eng., Lit. *wétra* storm, cf. Lat. *ventus*, Got. *vinds* wind Eng., ἄημι. 1. 23. 31.

αὐτο-κάβδαλος slovenly : κόβαλος. 10. 6.

αὐτό-ματος of oneself : cf. ἠλέ-ματος.

αὐτός ipse : Hesych. αὖς (αὐτός formed from Gen., cf. Lat. *cujus* Adj.), αὖθι there, αὖ.

αὐχέω = εὔχομαι. 9.

αὐχήν neck : Aeol. αὔφην ἄμφην, Got. *hals-agga* : 17.

αὔω A. light a fire : εὕω. 9.

αὔω B. shout : Lat. *ovo*, Ags. *eōvle* owl Eng. 9.

(ἀφάκη vetch : φακός.)

ἄφαρ straightway : ἄφνω + ἄρ, ἄρα. 29.

ἀφαρεύς fin :

ἀφάρκη privet :

ἀφαυρός feeble : φλαῦρος. 1. 35.

ἀ-φελής smooth : ἀ- neg., φέλλια.

ἄφενος wealth, ἀφνειός wealthy : ἀ- copul., Lit. *gana* enough. 27. 2.

ἄφθαι ulceration : Lat. *asper :* 6.

ἀφία a plant :

ἄφλαστον stern :

ἀφλοισμός ἀφρός foam : NHG. *seifer :* 35. 25.

ἄφνω suddenly : ἰάπτω. 33. 21.

ἀφύη anchovy : ἀφύω.

ἀφυσγετός mud : *ἀσπυϜετός πτύω?

ἀφύσσω draw water : λαφύσσω. 10.

ἀφύω become white :

ἀχαίνης brocket :

(ἀχάνη a measure : Persian.)

ἀχαρνώς a sea-fish :

ἀχάτης agate : river Achates in Sicily.

ἄχερδος = ἀχράς. 24.

ἀχερωίς poplar : Ἀχελώιος, 'growing by rivers'.

ἀχηνία want : Lat. *egeo,* Lit *aikstyti* to desire, Sk. *ih.* 10.

ἄχθος load : ἄγω.

ἀχλύς mist : Lat. *aquilus op-ācus,* Lit. *áklas* blind *úkas* mist, ὠχρός. 8.

ἄχνη A. froth : χνόος. 1.

ἄχνη B. chaff : O Lat. *agna,* Got. *ahana* Eng. *awn,* ἀκοστή. 21.

ἄχος pain : O Ir. *agathar* timet, Got. *agis* fear *aglo* anguish Eng. *awe
ail ugly,* Sk. *agham* evil, ἄγχω. 32.

ἀχράς wild pear :

ἄχρι = μέχρι. 10.

ἄχυρα chaff, ἄχωρ scurf : Got. *ahs* ear (of corn) Eng., ἄχνη B. 29.

ἄψ back : ἀπό (cf. ἐξ).

ἀ-ψεφής careless : ψέφος gloom.

(ἀψίνθιον ἀσπίνθιον wormwood : foreign.)

ἄψ-ορρος back : Lat. *erro,* Got. *ur-reisan* rise Eng., cf. ἄλη. 19.

ἀών a fish :

ἄωρος sleep, ἀωτέω I sleep : ἄημι, 'breathe, snore'. 7.

ἄωτος fleece : ἄημι, 'blown about' (cf. Lat. *plūma* πλέω, Ags. *fnacs*
'fringe' πνέω, Eng. down 'plumage' θύω θύσανος). 7.

βᾶ = βασιλεῦ (cf. βρῖ δῶ κρῖ λί λίς μᾶ ρᾶ).

βᾶ βαβαί βαβαιάξ Interj. : Lat. *babae.*

βαβάκτης reveller, βάβαξ chatterer : βαμβαίνω.

βαβράζω chirp : Eng. *purr.*

βάζω speak :

βάθος = βένθος. 10.

βαίνω walk : *γFέμ-jω, Lat. *venio*, Got. *qiman* come Eng., Sk. *gam* go : cf. Lat. *bēto*, Ir. *béim* step, Lett. *gáju* I went, Sk. *gā* go. 27. 9. 17. 19.

βαιός little : Lit. *gaiszti* disappear. Hence βαιών blenny. 27. 34.

βαίτη coat : Got. *paida* Eng. *pea-jacket* :

(βάκηλος eunuch : Phrygian, Lat. *babaecalus.* Petron. 37 fin.)

(βάκκαρις nard : Lydian, Ir. *bachar* lady's-glove.)

βάκτρον staff : Lat. *baculum*, cf. βαίνω.

βάλαγρος a fish :

βαλανείον bath (Lat. *balneum*) : 'vapour-bath', Sk. *galanas* dropping, βάλλω.

βάλανος acorn : Lat. *glans*, Lit. *gille* : 'dropt', βάλλω. 27.

βαλβίς starting-point : *φλαγFίς, Lat. *sufflāmen*, Ags. *balc* beam Eng. *baulk*, βλάβη φάλαγξ. 19. 24. 27.

βάλε utinam : βούλομαι. 11.

(βαλήν king : Phrygian, Carian γέλαν βασιλέα, O Slav. *golěmŭ* great, πάλμυς.)

βαλιός dappled : βάλλω (cf. Sk. *asitas* 'black' as 'throw').

(βαλλάντιον purse : foreign.)

(βαλλίζω dance : Italian, late Lat. *ballo* dance (Eng. *ball ballet*), Sk. *bal* whirl.)

βαλλιρός a fish :

(βάλλις a plant : foreign.)

βάλλω throw : NHG. *quellen* gush, Lit. *gullěti* to lie, Sk. *gal* drop. 27. 11.

(βάλσαμον balsam : Heb. *besem.*)

βαμβαίνω chatter : onomatopoeic, Lat. *babulus* App. Met. 4. 14 babbler, Eng. *babble boom*, Sk. *bababā* crackling, βόμβος.

(βαμβραδών anchovy : βεμβράς μεμβράς, foreign.)

βάναυσος vulgar :

βάπτω dip : O Nor. *kaf* diving, Sk. *gambhan* depth, cf. βάθος. 27.

βάραγχος = βράγχος. 2.

βάραθρον pit : Arcadian ζέρεθρον, Lat. *gurges*, Lit. *prá-garas*, βορά. 27. 11.

βάραξ = γοῦρος. 27. 11.

βάρβαρος foreign : Lat. *balbus blatero*, O Ir. *balb* dumb, Lit. *birbti* hum Sk. *balbalā* stammer, βληχή.

(βάρβιτος lyre : Aeol. βάρμιτον, mariandynian βώριμος song Pollux 4. 54.)

(βᾶρις boat : Coptic *bari.*)

βαρύς heavy : Lat. *gravis*, Got. *kaurus*, Sk. *gurus.* 27.

(βάρωμος Sappho 154 = βάρβιτος.)

(βάσανος touchstone : Lit. *bandyti* prove, Lydian.)

βασιλεύς king : diminutive of *βάσιλος cf. βασίλη :

βάσκανος slanderous : Lat. *fascino* :

(βασκάς duck : φασκάς, foreign.)

(βασσάρα fox : Coptic bashar.)

βαστάζω lift : O Nor. kasta throw Eng. cast.　27.

βάταλος ānus :

βατάνη = πατάνη, Sicilian.

(βατιακή cup : βατιανή βατιατική, foreign.)

βατίς βάτος A. a fish ('wriggling'), B. bush : Lat. vatius, Sk. jat twist.
　27.

(βάτραχος frog : βάθρακος βρόταχος, NHG. kröte toad.)

βατταρίζω stammer :

βατύλη dwarf : Proper Name?

βαυβάω fall asleep ('snore', cf. ἀωτέω), βαΰζω bark (*βαϜ-ύζω) : Lat.
　baubor, Lit. bubauti roar.　5. 34.　So βαυκός prudish (cf. ὅλολυς).

βδάλλω milk : 'make to drop', βάλλω.　Hence βδέλλα leech.　6.

βδέω visio : *γϜέσω, Lat. vīsio, Lit. bezëti βδεῖν.　27. 6. 34.

βέβαιος sure, βέβηλος unconsecrated : βαίνω.　5.

βέβρός stupid : Hesych. βεμβρός, βαμβαίνω.

(βέδυ air : Phrygian.)

βείομαι vivam : *γϜείϜομαι, Lat. vīvo, Welsh byw alive, Got. qius Eng.
　quick, Lit. gywas, Sk. jīv to live.　27. 34.

(βεκός bread : Phrygian, φώγω.)

βέλεκοι pulse ;

(βελένιον a plant : Persian?)

βέλος dart : βάλλω.

βέλτερος better : Hesych. ἰξέλα good luck (Macedonian), βούλομαι.　7.

βέμβιξ top : Lett. bamba ball, Sk. bimbikā :

(βεμβράς = βαμβραδών.)

βένθος depth : Ir. badad drowning, Sk. gadhas a cleft.　27.

(βέρβερι mother-of-pearl : Indian.)

(βερβέριον coat : foreign.)

βερέσχεθος booby :

(βεῦδος βεῦθος gown : foreign.)

βῆ cry of sheep : Lat. bee, Eng. baa.

βηλός threshold : βαίνω.　17.

βήξ cough :

βῆσσα glen : *βένθ-ja βένθος.　17. 19.

βία strength : Lat. viĕtus, Sk. ji conquer.　27.

(βίβλος βύβλος papyrus-bark : Egyptian.)

βιβρώσκω eat : βορά.　24.

(βῖκος jar (Eng. beaker, pitcher) : Heb. baqbūq flask.)

βīνέω coeo : *γϜεν-νέω γυνή?

βίος life : βείομαι.　31.

βιός bow : Lat. *filum hīlum*, Welsh *giau* sinews, Lit. *gija* thread, Sk. *jyā* bowstring. 27.

βιπτάζω = βάπτω. 13.

(βίττακος = ψιττάκη.)

βλάβη damage : βαλβίς.

βλαισός bandy-legged :

βλάξ lazy : Lat. *flaccus*, Lit. *blúkti* to become weak. 19.

βλαστάνω grow : Ags. *brant* high, O Slav. *brŭdo* hill. 19. 25. 20.

βλάσφημος slanderous :

βλαύτη slipper : foreign ?

βλεμεαίνω exult :

βλέννα mucus, βλέννος a fish :

βλέπω see, βλέφαρον eyelid : γλέφαρον. 27. 29.

βλῆρ = δέλεαρ (cf. κῆρ κέαρ). 27. 2. 24.

βληχή bleating : Lat. *bālo*, OHG. *blāzan* bleat Eng., O Slav. *bléjati*, βάρβαρος.

βληχρός languid, βλῆχρος a plant : βλάξ. 21.

βλήχων = γλήχων. 19.

βλῑμάζω squeeze : *βλεδ-μάζω (cf. δρυμάζω), ἀμαλδύνω. 19. 17.

(βλιτάχεα = βρίγκοι.)

βλίτον a plant : NHG. *melde* orach : 19. 24.

βλίττω take honey : μέλι. 19. 31.

βλιχώδης snivelling :

βλοσυρός stout : *βλοθ-συρός βλαστάνω (cf. ἀή-συρος). So βλωθρός tall. 35. 30.

βλύω see ἀναβλύω.

βλωμός see ὀκτάβλωμος.

βλώσκω go : Lat. *re-meligo* hinderer, μολεῖν. 19. 24.

βοή shout : Lat. *boere bovāre*, γόος. 27.

βόθρος trench : Lat. *fodio*, Lit. *bedéti* dig. 20.

βοῖ = βαβαί.

βολβός onion (Lat. *bulbus*) : Lat. *globus glomus*, O Nor. *kólfr* bulb, βῶλος. 27. 5. So βόλιτον dung (cf. σφυράδες). 30.

(βόλινθος wild ox : foreign.)

βόμβος buzzing, βόμβυξ A. flute : βαμβαίνω.

(βόμβυξ B. silkworm : Pers. *pamba* cotton.)

(βόνασος = μόναπος.)

βορά food : Lat. *voro*, O Ir. *gelid* consumit, Lit. *gérti* to drink, Sk. *gar* devour. 27.

βόρβορος mud :

βορβορυγμός rumbling : βρυχάομαι. 5. 2.

(βορέας north wind : O Nor. *byrr* a fair wind, Lit. *búris* shower, φύρω, Thracian, cf. βρῦτον.)

βόσκω feed : Lat. *vescor.* 27. Hence βοσκάς = βασκάς, popular etymology.

(βόστρυχος βότρυχος curl, βότρυς bunch of grapes : foreign.)

βουβάλια bracelets :

(βούβαλις antelope : Sk. *gavalas* buffalo, βοῦς.)

βουβών groin : βομβών, Lat. *boa* swelling, O Nor. *kaun* a sore, Sk.
gavīnis groin. 27. 17. 5.

βου·γάιε braggart : 'great ox' (cf. βού-βρωστις), Hesych. γαῖος ox, γῆ.

βού·κολος cowherd : κέλλω.

βούλομαι wish : Lat. *volo,* Lit. *galéti* be able. 27.

βουνός hill : γύαλον. 27.

βοῦς ox : Lat. *bōs,* Ir. *bó* cow, Ags. *cū* Eng., Lett. *góws :* βοή (cf. Lat.
vacca vagio, Eng. bull bellow). 27.

βραβεύς umpire : 'taking the stakes', Got. *greipan* seize Eng. *grip
grasp,* Lit. *grébti.* 27. 11.

βράγχος sorethroat : βρόγχος. 11.

βραδύς slow : *βραθύς cf. βράσσων, Lat. *bardus,* Sk. *jalhus* (=*jardhus).
27. 24. 28.

βράκανα herbs :

βράκος robe : Aeol., = ῥάκος (cf. λώπη).

βράσσω winnow : *φράκ-jω, cf. φύρω. 19.

βράχε rattled : Lat. *frigo* squeak, Ags. *beorcian* bark Eng., Lit. *brizgéti*
bleat, Sk. *barh* roar. 19.

βραχίων arm : Lat. *bracchium,* sq., 'shorter' than the leg.

βραχύς short : Lat. *brevis,* Got. *ga-maurgjan* shorten. 19. 24.

βρέγμα cranium : Ags. *bregen* brain Eng., φράσσω. 19.

βρεκεκεκέξ cry of frogs.

βρέμω roar : Lat. *fremo,* OHG. *breman* NHG. *brummen.* 19.

(βρένθος βρίνθος a bird : foreign.)

βρενθύομαι strut : βρίθω. 17.

βρέτας image : Sk. *mūrtis* figure, βρότος. 19. 7.

βρέφος babe : Lat. *germen,* Got. *kalbo* calf Eng., O Slav. *žrébe* young,
Sk. *garbhas* embryo, δελφύς. 27. 24.

βρεχμός = βρέγμα.

βρέχω wet : O Slav. *grạziti* drip. 27.

βρῖ (cf. βᾶ) βριαρός strong : Sk. *jri* overpower. 27.

(βρίγκος a fish : βρύσσος.)

βρίζω slumber : sq., 'am heavy with sleep'.

βρίθω am heavy : Got. *braids* broad Eng., πάρθενος. 19. So βρῑμάομαι
am angry, βρῑμη weight.

βρίκελος a mask : Proper Name?

βρόγχος windpipe : O Nor. *barki,* βράχε.

βρόμος A. stink :

βρόμος B. βόρμος oats. 24.

βροντή thuñder : βρέμω. 7. 19.

βρόξαι to swallow : βρύχιος.

βρότος gore : Sk. *mūrtas* coagulated. 19.

βροτός mortal : Sk. *mrtas* dead *mar* die, μαραίνω. 19. 24.

(βροῦκος βροῦχος locust : foreign.)

βρόχος noose : O Nor. *kringla* ring, Lit. *grenszti* twist. 27.

βρναλίκτης dance : βρύω *βρύαλος (cf. αἰγίλωψ) *βρυαλίζω.

βρύκω βρύχω grind the teeth : Got. *kriustan*, O Slav. *gryzą* I bite. 27.

βρῦν drink : βορά.

(βρύσσος sea-urchin : foreign.)

(βρῦτον beer : Thracian, Ags. *beor* Eng., φύρω.)

βρυχάομαι roar : βράχε. 11.

βρύχιος deep : βρέχω. 11.

βρύω am full : φρέαρ. 19.

βρωμάομαι bray : βρέμω (intensive, cf. εὐωχεω νωμάω πωτάομαι).

βύας owl : βοή. 15.

(βύβλος = βίβλος.)

βυθός βυσσός depth : βάθος. 14. 19.

βύκτης howling : Lat. *bucca*, NHG. *pfauchen* snort, O Slav. *bučati* roar, Sk. *bukk.*

βύρσα hide : Hesych. βερρόν thick, Ags. *crusen* pelliceus. 27.

(βύσσος linen : Heb. *buts.*)

βύσταξ = μύσταξ (cf. ἀμάμαξυς).

βύω stuff up : *γΫύω cf. Perf. ζέβυται, O Nor. *púss* purse. 27.

βῶλος clod : Lat. *glēba*, Eng. *clue clod*, Sk. *gōlas* ball, γαυλός. 27.

βωμός altar : βῆμα βαίνω. 8.

γάγγαμον net : γέντο. 5. 11.

γάγγλιον tumour : OHG. *klenken* to tie. 35. 11.

γάγγραινα gangrene ; γράω gnaw, Sk. *gras.* 5. 34.

(γάδος hake : foreign.)

(γάζα treasure : Persian.)

γαῖα earth :

γαίων exulting : Lat. *gau*, O Nor. *kátr* merry. 34.

γάλα milk : *γλάκτ, γλάγος. 2. Hence γαλα-θηνός suckling, θῆσθαι.

(γαλάδες γάλακες mussels : foreign.)

γαλέη weasel :

γαλήνη calm : Hesych. γελεῖν shine, Sk. *jval.* 11.

γάλοως sister-in-law : Lat. *glōs*, O Slav. *zlŭva* :

(γάμμα G : Heb. *gimel.*)

γάμος marriage : Lat. *gener* γαμβρός (*genero* = *gem-ro), Sk. *jāmā* daughter-in-law : 'seizing', γέντο. 11.

γαμφηλαί jaws : O Ir. *gop-chóel* lean-jawed, Ags. *camb* comb Eng., Lit. *gembe* hook, Sk. *jambh* snap. 11.

γαμψός curved : Lat. *gibbus*, Lit. *gumbas* tumour.

γάνος A. joy : γλήνεα. 10.

(**γάνος** B. **γλάνος** hyena : Phrygian.)

γάργαλος tickling : ἐγείρω excite. 11. 5.

γάργαρα heaps : ἀγείρω. 5. 11.

γαργαρεών uvula : Lat. *gurgulio gula*, O Nor. *kverkr* throat, βορά. 5. 11.

(**γάρος** caviar : Sk. *garas* drink, βορά.)

γαστήρ belly : *γϜενστήρ, Lat. *venter*, Got. *qithus* Eng. *kid-ney* NHG. *wanst*, Sk. *jatharas* (=*jastaras) : 32. 10.

γαῦλος merchantman : Ags. *ceol* ship, γογγύλος. So **γαυλός** pail, Sk. *gōlā* jug. 9.

γαῦρος exulting : γαίω. 23.

γαυσός = γαμψός. 17. 32.

γὲ at least : Got. *mi-k* me, Lit. *tas-gi* the same ; cf. Lat. *hic*, Sk. *gha* at least (cf. γένυς ἐγώ μέγας τρώγλη).

γέγειος ancient : γῆ (cf. αὐτόχθων). 5. 30.

γέγωνα call out :

(**γεῖσον** cornice : Carian γίσσα stone, OHG. *kis* gravel.)

γείτων neighbour : γῆ (cf. Lat. *vicinus*). 30.

γελάω laugh : γαλήνη.

γέλγη = γρύτη. 25. 5.

γέλγις garlic : Sk. *grnjanas :*

γέμω am full : Lat. *gemma gemursa gumia gemo*, O Slav. *žĭmą* I compress.

γένος race : Lat. *genus nascor*, Ir. *gein* birth, Got. *keinan* germinate *kuni* kin Eng., Lit. *gimti* be born, Sk. *jan* generate.

γέντο he grasped : *γέμ-το : 19.

γένυς jaw : Lat. *gena genuīnus* B., Welsh *gen*, Got. *kinnus* cheek Eng. *chin*, Lit. *žándas* jawbone ; cf. Sk. *hanus* (cf. γὲ).

γέρανος crane : Lat. *grus*, Welsh *garan*, Ags. *cran* Eng., Lit. *gérwe* Armen. *krē :* Welsh *garan* shank (Eng. *garter) :*

γέρας privilege : Sk. *garvas* pride.

(**γέργῡρα γόργῡρα** = κάρκαρον.)

γέρρον wickerwork : γυργαθός.

γέρων old man : O Slav. *zrěti* ripen, Sk. *jaras* old *jar* wear out.

γεύω give to taste : Lat. *gusto*, O Ir. *to-gu* choice, Got. *kausjan* to taste *kiusan* approve Eng. *choose* Ags. *cyssan* kiss Eng., Sk. *jush* be pleased. 34.

(**γέφυρα** bridge : Lac. διφοῦρα Theban βλέφυρα, Asiatic.)

γῆ = γαῖα.

γηθέω rejoice : Lat. *gaudeo*, γαίων. 17.

(γήθυον γήτειον leek : Sk. *gandholi* a plant.)

γῆρας age : γέρων. 30.

γῆρυς voice : Lat. *garrio*, Ir. *gair* cry, O Nor. *kalla* to call Eng., Lit. *garsas* voice, Sk. *jar* call.

γίγαρτον grape-stone : Lat. *grānum*, γέρων, 'rubbed'. 5. 11.

γίγγλυμος joint : γάγγλιον. 11.

(γίγγρας flute : Heb. *kinnour* harp, κινύρα.)

γίγνομαι am born : Lat. *gigno*, γένος. 31.

γιγνώσκω know : Lat. *nosco*, O Ir. *er-gna* intellect, Got. *kunths* known Eng., Lit. *žinóti* know, Sk. *jnā :* praeced., 'produce in thought'.

(γίννος mule : ἴννος, Ligurian γυγήνιος Strabo 4. 6. 2.)

γλάγος milk : *μλάγος ἀμέλγω. 19. 24.

γλάζω sing : O Nor. *klaka* twitter. 19.

γλακτο-φάγος living on milk : γάλα.

γλάμων blear-eyed (Lat. *gramiae*) : Got. *qrammitha* moisture : 25.

(γλάνις shad : Phoenician.)

γλαρίς chisel :

γλαυκός bright : O Slav. *glavija* firebrand, Sk. *jūrv* burn, cf. γαλήνη.

γλάφω carve : *σκλάφω Lat. *scalpo*, cf. σκάλλω. 19. 24.

γλέφαρον eyelid : O Slav. *glipati* see. 29.

γλήνεα shows, γλήνη eyeball : Ir. *glan* clean, Ags. *claene* Eng., 'bright', γαλήνη.

γλήχων pennyroyal : μαλάχη. 19.

(γλῖνος γλεῖνος maple : κλινότροχος.)

γλίσχρος sticky, greedy : Lat. *glittus* smooth *glis* clay, Lit. *glittus* smooth, sticky. 19.

γλίχομαι desire : *γλέθ-σκομαι, O Slav. *gladŭ* hunger, Sk. *gardh* be eager. 11. 35.

γλοιός Subst. oil : Lat. *glūten*, Ags. *clifian* cleave to Eng. Hence γλοιός Adj. vicious, 'slippery'.

γλουτός nates :

γλυκύς sweet : *ὁλυκύς Lat. *dulcis :* 19. 24.

γλύφω carve : *σκλύφω Lat. *sculpo*, cf. σκύλλω (cf. γλάφω).

γλῶσσα tongue, γλωχίς point : O Slav. *gložije* thorn. 19.

γνάθος = γένυς. 24.

γναμπτός curved : O Nor. *kneif* pincers Eng. *knife nip*, Lit. *žnypti* pinch. 11.

γνάφαλος a bird : γνάπτω New Att. for κνάπτω.

γνήσιος legitimate : γένος. 24.

γνύξ on the knee : γόνυ.

γόγγρος A. = γρῦλος. 5.

γόγγρος B. excrescence on trees : γίγαρτον, 'rubbing'. 5. 24.

γογγύζω see περιγογγύζω.

γογγύλος round : γυρός. 5. 25.

γόης enchanter : γόος.

γόμφος bolt : γαμφηλαί.

γόνυ knee : Lat. *genu*, Got. *kniu* Eng., Sk. *jānu* : 2.

γόος groan : O Ir. *guth* voice, OHG. *chuma* complaint, Lit. *gauti* howl, Sk. *gu* shout.

γοργός A. grim : Ir. *garg* fierce, O Slav. *groza* horror : Sk. *garj* bellow (cf. Eng. grim, χρεμετίζω).

γοργός B. swift : ἀγείρω. 7. 5.

γουνός = γωνία. 17.

γοῦρος cake :

(γράσος smell : Lat. *hircus*.)

γραῦς old woman, scum (= slough γῆρας) : γέρων. 24.

γράφω scratch : *σκράφω, Lat. *scribo*, σκαριφισμός (cf. γλάφω).

(γραψαῖος crab : Ags. *crabba* Eng., κάραβος.)

γρῖφος weel : *σκρῖφος, Lat. *scirpus* (cf. γλάφω) :

γρομφάς sow : *σκρομφάς, Lat. *scrōfa* (cf. γλάφω) : γράφω, 'scratching, rooting'.

γρῦ morsel : γίγαρτον. 24.

γρύζω A. mutter : Lat. *grundio*, O Nor. *kretta* murmur. 19.

γρύζω B. melt :

γρῦλος conger : Sk. *gargaras* a fish : βορά, 'drinker'. 24.

γρῡμέα γρύτη frippery : Lat. *scrūta*, Ags. *scrūd* dress, σκύλλω (cf. λώπη).

γρῡπός curved : Ags. *crumb*, cf. γυρός. So γρύψ griffin, 'hook-nosed'.

γύαλον hollow, γύης A. plough-tree, γυῖον limb, γυιόω lame ('bend') :

γύης B. field : Sk. *jyā* earth.

γύλιος wallet : OHG. *kiulla*, γαυλός. 31.

γυμνός naked : *νυγϜ-νός, Lat. *nūdus*, Ir. *nocht*, Got. *naqaths* Eng., Lit. *nūgas*, Sk. *nagnas* : 19. 27.

γυνή woman : Boeotian βανά, Ir. *ben*, Got. *qens* Eng. *quean queen* : 11.

(γύννις effeminate : γίννος.)

γυργαθός weel :

γῡρός round : Lat. *būris* plough-tail. 32.

(γύψ vulture : Egyptian ?)

(γύψος chalk : Pers. *jabs* gypsum.)

γωλεός hole : 'lair', βάλλω (cf. Lat. jaceo jacio). 7.

γωνία corner : ἀγοστός, 'hiding-place'. 17.

(γωρῡτός bow-case : κώρυκος.)

δα- = ζα-. 32.

δᾶ earth : Cyprian ζᾶ, γῆ. 26.

δαήμων skilful : Zd. *dā* know.

δᾱήρ brother-in-law : Lat. *lēvir*, Ags. *tācor*, Lit. *dёweris*, Sk. *dēvar-* :
δαί = δή.
δαῖ battle : δαίω A.
δαίδαλος variegated : Ags. *tāt* gay :
δαίμων deity : δαίω B.
δαίρω = δέρω.   9.
δαίω A. burn : O Ir. *dóthim* I burn, Sk. *du* burn.
δαίω B. divide : Ags. *tīd* time Eng. *tide*, *tīma* time Eng., Sk. *dā* cut off.
δάκνω bite : Got. *tahjan* to tear Eng. *tongs*, O Slav. *desna* gum, Sk. *dạç* bite, cf. praeced.
δάκρυ tear : Lat. *lacruma*, Welsh *dagrau* tears, Got. *tagr* tear Eng. : praeced., 'bitter' (cf. Sk. açru 'tear' ἀκίς).
δάκτυλος A. finger : *δέγκτυλος, Lat. *digitus* (=*dencitus), Ags. *tā* Eng. *toe* : δέκομαι.   10.
(δάκτυλος B. date (Eng.) : Phoenician.)
δαλερός hot : δαίω A.
δαμάζω tame : Lat. *domo*, O Ir. *damim* I endure, Got. *ga-tamjan* to tame Eng., Sk. *dam*.   11.
δανείζω lend : δάνος gift, δαίω B.
δανότης misery : δαίω A., cf. δύη.
δαπάνη expense, δάπτω devour : Lat. *dapes*, cf. δαίω B.
δά-πεδον floor : δα-.
(δάπις = τάπης.)
δαρδάπτω devour : *δαρδάρπτω, δρέπω.   5. 11. 35.
(δᾱρεικός a coin : Pers. *dār* holder = king.)
δαρθάνω sleep : Lat. *dormio*, O Slav. *drěmati* to sleep, Sk. *drā*.   11.
δά-σκιλλος a fish : σκίλλα, = σχινοκέφαλος.
δα-σπλῆτις fearful : Lat. *splendeo*, Lit. *splendĕti* shine ?
δασύς thick : Lat. *densus dusmus dūmus :*   10.
(δαῦκος parsnep : Ags. *docce* dock Eng. : Celtic ?)
δαυλός thick : δασύς ?
δαύω sleep : διά + *l*-ανω.   32.
(δάφνη bay : Thessalian δαύχνη, Pergaean λάφνη, Lat. *laurus*.)
δαψιλής plentiful : δαπάνη.
δέ but : Lat. *quī-dam qui-dem*, Zd. *da* he, δή ὅδε.
δέατο seemed : *δεί-ατο, Sk. *dī* shine, cf. δῖος.   34.
δέδαα nōvi, δέδαε docuit : δαήμων.
δέελος conspicuous : δέατο.   34.
δεῖ oportet : δεύομαι.   34.
δειδίσκομαι welcome : *δει-δέκ-σκομαι δέκομαι.   5. 13. 35.
δείδω fear : *δέδδοα *δέ-δϝοια, Zd. *dvaētha* fear.   17. 34.
δείελος vespertinus : δύω set.   34.
δεικανάομαι welcome : δέκομαι.   17.

δείκνυμι show : Lat. *deico indico dicio*, O Ir. *decha* dicat, Got *ga-teihan* announce Eng. *token*, Sk. *diç* shew.

δείλη afternoon : δείελος.

δεῖνα some one : Pruss. *dei* one, Zd. *di* he, δέ.

δεῖνος = δῖνος, Cyrenaic.

δεῖπνον dinner : δάπτω. 17.

δειρή neck : Lat. *dorsum*, Ir. *druim* back : 17.

δείς one : δεῖνα, on analogy of εἷς.

δέκα ten : Lat. *decem*, Ir. *deich*, Got. *taihun* Eng., Lit. *deszimtis*, Sk. *daçan :*

δεκάζω bribe, δέκομαι receive : Sk. *dāç* grant, δοκέω. 7.

δέλεαρ bait : βορά. 26. 25.

(δέλτα D, δέλτος tablet : Heb. *daleth* D, tablet.)

δέλφαξ porker, δελφίς dolphin, δελφύς womb : βρέφος. 26.

δέμας person, δέμνια bed, δέμω build : Got. *timrjan* Eng. *timber*, cf. δέω.

(δενδαλίς barley-cake : δανδαλίς, foreign.)

δενδίλλω glance : Ags. *til* aim Eng. *till* Prep., Lit. *dyrěti* peep out, Sk. *ā-dar* observe. 5. 11. 25.

δένδρον tree : δρῦς. 5.

δέννος reproach : δονέω (cf. διασύρω). 7.

δεξαμενή tank : δέκομαι.

δεξιός right : Lat. *dexter*, O Ir. *dess*, Got. *taihsva*, Lit. *deszine* right hand, Sk. *dakshinas* right : δέκομαι, 'the hand of welcome'.

δέπας cup : δάπτω, 'a measure'. 10. 32.

δέρκομαι see : Lat. *larva*, O Ir. *derc* eye, Got. *ga-tarhjan* point out, Sk. *darç* see, cf. δενδίλλω.

δέρω flay : Welsh *darn* piece (Eng.), Got. *ga-tairan* to tear Eng., Lit. *dirti* flay, Sk. *dar* tear.

δεσ-πότης master : Lit. *gaspadórus*, Sk. *jāspatis*, γένος + πόσις. 26. 32. So δέσ-ποινα lady, Lit. *pona*, πῶν.

δεύομαι want : Ags. *tōm* empty, Sk. *dūras* far, δύω. 31.

δεῦρο δεῦτε hither : Lit. *guiti* drive, Sk. *jū* quick. 26.

δεύτερος second, δεύτατος last : δεύομαι, 'further, furthest'.

δεύω wet : OHG. *zawa* dyeing.

δέφω δέψω knead : MHG. *zispen* tread. 32. 24.

δέχομαι = δέκομαι. 29.

δέω bind : Sk. *dā*.

δή indeed : δέ.

δηλέομαι injure : Lat. *doleo*, δέρω. 25.

δήλομαι = βούλομαι. 26.

δῆλος = δέελος.

δῆμος land : δαίω B.

δημός fat : δαίω A., 'burnt' at sacrifice.

δήν long : *δεϝάν, O Slav. *davino* formerly, δεύομαι.

δήνεα plans : δαήμων.

δῆρις fight : δέρω.

δῆτα indeed : = δὴ εἶτα (as χρῆναι = χρὴ εἶναι).

δήω inveniam : δαήμων.

διά through : δύο. 32.

δι-άζομαι begin to weave : ἄττομαι. 28.

διαίνω = δεύω. 12.

δί-αιτα maintenance : αἴνυμαι. *αυ ζιτε?*

διάκονος servant, διάκτορος conductor : διώκω. 8.

διάκόσιοι 200 : δύο + ἐκατόν, on analogy of τρια-κόσιοι.

δια-μυλλαίνω make mouths : μυλλός awry :

δια-πρύσιος piercing : πείρω. 24. 22.

δια-σφάξ ravine : σφίγγω.

δι-αττάω sift through : ἄττομαι, 'separate'.

δια-φρέω let through : φέρω.

διδάσκαλος teacher, διδάσκω teach, διδαχή teaching : *δι-δέγκ-σκω, Lat. *doceo disco* (= *dec-sco), Zd. *dakhsh* teach. 5. 10. 35. 29.

διδράσκω see ἀποδιδράσκω.

δίδυμος double : δύο + γένος?

δίδωμι give : Lat. *do*, Ir. *dán* treasure, Lit. *dúti* give, Sk. *dā*, δαίω B. 8.

δίεμαι hasten, διερός A. swift : Ir. *dian*, Lett. *dit* to dance, Sk. *dī* swing.

διερός B. liquid : διαίνω.

δίζημαι seek : ζητέω. 5.

δίζω doubt : δύο. 32.

δι-ηνεκής continuous : ἠνεκέως.

διήρης upper : δύο + ἀραρίσκω. 32.

(διθύραμβος hymn to Dionysos : foreign.)

(δίκαιρος a bird : Indian.)

δικεῖν to throw :

δίκελλα mattock : δύο + κέλλω, cf. μά-κελλα. 32.

δίκη custom : δείκνυμι. 31.

δίκροος forked : δύο + κυρέω, cf. ἀντι-κρύ.

δίκτυον net : δικεῖν.

δῖνος whirling, cup : δίεμαι.

δῖος divine : Lat. *deivus deus dies*, Ir. *dia* god, day, O Nor. *tivar* gods Ags. *Tivesdäg* Tuesday Eng., Lit. *dëwas* god *dëna* day, Sk. *div* shine. 34.

δίπλαξ διπλόος double : δύο + πλεῖος, Lat. *duplex duplus*, Got. *tveifls* doubt.

διπλάσιος double : δύο + πλάσσω, Got. *ain-falths* single *manag-falths* manifold Eng. 22.

δίς twice : Lat. *bis*, Sk. *dvis*, δύο. 32.

δίσκος quoit : δικεῖν. 35.

διστάζω doubt : δύο + ἵστημι.

δῑφάω seek :

διφθέρα hide : δέφω. 13. 6.

δίψα thirst : Ir. *dibhe*, διφάω. 30.

δίω = δείδω. 31.

δι-ώκω pursue : *ι-ωκή*.

δι-ωλύγιος vast : ἠλύγη, 'dismal'. 8.

δνοπαλίζω shake : κάμπτω (cf. δνόφος σκέπας : cf. αἰγίλωψ). 19. 24.

δνόφος darkness : γνόφος κνέφας. 19. 7.

δοάν = δήν. 7. 34.

δοάσσατο = δέατο. 7.

δοθιήν boil :

δοῖδυξ pestle : δοκός. 5. 14.

δοκεύω watch : δέκομαι. 7.

δοκέω think, seem : O Ir. *doich* likely, δέκομαι. 7.

δοκός beam :

δολιχός long : O Nor. *tjálgr* prong, O Slav. *dlŭgŭ* long, Sk. *dîrghas*: Sk. *dhrāgh* be able, cf. *dhar* hold θρῆνυς. 20. 25. 2.

δόλος snare : Lat. *dolus*, O Nor. *tál* bait :

δόμος house : Lat. *domus*, O Ir. *dom*, O Slav. *domŭ*, Sk. *damas*, δέμω. 7.

δόναξ reed : Lett. *dónis :*

δονέω shake :

δόρπον supper : δρέπω. 7.

δόρυ shaft : δρῦς. 2.

δοῦλος slave : Sk. *dāsas*, *dās* give, cf. δίδωμι?

δοῦπος crash : ἐρί-γδουπος, κτύπος. 19. 32. 17.

δόχμιος aslant : Sk. *jihmas :* 26.

δράκων snake : δέρκομαι, 'bright-eyed'. 24.

δραμεῖν to run : Sk. *dram* run about, cf. ἀποδιδράσκω. 11. So δρᾱπέτης runaway.

δράσσομαι grasp : cf. δέρω. 19.

δραώ do : Lit. *daryti*, ἀποδιδράσκω (cf. πράσσω and Lat. ago).

δρέπω pluck : Bohem. *drápati* pull, δράσσομαι. 27.

δρῑμύς keen : δρυμάζω tear, δέρω (cf. Eng. tart, to tear). 24.

δριός thicket : δρῦς. 32.

δρίφος chariot : δίφρος, δύο + φέρω. 24.

δροίτη tub :

δρόμος course : δραμεῖν.

δρόσος dew : Got. *ufar-trusnjan* sprinkle, cf. Sk. *dru* run, melt, ἀποδιδράσκω.

δρύπτω tear : δρέπω. 11.

δρῦς oak : O Ir. *daur*, Got. *triu* tree Eng., O Slav. *drěvo*, Sk. *drus*: δέρω, 'fissile' (cf. Eng. wood Lat. di-vido). 24. Hence δρύ-φακτος lattice, φράσσω. 35.

δρώπτω watch : OHG. *zorft* clear, cf. δενδίλλω. 24.

δύη pain : Lit. *dowiti* to torment, δαίω A. 15.

δύναμαι am able : *γνά-μαι γιγνώσκω, Eng. *can?*

δύο δύω two : Lat. *duo*, O Ir. *dá*, Got. *tvai* Eng., Lit. *du*, Sk. *dva* : δύω, 'going on'?

δύπτω dive : βάπτω. 26. 14.

δύρομαι lament : δέρω, 'tear oneself'. 11.

δυσ- ill- : O Ir. *du-*, Got. *tuz-* NHG. *zer-*, Sk. *dus-*.

δυσ-ηλεγής cruel : ἀλέγω.

δύσ-κηλος hopeless : κηλέω, on analogy of εὔ-κηλος.

δύσ-κολος unpleasant : κέλλω.

δυσ-πέμφελος stormy : πέμπελος shaking, Sk. *cancalas* moving, κέλλω. 27. 29.

δύστηνος wretched : δυσ- + ἵστημι. 35.

δύσ-χιμος terrible : χεῖμα, 'stormy'. 31.

δύω enter : Got. *taujan* do, Sk. *du* go, cf. δίεμαι.

δῶ (cf. βᾶ) δῶμα house : δέμω. 17.

δωμός = ζωμός, Laconian.

δῶρον palm : Ir. *dearna*, Lit. *delna* :

ε Interj. : Lat. *ei*.

ε himself : Lat. *sē*, O Ir. *fo-déine*, Got. *sik* Eng. *ba-sk bu-sk*, *si-lba* self Eng., O Slav. *sę* himself, Sk. *svas* one's own : ὁ. 32.

ἐανός fine : *Fεσ-αννός ἔννυμι. 17. So ἐανός robe, *Fεσ-ανός. 18. 34.

ἔαρ spring : *Fέσαρ, Lat. *vēr*, Welsh *gwianwyn*, O Nor. *vár*, Lit. *wásara* summer, Sk. *vasantas* spring. 33. 34.

ἰάφθη Il. xiii. 543 it was thrown : Sk. *vap* throw down, ἀποεπής. 18. 34.

ἐάω leave alone : *σεFάω, O Lat. *de-sivāre* cease. 33. 34.

ἕβδομος seventh : *ἕπτ-μος ἑπτά. 19. 2.

(ἔβενος ebony : Heb. *hobnīm*.)

ἐγ-γύη pledge : Lit. *gáuti* get, Zd. *gāo* hand.

ἐγγυ-θήκη stand : ἄγγος. 11.

ἐγγύς near : *ἐγγκύς, ἐνεγκεῖν, Got. *nehv* nigh Eng. 31. 35.

ἐγείρω wake : Sk. *gar* (cf. ἐθέλω ἐκεῖνος ἐμέ).

ἐγ-κάρσιος slantwise : Lat. *cerrītus*, Lit. *skersas*. 32. 11.

ἔγκατα entrails : *ἔγκστα, Lat. *exta*, Lit. *inkstas* kidney : 32. 2.

ἐγ-κοληβάζω Ar. Eq. 264 devour :

ἐγ-κομβόομαι am wrapt in : κόμβος band, Lat. *cingo*, Ags. *hōc* hook Eng., Lit. *kibti* stick fast. 27.

ἐγκονέω hasten : 'bend', ἀγκάλη.

ἐγ-κουράς painting on a ceiling :

ἐγκρίς pancake :

ἐγκυλιδωτός with a handle : ἀγκύλη = ἀγκάλη. 11.

ἐγ-κυτί close : Lat. *cutis*, Ags. *hȳd* hide Eng., σκῦτος. 32. 30.

ἔγχελυς eel : Lat. *anguilla*, O Ir. *esc-ongu* 'water-snake (?)', Ags. *ael* Eng., Lit. *ungurys*, ἔχις. 32.

ἐγχεσί-μωρος devoted to the spear : μέριμνα. So ἰό- σινά- ὑλακό-.

ἔγχος spear : O Slav. *nožĭ* sword, νύσσω. 24.

ἐγώ I : Lat. *ego*, Got. *ik* Eng., Lit. *asz*, cf. Sk. *aham* :

ἐδανός sweet :

ἔδαφος bottom, ἔδεθλον floor : οὖδας. 7.

ἔδνα ἔεδνα nuptial gifts : Welsh *dy-weddi* bride, Lit. *wedu* I marry, cf. Sk. *vadhutĭ* girl. 18. 1.

ἔδος seat : Lat. *sedeo sēdes*, O Ir. *sedait* sedent, Got. *sitan* sit Eng., Lit. *sėdėti*, Sk. *sad*. 18.

ἔδω eat : Lat. *edo*, Got. *itan* Eng., Lit. *ėdmi* I devour, Sk. *ad* eat.

ἐέλσαι = ἔλσαι, εἱλέω. 1.

ἔθειρα hair :

ἐθείρω till :

ἐθέλω wish : Got. *gailjan* rejoice Eng. *gallant*, Lit. *gailus* passionate, χαίρω (cf. ἐγείρω). 26. 25.

ἔθνος tribe, ἔθος custom : Got. *sidus*, Sk. *svadhā* : ἒ (cf. Lit. *suesco*) + τίθημι. 35.

εἰ if : Osc. *svai* Lat. *sei*, ἔ. 33.

εἶα εἶεν Interj. : Lat. *ēja*.

εἰαμενή meadow : *ἠσαμενή ἧμαι, 'low-lying'. 34.

εἴβω pour : false formation from δάκρυον εἴβων = δάκρυα λείβων, cf. αἶα. (Sayce.)

εἶδαρ food : *ἔδ-Fαρ, ἔδω. 17.

εἶδον saw : Lat. *video*, Got. *vitan* to watch, Lit. *weidas* sight, Sk. *vid* perceive. 33.

εἶθαρ forthwith : *ἔνθαρ, εὐθύς. 17.

εἰκῆ heedlessly : *ἐγκῆ, ἧκα, 'calmly'. 17.

εἴκοσι ἐείκοσι twenty : *Fει-κεν-τι (on analogy of τριά-κοντα, cf. Laconian βείκατι), Lat. *vīginti*, O Ir. *fiche*, Sk. *viçati* : δύο + δέκα. 33. 1. 22.

εἴκω yield : ἑκών. 33.

εἰκών image : Lit. *wykti* take place. 33.

εἰλαπίνη feast : *ἐFλαπίνη, ἐλπίς, Lat. *voluptas*. 1. 17. 24.

εἶλαρ shelter : *Fέλ-Fαρ, εἰλέω. 17.

εἰλεός colic : εἰλύω, 'turning'.

εἰλέω press : *Fελ-νέω, Ir. *fál* hedge, Got. *varjan* hinder, Lit. *wérti* to open, Sk. *var* cover, keep off. 33. 17. 25. Hence εἴλη troop, *ἐFλη, Lit. *walyti* collect. 1. 17.

εἴλη sunlight : *Fέλ-Fη, Got. *vulan* be hot, O Slav. *varŭ* heat, Sk. *ulkā* firebrand. 18. 17.

εἰλύομαι crawl, εἰλύω envelop : *ϜελϜω, Lat. *volvo*, Welsh *olwyn* wheel, Got. *af-valvjan* roll away Eng. *wallow*, Lit. *wóloti* revolve, Sk. *varas* circle. 33. 3. 23. 5.

εἶμα dress : *ἔσμα, ἕννυμι. 17.

εἱμαρμένη fate : ἔμμορε, μέρος. 4. 17. 11.

εἶμι go : Lat. *eo*, Got. *i-ddja* ivi, Lit. *eimi* I go, Sk. *i* go.

εἰμί am : *ἐσ-μί, Lat. *sum*, O Ir. *am*, Got. *im* Eng., Sk. *asmi*. 17.

εἰνάτερες sister-in-law : Lat. *janitrīces*, O Slav. *jętrŭvĭ* sister-in-law, Sk. *yātar:* 33.

εἵνεκα on account of : *Ϝέσνε-κα, ὠνή, 'at the price of'. 18. 17.

εἰνοσί-φυλλος leafy : ἔνοσις. 17.

εἷος while : *ἦ-Ϝος, ὅς.

εἰπεῖν to say : ἔπος.

εἴργω ἑέργω ἔργω shut out, shut in : Lat. *urgeo*, O Ir. *braig* chain (?), Got. *vrikan* pursue Eng. *wreak wretch*, Lit. *wargas* distress, Sk. *varj* press, exclude, cf. εἰλέω. 1. 33.

εἴρερος slavery : εἴρω A.

εἴρη assembly : *Ϝέρ-Ϝη, εἴρω B. So εἰρήνη peace, cf. ὄαρος. 17.

εἴρην ἱρήν youth : ἄρσην. 17.

εἶρος wool : Lat. *vellus*, Ir. *olann*, Got. *vulla* Eng., Lit. *wilna*, Sk. *ūrnam:* 'covering', εἰλέω. 33.

εἴρω A. fasten together : *ἔσρω, σειρά. 1. 17. 31.

εἴρω B. say, εἴρων dissembler : *Ϝέρ-jω, Lat. *verbum*, Got. *vaurd* word Eng., Lit. *wardas* name, Zd. *var* teach. 33. 17.

εἰς into : *ἐν-ς, ἐν (cf. ἐξ ἄψ). 17.

εἷς one ; *σέμ-ς, ἅμα. (ἑνός etc. from ἕν =*ἔμ, cf. χιών.) 18. 17.

ἴση equal : ἴσος. 1.

εἴσκω make like : *ἐϜίκ-σκω, εἰκών. 1. 35.

εἶτα then : Lat. *is*, Lit. *jis* he, + τό.

ἐκ out of : Lat. *ec- ex ē*, O Ir. *ass*, Lit. *isz*.

ἑκάς far : ἕ (cf. ἀνδρα-κάς), 'by oneself'.

ἕκαστος each : ἁ- (ἑ- on analogy of ἕν) + κοῦ, cf. Ir. *cách*.

ἑκατόν hundred : *ἑ-κεν-τόν, ἁ- (cf. praeced., cf. Sk. *sa-hasra* χίλιοι) + δέκα (cf. εἴκοσι), Lat. *centum*, Welsh *cant*, Got. *hund* Eng., Lit. *szimtas*, Sk. *çatam*. 10.

ἐκεῖ there, ἐκεῖνος he : Lat. *cis*, Got. *hina* this, Ags. Eng. *he*, Lit. *szis* this, καί κὲ (cf. ἐμέ).

ἕκηλος quiet, ἕκητι by means of : ἑκών.

ἔκ-παγλος fearful : πλήσσω. 35.

ἑκυρός father-in-law : Lat. *socer*, Welsh *chwegrwn*, Got. *svaihra*, Lit. *szészuras*, Sk. *çvaçuras:*

ἑκών willingly : Sk. *vaç* wish. 18.

ἐλαία olive, ἔλαιον oil (Lat. *olīva olīvum* = Got. *alev* oil Eng., Lit. *aléjus*) :

(ἐλασᾶς grosbeak, ἐλέα reedwarbler, ἐλεᾶς ἐλεός B. owl, ἐλειός ἐλειός B. falcon : foreign.)

ἐλάτη pine : Lat. *linter*, Lit. *lenta* plank. 1. 10.

ἐλαύνω drive : *ἐλα-νύω, ἔρχομαι. 25. 2. 17.

ἔλαφος deer : *ἔλνο-φος, Lit. *élnis* : 10.

ἐλαφρός light, ἐλαχύς small : Lat. *levis*, O Ir. *laigiu* smaller, Got. *leihts* light Eng., Lit. *lengwas* easy, Sk. *raghus* light, quick, ὀρχέομαι. 1. 25. 10. 27.

ἔλδομαι ἐέλδομαι wish : cf. ἦρα. 33. 25. 1.

(ἔλεγος lament : Phrygian? Hence ἐλεγῖνος a fish, cf. βόαξ.)

ἐλέγχω convict : Ir. *lochd* fault, ἐλαχύς, 'make light of'.

(ἐλεδώνη ἐλεδώνη polypus : foreign.)

ἐλεῖν to seize : αἱρέω. 18. 25.

(ἐλειός ἐλειός A. dormouse : foreign.)

ἐλελεῦ Interj. : ἀλαλαί.

ἐλελίζω shake : *ἐ-λε-λέγ-jω, Got. *laikan* leap, Lit. *laigyti*, Sk. *raj* be agitated. 1. 5. 11.

ἐλελί-σφακος sage :

ἐλένη basket :

ἔλεος pity :

ἐλεός A. board :

ἐλεύθερος free : Lat. *liber*, λίπτομαι, dialectic (cf. θήρ). 1. 12.

ἐλεφαίρομαι cheat : *ἐϜλεφαίρομαι, Lit. *wilbinti* allure. 1. 35. 24.

(ἐλέφας ivory, ἐλεφιτίς a fish : Heb. *aleph* bull.)

ἐλθεῖν to come : ἔρχομαι. 25.

ἐλίκη willow : Lat. *salix*, Ir. *sail*, Ags. *sealh* Eng. *sallow* : 18.

ἐλινύω rest : *ἐλεν-νύω, Lat. *lēnis lentus*, Got. *af-linnan* yield. 1. 11. 17.

ἐλίσσω roll : cf. εἰλύομαι. 18.

ἐλίχρυσος a plant : *ἐλικό-χρυσος, 'with golden tendrils'. 35.

ἔλκος wound : Lat. *ulcus*.

ἕλκω drag : Lit. *wilkti*, cf. ἀπαυράω. 18.

(ἐλλέβορος ἑλλέβορος hellebore : foreign.)

ἐλλεδανοί bands : *ἐϜλεδανοί, εἰλέω. 1. 19. 24.

ἐλλό-ποδες young animals : ἑλλός Adj., 'going softly'?

ἐλλός fawn : ἔλαφος. 19.

ἑλλός Adj. ἔλλοψ dumb :

(ἔλλοψ ἔλοψ sturgeon : foreign.)

ἕλμινς worm : Lat. *vermis*, Got. *vaurms* snake Eng. 18.

ἕλος marsh : Lat. *vallis*, O Nor. *völlr* field : εἰλέω, 'depression'. 18.

ἐλπίς hope : cf. ἔλδομαι. 33.

ἔλυμος A. millet :

(ἔλυμος B. flute : ἰάλεμος.)

ἕλωρ prey : ἐλεῖν.

ἐμβραμένα = εἱμαρμένη. 19. 24.

ἐμέ me: Lat. *mē*, Ir. *me*, Got. *mik* Eng., O Slav. *mę*, Sk. *mām:* cf. ἐγείρω.

ἐμέω vomit: Lat. *vomo*, O Nor. *vaema* nausea, Lit. *wémti* to vomit, Sk. *vam.* 33.

ἐμ-μαπέως quickly: μαπέειν.

ἐμ-πάζομαι care for: O Nor. *spakr* wise, O Slav. *paziti* attend. 32. 19.

ἔμ-παιος experienced: τίω. 27. 9.

ἔμ-πεδος sure: Ags. *fäst* fast Eng., πούς.

ἔμπης nevertheless: ἐν πᾶσι (cf. πύξ).

ἐμπίς gnat: Lat. *apis*, OHG. *imben* bees.

(ἐμύς ἐμύς tortoise: foreign.)

ἐν ἐνί in: Lat. Ir. Got. Eng. Lit. *in*, Sk. *antar.*

ἔν-αγχος lately: ἄγχι.

ἐναίρω destroy: ἀνύω (cf. Lat. conficio). Hence ἔναρα spoils, Sk. *sanara.* 33.

ἐν-αργής visible: ἀργός.

ἐν-δελεχής continuous: δολιχός. 7. 2.

ἔν-δῖος at noon: δῖος.

ἐν-δυκέως heartily: Hesych. δεύκει φροντίζει, δοκέω. 12.

ἐνεγκεῖν to bring: Lat. *nanciscor*, Lit. *neszti* carry, ἀνάγκη. 1.

ἐνενήκοντα ninety: Lat. *nōnāgintā*, *ἔν(ν)ε-νος ἐννέα cf. ἑβδομή-κοντα. 35.

ἐνεός dumb:

ἔνερθε beneath, ἔνεροι those below: νέρτερος (cf. ἀνακῶς). 1.

ἔνη Ar. Ach. 610 = ἦν.

ἐν-ηής gentle: ἠύς.

ἔνθα there: ἐν.

ἐνιαυτός year: sq. + ἔτος. 9. 23.

ἔνιοι some: Got. *anthar* other Eng., Sk. *anyas:* ἀνά, 'there'.

ἐν-ίπτω A. ἐν-ίσσω rebuke: ἶπος. 19.

ἐν-ίπτω B. relate: ἔπος, false resemblance to praeced.

ἐννέα nine: Lat. *novem*, O Ir. *nói*, Got. *niun* Eng., Pruss. *newints* ninth, Sk. *navan* nine: *ἐσνέα, νέος, 'the new number' after two quaternions. 1. 19. 34.

ἐννέπω say: *ἐν-(σ)Fέπω cf. ἔνισπε ἔσπετε, Lat. *insece signum*, Ir. *insce* discourse, Ags. *segan* say Eng., Lit. *sakyti.* 32. 19. 27.

ἔννηφιν perendie: *ἔνjη-φιν, ἔνος. 19.

ἐννοσί-γαιος earth-shaking: ἔνοσις. 19.

ἔννυμι clothe: ἐσθής. 18. 19.

ἐν-οπή cry: ὀγκάομαι. 27. 32.

ἔνος ἔνος old, ἔνη perendie: Lat. *senex*, Ir. *sén* old, Got. *sineigs* Eng. *sene-schal*, Lit. *sénas*, Sk. *sanas.* 33. 18.

ἔνοσις shaking: *ἔν-Fοθ-σις, ὠθέω. 35. 30.

ἔντεα armour, ἐντύνω prepare : ἀνύω.

ἕξ six : Lat. *sex*, Welsh *chwach*, Got. *saihs* Eng., Lit. *szészi*, Zd. *khshvas*, Sk. *shash* : 32.

ἔξ-αιτος choice : αἴνυμαι.

ἐξ-αμ-βρόσαι Aesch. Eum. 925 to bring out of : βλαστάνω.   35.

ἐξ-αμπρεύω haul out : ἄμπρος rope, ἄντλος.   27.

ἐξ-απίνης suddenly : ἄφνω.   2.

ἔξ-αστις selvedge : ἄττομαι.

ἐξ-αυστήρ flesh-hook : Lat. *haurio* (= *ausio), O Nor. *ausa* to pump.

ἑξῆς in order : ἔχω.   18.

ἐξ-ούλη ejectment : εἰλέω.   7. 17.

ἔοικα seem : εἰκών.   7.

ἐόλει troubled : εἰλέω.   34.

(ἑορτή ἔροτις festival : foreign, Pamphylian ἐϝοταις = ἑορταῖς.)

ἐπ-āλής sunny : ἀλέη.

ἐπ-ασσύτερος thronging : ἄττομαι.

ἐπ-αυρίσκω enjoy : ἀπ-αυράω.

ἐπ-είγω press : αἰγανέη.

ἐπ-εν-ήνοθε see ἀν-ήνοθε.

ἐπ-εντρώματα dainties :

ἐπή-βολος possessing : ἐπί (cf. ὑπερή-φανος), on analogy of παντί πάντη.

ἐπ-ηγκενίδες planks : ἐνεγκεῖν.   3. 24.

ἐπ-ηετανός abundant : αἰεί.   17.

ἐπ-ήρεια abuse : ἀρά, 'cursing'.

ἐπ-ητής courteous : ἀίω B., 'observant'.   17.

ἐπί on : Lit. *apé* around, Sk. *api* further, ἀπό.

ἐπί-βδā morrow : βαίνω.   6.

ἐπι-ζαρέω press on : βαρύς.   26.

ἐπι-ζάφελος violent : *ζάχ-ϝελος, ἀζηχής.   30. 27.

ἐπι-κάρσιος = ἐγ-κάρσιος.

ἐπι-κοκκάστρια mocker : κοκκο-βόας.

ἐπί-ξηνον block : ξέω.   17.

ἔπι-πλα furniture : πέλω (= ἐπ-όντα).   31.

ἐπί-πλοον caul, ἐπι-πολῆς superficiei : Lat. *pellis*, Got. *filleins* of leather Eng. *fell*, Lit. *plene* skin.   24.

ἐπι-ρράσσω burst on : ῥάσσω.

ἐπί-ρροθος helper, abusive : ῥόθος (cf. βοη-θόος).   19.

(ἐπίσειον ἐπίσιον pubes : al. ἐπείσιον, foreign.)

ἐπι-σκύνιον eyebrow : σκῦτος.

ἐπι-σμυγερός gloomy : Ir. *much* grief.

ἐπί-σσωτρον tire : σῶτρον felloe, σεύω.   19.

ἐπί-σταμαι know : ἵστημι, cf. Eng. under-stand.

ἐπ-ιτάρροθος helper : *ἰέναι* + *ῥόθος,* cf. *ἐπίρροθος.*

ἐπι-τηδές on purpose : *τείνω,* Lat. *intente.* 17.

ἐποποῖ ποποποῖ cry of hoopoe, *ἔποψ.*

ἔπος word : Lat. *voco vōx,* O Ir. *faig* dixit, OHG. *ga-wahan* mention, Pruss. *wákis* cry, Sk. *vac* say. 33. 27.

(ἔποψ hoopoe (French *huppe,* Eng.) : Hesych. *ἀπαφός,* Lat. *upupa, opunculo* a bird.)

ἑπτά seven : Lat. *septem,* Ir. *secht,* Got. *sibun* Eng., Lit. *septyni,* Sk. *saptan.* 18.

ἕπω prepare, ἕπομαι follow : Lat. *sequor,* Ir. *sechur* I follow, Lit. *sekti* follow, Sk. *sac.* 18. 27.

ἔρα-ζε to earth : Got. *airtha* earth Eng., *ἀρόω.*

ἔραμαι ἐράω A. I love, ἔρος ἔρως love, ἔρανος picnic : *ἀραρίσκω.*

ἐράω B. pour, see *ἀπ-εράω.*

ἔργον work, ἔρδω do : O Welsh *guerg* efficax (Rhys), Got. *vaurkjan* to work Eng., Zd. *varez* work, *εἴργω.* 33. 19.

(ἐρέβ-ινθος chick-pea : *ὄροβος.*)

(ἔρεβος darkness : Heb. *erebh* evening.)

ἐρέθω provoke : Lat. *in-rito,* Lit. *érzdinti* growl, *ἔρις.*

ἐρείδω lean : Lat. *ridica* prop. 1.

ἐρείκη heath : Ir. *froech :* 1. 35.

ἐρείκω tear, ἐρείπω dash down, ἐρέπτομαι graze on : Lat. *ringor rīma,* Welsh *rhych* furrow, O Nor. *rifa* to tear Eng. *rift,* Lit. *rěkti* cut, *ἁρπάζω.* 1. 17. 27.

ἐρέσσω row, ἐρετμόν oar : Lat. *ratis rēmus,* Ir. *iom-raim* I row, Ags. *rōvan* row Eng., *rōdor* rudder Eng., *ār* oar Eng., Lit. *irti* row, Sk. *aritar-* rower, *ἔρχομαι.* 1. 24. 19.

ἐρεσχελέω ἐρισχηλέω jest :

ἐρεύγομαι disgorge, roar : Lat. *ructo ē-rūgo rūmino,* Ags. *rocetan* belch, Lit. *rúgti.* 1.

ἔρευνα search : Got. *runa* mystery. 1.

ἐρέφω roof :

ἐρέω will say : *εἴρω* B.

ἐρῆμος lonely : Got. *arms* poor, Sk. *armakas* narrow. 1. 24.

ἐρητύω check : *εἰλέω.*

ἐρι- very : Ir. *ur,* *εὐρύς.* 33.

ἐριθάκη bee-bread : 'web', *ἐρῖθακίς* Theocr. 3. 35 = *ἔρῖθος* weaver.

ἐρίθακος ἐρῖθεύς redbreast : 'busy' at building a nest, sq.

ἔρῖθος labourer : Got. *ga-redan* apply oneself to, Lit. *ródas* counsel, *ἀλθαίνω.* 1. 24.

(ἐρῖνεός wild fig-tree : *ὄλυνθος.*)

ἔριον = *εἶρος.*

ἐρι-ούνιος helpful : *ὀνίνημι.* 3.

ἔρις strife : O Slav. *jarŭ* austere, Sk. *irasy* be angry, *ὄλλυμι.*

ἐρι-σφάραγος roaring : Ags. *sprecan* speak Eng., Lit. *sprageti* to rattle, Sk. *sphurj* hum : σφαραγέομαι (cf. Lat. fragor frango).

ἔριφος kid : O Ir. *heirp :*

ἐρι-ωλή hurricane : εἰλέω. 7.

ἕρκος fence : εἰλέω. 18.

ἕρμα A. support : Lit. *remti* to support. 4. 24.

ἕρμα B. Il. iv. 117 source : = ἀφορμή, ὁρμή. 7.

ἕρμαιον godsend : Ἑρμῆς.

ἑρμηνεύς interpreter : Lat. *sermo*, εἴρω A. 18.

ἔρνος shoot : Lat. *ornus*, Sk. *arnas* teak-tree, ὄρνυμι. 7.

ἔρομαι ask :

(ἔρπις wine : Coptic *ērp*.)

ἕρπω crawl : Lat. *serpo*, Sk. *sarp*, cf. ὁρμή. 18.

ἐρρηνο-βοσκός shepherd : ἄρνα. 1. 19. 24.

ἔρρω stray : ἐρύω, 'drag oneself about'. 19.

ἔρσαι young lambs : Hesych. ὄρσοι, ὄρρος, 'tail-end': popularly derived from sq., and so δρόσοι ψάκαλα. 4. 7.

ἔρση ἐέρση dew : Ir. *fras* a shower, Sk. *varshas* rain. 18. 1.

ἐρυθρός red : Lat. *ruber rūfus rōbus*, O Ir. *ruad*, Got. *rauds* Eng., Lit. *rudas*, Sk. *rudhiras*. 1.

ἐρύκω restrain, ἐρύομαι guard : εἰλέω. 1. 24. 35.

ἐρυσίβη mildew : Lat. *rūbīgo*, Ags. *rust* Eng., Lit. *rudis*, ἐρυθρός. 22.

ἐρύσιμον hedge-mustard : 'drawing blisters', ἐρύω.

ἐρυσί-πελας erysipelas : ἐρυθρός + πέλλα hide, ἐπίπλοον. 22.

ἐρυσί-χαιος with a staff : ἐρύω 'trail'+ χαῖος staff, Gallic *gaesum* spear Ir. *gái*, Ags. *gār* Eng. *gar-lic, to gore*. 34.

ἐρύω drag : Lat. *verro*, cf. ἀπαυράω. 33. 2. 34.

ἐρχατάομαι am cooped up : εἴργω. 29.

ἔρχομαι come : NHG. *eilen* hurry, Sk. *ar* go.

ἐρωδιός = ῥωδιός. 1.

ἐρωή A. impetus : Ags. *raes*, ῥώομαι. 1.

ἐρωή B. rest : Ags. Eng. *rest*, Sk. *ratis*, ἔραμαι. 1. 24.

ἔρως see ἔραμαι.

ἐρωτάω = ἔρομαι.

ἐσθής clothing : Lat. *vestis*, Welsh *gwisg* garment, Got. *vasti*, Sk. *vas* put on. 33.

ἐσθίω = ἔδω. 20.

ἐσθλός good : εἰμί, 'real'.

ἕσμα stalk, ἑσμός swarm :

ἕσπερος evening : Lat. *vesper*, O Ir. *fescor*, Lit. *wákaras*. 18. 27.

ἑστία hearth : εὕω. 18.

ἕστωρ peg :

ἐσχάρα hearth : NHG. *schart* frying-pan, Lit. *skarwada*, Sk. *kharas* hearth : Hence ἔσχαρος sole, 'fit for broiling'. 1.

ἔσχατος furthest : ἐξ. 24.

ἐτάζω examine : * (ἐ)σετάζω, εἰμί. 31. 33.

ἐταῖρος comrade : ἑτοῖμος.

(ἔτελις a fish : Lat. *attilus.*)

ἐτεός true : O Ir. *saith* treasure, Ags. *sōð* true Eng. *sooth*, Sk. *satyas*, ἐτάζω.

ἕτερος other : ἁ- (ἑ- as if from ἕν : Dor. ἅτερος, cf. Att. θάτερον.)

ἔτης clansman : O Slav. *svatŭ* connexion, ἕ. 33.

ἐτήτυμος = ἔτυμος. 5. 3.

ἔτι still : Lat. *et at-avus*, O Ir. *aith-scribend* rescriptum, Sk. *ati* over.

ἔτνος soup : O Ir. *ith* pulse : Sk. *yat* join, sq., (cf. ζωμός). 33.

ἑτοῖμος ready : Sk. *yat* join. 18.

ἔτος year : Lat. *vetus*, Lit. *wétuszas*, Sk. *vatsas* (and ἰταλός calf, Lat. *vitulus veterīnus*, Got. *vithrus* wether Eng.). 33.

ἐτός idly : Sk. *svatas* of oneself, ἕ. 33.

ἔτυμος = ἐτεός.

εὖ well : ἐΰς.

εὐ-ᾱγής clear : ἀγής.

εὐαί εὐάν Interj. : Lat. *euax.*

εὐ-δείελος = δέελος.

εὐ-διεινός εὔ-διος sunny : δέατο. 31.

εὕδω sleep : ἄστυ. 4. 24.

εὐ-θηνέω thrive : τίθημι.

εὐθύς straight : *σενθύς, Ags. *ge-sund* healthy Eng. *sound*, O Slav. *sądu* thereon, Sk. *sādhus* straight. 33. 17.

εὐθύ-ωρον straight :

εὔκηλος secure : ἔκηλος. 24.

εὐλάκᾱ plough-share : ἕλκω. 1. 23. 2.

εὐλή maggot : εἰλύω. 1. 23.

εὔληρα reins : Lat. *lōra*, εἰλύω, 'twisted'. 1. 23.

(εὔμᾱρις shoe : Persian ?)

εὐνή bed, εὐναί anchor-stones : Ags. *vunjan* dwell Eng. *wont*. 24.

εὖνις bereft : Got. *van* want Eng., Ags. *vanian* wane Eng., Sk. *ūnas* deficient. 24.

εὐοῖ = εὐαί.

εὐράξ Ar. Av. 1258 sideways : εὐρύς.

εὑρίσκω find : Ir. *fuaras* I found. 18.

εὖρος S. E. wind : εὕω, 'hot'.

εὐρύς wide : O Ir. *ferr* better, Sk. *urus* wide, *var* cover, εἶρος. 24.

εὐρώς mould : Sk. *var* cover, praeced. ?

ἐΰς = ἠΰς. 30.

εὖτε when : ἠΰτε (cf. εὖ ἠΰς). 30.

εὔχομαι vow : *εὖν-σκομαι, Ags. *vūsc* wish Eng., Sk. *vānch* to wish, cf. ὄνησις. 24. 32.

εὕω singe : Lat. *ūro,* Ags. *ysla* ashes, Sk. *ush vas* burn.　4. 24. 34.

εὐ-ωχέω entertain : ἔχω (cf. βρωμάομαι).

ἔφλαδον they burst : φλέω.　11.

ἐχε-πευκής sharp : πευκεδανός.

ἔχθος hatred :

ἐχῖνος hedgehog : NHG. *igel,* Lit. *ežys :*

ἔχις viper : Lat. *anguis,* NHG. *unke,* Lit. *angis :* 32.

ἔχραε assailed : χραίνω.

ἔχω hold : *σέχω (cf. ἕξω ἔσχον), Got. *sigis* victory, O Nor. *segl* sail Eng.
　'supporting the wind', Sk. *sah* to support.　35.

ἐψιά pastime : *jεκϜ-ιά, Lat. *jocus,* Lit. *jūkas* jesting, ἰάπτω.　18. 27. 22.

ἔψω boil : ἔπω.

ἐῶμεν Il. xix. 402 we be sated : *ἄομεν (cf. 'Ατρείδεω 'Ατρείδᾱο), ἆσαι.　4.

ἐώρα = αἰώρα.

ἕως A. = ἠώς.　4. 30.

ἕως B. = εἷος.　34.

ζα- very : διά.　19.

ζάγκλον sickle : διά + ἀγκάλη.

ζά-θεος sacred : θεός.

ζάκορος priest : διάκονος.　19. 30.

ζάλη spray : *ϝέλλη *ϝέσλη, ζέω.　10. 19.

ζα-χρηής violent : χραίνω.

ζάψ sea : βάπτω.　26.

ζάω live : *γ(Ϝ)ιαω βίος.　32. 19.

ζειά spelt : *jεϜ-ιά, Ir. *eo-rna* barley, Lit. *jáwas* corn, Sk. *yavas :* 34.

(ζειρά cloak : Thracian, Lat. *horreo,* Sk. *harsh* stiffen.)

(ζέλα wine : Thracian, χάλις.)

ζεύγνυμι yoke : Lat. *jungo,* Lit. *jungti* to yoke, Sk. *yuj,* cf. ζώννυμι.

ζέφυρος W. wind : ζόφος, 'from the dark quarter'.　7.

ζέω boil : Ags. *gaestan* bubble up Eng. *yeast,* Sk. *yas* bubble.　34.

ζῆλος rivalry : praeced., Dor. ζᾶλος cf. ζάλη.

ζημία loss : Sk. *yam* hold, restrain.

ζητέω seek :

ζητρεῖον prison : Hesych. ζητρός executioner, ζειά (cf. Lat. pistrinum).

(ζιγνίς lizard : foreign.)

ζόφος = δνόφος.　6.

ζυγία hornbeam : sq., 'fit for making yokes'.

ζυγόν yoke : Lat. *jugum,* Welsh *iau,* Got. *jukuzi* Eng., Lit. *jungas,*
　ζεύγνυμι.　31.

(ζῦθος beer : Egyptian.)

ζύμη leaven, ζωμός broth : Lat. *jūs,* Lit. *júsze,* Sk. *yūs, yu* bind.　17.

ζώννυμι gird : Lit. *jósta* girdle, Zd. *aiw-yâçtō* girt, cf. praeced.　19.

ζωντεῖον dungeon : ζάω, 'place of living'.
ζωρότερον stronger (of wine) : ζωμός, 'a better mixture'.

ἦ A. Interj.
ἦ B. = ἠέ (cf. ἥλιος ἦρι).
ἦ truly : Got. *ja* yea Eng., Lit. *je*, εἶτα. 33.
ἠβαιός = βαιός, for ἦ βαῖος.
ἥβη youth : Lit. *jėgti* be strong. 18. 27.
ἠγά-θεος holy : ἄγαν + θεός. 3.
(ἤγανον = τήγανον, cf. ἀνθρήνη.)
ἠγέομαι = ἄγω. 4. 30.
ἧδος pleasure, ἡδύς sweet : Lat. *suāvis*, Got. *suts* pleasant Eng., ἀνδάνω.
   33. 32.
ἠέ or : ἦ + Lat. *-ve*, Sk. *vā*. 34.
ἠέλιος sun : Cretan ἀβέλιος, ἠώς.
ἠερέθονται they wave : ἀείρω. 3.
ἠέριος early : ἠώς.
ἠθεῖος honoured : ἦθος.
ἠθέω filter : ἠθμός, ἵημι. 35.
ἦθος haunt, custom : ἔθος. 30.
ἥϊα chaff, provisions : *ἀϜέσια, Lat. *avēna* oats, Lit. *awižos*, Sk.
   avasam food. 17. 34. 31.
ἴθεος youth : 'un-married', ἰσθμός. 1. 3.
ἠϊόεις deep-mouthed (of a river), ἠϊών shore : Lat. *ōra* *ōs*, O Nor. *óss*
   mouth of a river, Lit. *osta*, Sk. *ās* mouth. 34.
ἤϊος archer : Sk. *āsas* bow, *as* throw, ὀστέον. 34.
ἦκα softly :
ἤκεστος fresh, ἀκή meeting-point : ἀκμή. 30.
ἥκιστα least : ἑκών εἴκω. 30.
ἥκω am come : ὠκύς. 4. 7.
ἠλακάτη distaff : Lit. *lanktis* reel, λέχριος, 'held obliquely'. 1. 3.
ἠλάσκω wander, ἠλεός distraught : ἄλη.
(ἤλεκτρον amber : Celtic, Scythian *sualiternicum* Plin. xxxvii. 11.)
ἠλέκτωρ sun : praeced.
ἡλιαία assembly : Dor. ἁλία, ἁλής.
ἠλίβατος lofty : Hesych. ἄλιψ rock : 3.
ἤλιθα = ἅλις. 33.
ἠλίθιος foolish :
ἥλιος = ἠέλιος. 4.
ἧλιξ comrade : ἕ.
ἧλος nail : Welsh *hoel* :
ἠλύγη darkness : λυγαῖος. 1. 17.

ἤλυθον came : ἔρχομαι. 25. 2.

ἧμαι sit : *ἧσ-μαι, Lat. *ānus āra,* Sk. *ās.* 4. 35.

ἠμαλάψαι to destroy : μάρπτω. 1. 25. 2.

ἧμαρ ἡμέρα day : Zd. *ayare,* ἰέναι (cf. τέκ-μαρ ἵ-μερος). 33. 18.

ἤμβλακον missed : ἀ- neg. + μάρπτω. 6. 19. 25. 24.

ἡμεῖς we : *ἀσμεῖς ἄμμες. 4. 17.

ἥμερος tame : ἧμαι.

ἠμί say, ἧ he said : *σαίνω, O Slav. *sę,* Sk. *sāman* song. 33.

ἡμι- half : Lat. *sēmi-,* Welsh *hanner,* Ags. *sām-,* Sk. *sāmi:* ὁμός, 'equal parts'. 18.

(ἡμιτύβιον cloth : Egyptian, Hdt. 2. 164 Ἑρμοτύβιες soldiers).

ἠμορίς lacking : ἀ- neg. + μοῖρα. 3.

ἧμος when : ὅς, cf. ἄ-μμες. 33. 17.

ἡμύω bow down : μύω. 1. 3.

ἤν Interj. : Lat. *en,* O Ir. *énde.*

ἠνεκέως continuously : ἐνεγκεῖν. 1. 3. 32.

ἡνία reins : O Slav. *po-jasŭ* girdle : 18. 17.

ἡνίκα when : *ἠ-νός ὅς, cf. αὐτίκα.

ἠνίπαπε he rebuked : ἐνίπτω A.

ἧνις yearling : ἀνύω.

ἠνορέη manhood : ἀνήρ. 1. 3. 7.

ἤνοψ bright :

ἤνυστρον stomach : ἀνύω, 'completing digestion'.

ἧπαρ liver : Lat. *jecur,* Welsh *iau* (Rhys), Lit. *jeknos,* Sk. *yakṛt,* ἴκτερος : 18. 27.

ἠπεδανός weak : ἤπιος.

ἤπειρος mainland :

ἠπερ-οπεύς deceiver : Got. *afar* after, Sk. *aparas,* ἀπό, + ὀπα.

ἠπήσασθαι mend :

ἠπιάλης nightmare, ἠπίαλος ague : 'weakening', ἤπιος.

ἠπίολος moth : Lat. *vappo,* Ags. *vifel* weevil Eng. (Lit. *wabalas* beetle): Ags. *väfer* unsteady. 33.

ἤπιος gentle : Lit. *opus* fragile.

ἠπύω call :

ἧρα kindness, ἤρανος friend : Got. *viljan* to will Eng., Sk. *var* wish. 33.

ἠρέμα gentle : Got. *rimis* peace, Lit. *ramas.* 1. 3.

ἦρι early : ἠέριος (cf. ἧ B.).

ἠρίον tomb : *Fηρίον : Sk. *var* cover εὐρύς?

(ἠρύγγιον ἠρίγγιον a plant : Gallic *arinca* rye, Ags. *ryge* Eng.)

ἥρως hero : Sk. *sāras* strength. 18.

ἥσυχος quiet : ἧμαι.

ἦτορ heart, ἦτρον abdomen : Ags. *ādre* vein, O Slav. *ǫtrova* belly, Sk. *antram* intestines. 17.

ἤτριον warp : ἅττομαι.

ἠΰς brave : Got. *avi-liud* grace, Sk. *avas* : ἀίω B., 'worthy of regard'.

ἠΰ-τε as : ἠέ *ἠϝέ. 23.

ἠχή noise : Lat. *vāgio.* 33.

ἠώς dawn : Aeol. αὔως, Laconian ἀβώ early : ἄημι, from the morning breeze, cf. Lat. *aur-ōra.* 17.

θαάσσω sit, θᾶκος seat : *θεϝάκ-jω, cf. τίθημι.

θαιρός hinge : θύρα. 32.

θαλάμη den, θάλαμος chamber : θόλος. 11.

θάλασσα sea : θράσσω. 2. 25. 19.

θαλλός branch, θάλλω flourish, θαλύσια first-fruits : χλιαίνω (cf. sq.). 26. 24.

θάλπω warm : τρέφω. 24. 11. 25.

θαμά thickly : θωμός, 'in heaps'. 11.

θάμβος amazement : *στάμφος, Lit. *stebëtis* be astonished, Sk. *stabh* stiffen, cf. Lat. *stupeo,* ἵστημι. 32. 19.

θάμνος bush : MHG. *tan* wood :

θάνατος death : Ags. *dvīnan* disappear Eng. *dwindle,* Sk. *dhvan* fall to pieces. 32.

θάομαι admire, θαῦμα wonder : *στάϝ-ομαι ἵστημι, cf. θάμβος. 32. 34. 23.

θάπτω bury : Welsh *dwfn* deep, Got. *diups* Eng., Lit. *dubus,* cf. τίθημι. 20.

θάρσος courage : Got. *ga-daursan* dare Eng., Lit. *drąsus* brave, Sk. *dharsh* be bold, cf. *dhar* hold, hold one's ground, θρῆνυς.

θέα sight : Dor. θάα cf. θηέομαι, θάομαι. 30.

θέειον θεῖον sulphur : *θεϝέσιον, θύω A. 34.

θειλό-πεδον drying-ground : θέρομαι. 3. 25.

θείνω strike : Ags. *dynt* blow Eng. *dint,* Sk. *dhanas* contest.

θεῖος uncle : Lit. *dëdas ;* formed from θεία aunt, θῆσθαι.

θέλγω charm : Got. *dragan* carry Eng. *draw,* Lit. *dryžóti* to touch, Sk. *dhranj* draw. 25. 20.

θελεμός gentle : θέλω χαίρω, 'pleasant'.

θέλυμνα foundations : στέλλω. 32.

θέλω = ἐθέλω.

θέμεθλα θεμείλια foundations : θεμόω.

θέμις law : Got. *doms* judgment Eng. *doom,* Sk. *dhāman* law, τίθημι.

θεμόω direct : Eng. *king-dom,* Sk. *dhāman* effort, τίθημι.

θέναρ palm of hand : OHG. *tenra* Ags. *denu* valley : θείνω (cf. ταπεινός), 'depression'.

θεο-πρόπος priest : *πρόκ-ϝος, Lat. *precor,* Got. *fraihnan* ask, Lit. *praszyti* beg, Sk. *praçnas* question. 27.

θεός god : φεός, cf. θέσ-φατος : 34.

θεουδής religious : *θεο-δδής δείδω. 17.

θεράπων servant : τρέφω. 24. 2.

θέρμος lupine :

θερμός warm : Lat. *formus*, Sk. *gharmas* warmth, cf. sq. 25.

θέρομαι grow warm, θέρος summer : Lat. *fornax furnus*, O Ir. *er-gorid* it bakes, O Slav. *goréti* be hot, χάρμη A. 26.

θέσκελος mighty, θεσπέσιος θέσπις divine : θεός + ἐννέπω. 35. 27. 31.

θεσμός law : τίθημι. 19.

θέσσασθαι pray for : θεός (cf. Lat. *veneror Venus*).

θέσφατος appointed : *θεσό-φατος, θεός + φημί.

θέω run : Sk. *dhav*, θύω A. 34.

θεωρός spectator : *θᾱο-ρός (cf. ἐῶμεν), θάομαι.

θήγω sharpen : Eng. *dagger*, Lit. *dégti* to sting.

θῆλυς A. female : θῆσθαι.

θῆλυς B. cold, loud : θάλλω.

θημών = θωμός. 7.

θήν surely : τίθημι.

θήρ = φήρ (dialectic, cf. θεὸς θλάω θοίνη θύλακος, ἐλεύθερος ψαθυρός).

θής labourer : Lat. *famulus*, τιθασός.

θησαυρός store : τίθημι.

θῆσθαι to milk : Lat. *felo femina*, Ir. *dith* suck, Got. *daddjan* suckle Eng. *dug*, O Slav. *doiti*, Sk. *dhā* suck.

(θῆτα Th : Heb. *teth.*)

θίασος procession : foreign ?

θιγγάνω touch : Lat. *fingo pollingo*, Got. *deigan* to mould Eng. *dough*, Sk. *dih* anoint. 20.

θίς heap : Ags. *dūn* hill Eng. *down*, cf. τίθημι.

θλάσπις cress : sq., its seed being bruised for a condiment.

θλάω θλίβω = φλάω φλίβω (cf. θήρ).

θνήσκω see θάνατος. 24.

θοίνη feast : Aeol. φοίνα :

θόλος vault : στέλλω. 32.

θολός mud : Ir. *dall* blind, Got. *dvals* dull Eng., Ags. *dvolme* chaos, Lit. *durmas* storm, 25.

θοός swift : θέω. 7.

θορός seed : Sk. *dhārā* drop, θέω.

θόρυβος tumult : τονθορύζω. 27.

θοῦρος furious : θολός. 17.

θρᾶνος = θρῆνυς.

θράσσω confuse : O Slav. *trézati* rend, Sk. *tarh* crush. 24.

θράττα a sea-fish : foreign ?

(θραύπαλος guelder-rose, θραυπίς θρυπίς goldfinch : foreign.)

θραύω break : Lat. *frustum fraus frustra*, Sk. *dhurv* bend.

θρέομαι cry :

θρεττανελό sound of lyre.

θρῆνος dirge : Got. *drunjus* a sound Ags. *drāne* drone Eng. cf. Hesych. θρώναξ, Sk. *dhran* sound, θρέομαι.

θρῆνυς bench : Sk. *dhar* support. 24.

θρησκεία worship : Sk. *dhar* keep up, praeced. ?

(θρίαμβος hymn (Lat. *triumphus*) : foreign, διθύραμβος.)

θριγκός cornice : Hesych. στριγχός, στραγγαλίς, 'pressing tight'. 32. 11. 20.

θρίδαξ lettuce : τρεῖς + ἀκίς, 'triply indented', cf. τετρ-ακίνη. 21.

θρίζω destroy : θραύω. 11.

θρῖναξ trident : τρεῖς *τρῖνός + ἀκίς. 21.

θρίξ hair :

θρῖον fig-leaf : τρεῖς, 'three-lobed'. 21.

θρίψ wood-worm : Lett. *tárps*: 21.

θρόμβος drop : Ags. *dropa* Eng., Lit. *dribti* to drop.

(θρόνα flowers : Hesych. τρόνα, Sk. *trna* grass.)

θρόνος = θρῆνυς. 24.

θρῡγανάω τρῡγανάω scratch at a door :

θρῦλος noise : θρέομαι.

θρύον rush, nightshade : στρύχνος. 32.

θρύπτω break : τρυφή. 24.

θρώσκω leap, θρωσμός uprising : Sk. *dhūr* move.

θυανία rutting, θυάω rut : θύω A.

θυγάτηρ daughter : *θύκτηρ, Got. *dauhtar* Eng., Lit. *dukte*, Sk. *duhitar-*, *duh* to milk, 'suckling'. 28. 2.

θυεία mortar, θυέστης pestle : θύω A.

θυία juniper : θύω B., 'used for incense'.

θυλάγροικος lege θῡμ-άγροικος.

θύλακος bag : Lat. *follis*, Ir. *bolg*, Got. *balgs* Eng. *bag bellows belly*, φλύκταινα (cf. θήρ). 2. 20.

θῡμάλ-ωψ hot coal : θύω A. *θύμαλος (cf. αἰγίλωψ) + ὦπα.

θύμβρα savory : τύφω. 24.

θύμος thyme : Lat. *fūmus*, Lit. *dūmas* smoke, Sk. *dhūmas*, θύω A.

θῡμός soul : Lit. *dumas* thought, θύω A.

θύννος θῦνος tunny : θύω A.

θυο-σκόος priest : θύω B. + Lat. *caveo cūra*, Got. *us-skavs* prudent Ags. *sceāvian* to look Eng. *shew*, ἀκούω κοέω. 34.

θύρα door : Lat. *fores*, Welsh *drws*, Got. *daur* Eng., Lit. *durrys*, cf. Sk. *dvār*: θύω A. (cf. Lat. *forum* court, Lit. *dwáras*; Zd. *dvara* door, palace ; Eng. wind-ow 'wind's eye').

θύρσος wand : στύραξ A. 32.

θύσανος tassel : sq. (cf. ἄωτος).

θόω A. rush : Lat. *sub-fīo*, Got. *dauns* smell Ags. Eng. *dust*, O Slav. *duchati* blow, Sk. *dhū* shake. So θύω B. θύω offer, 'cause smoke to rise'.

θωή penalty : τίθημι, cf. θέμις. 7.

θῶκος = θᾶκος. 8.

θῶμαι feast : θῆσθαι.

θῶμιγξ string : στήμων. 32. 8.

θωμός heap : τίθημι. 7.

θωνᾶσθαι to feast : θῶμαι.

θώραξ cuirass : Sk. *dhar* hold, θρῆνυς. 8.

θώς jackal, θωΰσσω cry :

θωχθείς drunk : θήγω. 8.

θώψ flatterer : τέθηπα, 'admirer'. 8.

ἴα one : Lat. *is*, Got. *is* he, Sk. *iyam* hoc, μίν.

ἰά voice : ἰωή.

ἰαί Interj.

ἰαίνω warm : Sk. *ish* animate. 34.

(ἰάλεμος dirge : Phrygian, O Nor. *jálmr* noise, ἔλυμος B.)

ἰάλλω send : Sk. *ish* set in motion, ἰαίνω.

ἴαμβος satire : ἐψιά ἰάπτω. 19.

ἰάομαι heal : ἰός B. 'potion' (cf. φάρμακον).

ἰάπτω send forth, assail (cf. βάλλω) : *ji-jáptω, Lat. *jacio*, O Nor. *jaga* move to and fro Eng. *yacht* NHG. *jagen* hunt. 5. 27.

ἰασιώνη convolvulus : Ἴασιος.

(ἴασπις jasper : Heb. *yash'pheh*.)

ἰατταταί ἰατταταιάξ Interj.

ἰαῦ Interj.

ἰαύω sleep : *Fι-Fα-ύω ἄημι, 'breathe, snore'. 5. 9.

ἰαχή cry : ἰά.

(ἴβις a bird : Coptic *hippen*.)

ἴγδις mortar : ἶπος. 19.

ἰγνύη ham : γόνυ. 1.

ἰδεῖν see εἶδον.

ἴδη wood :

ἴδιος private : ἕ. 33. 13.

ἰδνόομαι bend : ἰγνύη. 26.

ἶδος ἱδρώς sweat : Lat. *sūdo*, Welsh *chwys*, Ags. *svāt* Eng., Lett. *swīdri*, Sk. *svid* to sweat. 32. 33.

ἱδρύω ἵζω seat : ἕδος. 13.

ἵεμαι hasten : οἴσω. 18.

ἱέραξ hawk : foreign ?

ἱερός mighty, holy : Sk. *ishiras* strong, ἰαίνω. 4.

ἰεῦ ἰή Interj.

ἵημι send : Sk. *sāyakas* arrow. 5. 18. 34.

ἰθύς Subst. effort : ἵεμαι. 33.

ἰθύς Adj. straight : *εἰθύς εἰθαρ. 31.

ἱκανός sufficient : ἵκω. 30.

ἰκμάς moisture : NHG. *seihen* to filter, O Slav. *sīcati*, Sk. *sic* pour out. 33.

ἵκρια hatches : ἀκίς, 'pointed'. 13.

ἵκταρ near : ἴπος Lat. *ico* (cf. πλησίον πλήσσω).

ἵκτερος jaundice : Lat. *jecur*, ἧπαρ. 33. 13.

ἰκτῖνος kite : Armen. *tzin*, Sk. *çyēnas* hawk, sq., 'thief'. 1. 6.

ἰκτίς polecat : κτίδεος. 1.

ἵκω come : O Ir. *fecht* journey, Sk. *viç* enter. 18.

ἵλαος gracious, ἱλαρός gay : οὖλε. 18. 11.

ἵλη = εἵλη. 31.

ἵλιγγος dizziness : εἰλύω. 31.

ἱλλάς A. rope : εἰλύω, 'twisted'. 11.

(ἱλλάς B. ἱλιάς thrush : foreign.)

ἱλλός squinting, ἴλλω turn : εἰλύω. 11.

ἰλύς mud : ὑλίζω. 16. Hence ἰλυ-σπάομαι crawl : σπάω, 'go through the mud'.

ἱμάς thong, ἱμάσθλη whip, ἱμονία rope : Ir. *sin* collar, Ags. *sima* chain *sinu* sinew Eng., Lett. *sīt* bind, Sk. *sī*, cf. κασσύω. 18.

ἱμάτιον = εἷμα. 17. 11.

ἵμερος desire : *ἴσ-μερος, Sk. *ish* seek (= *ish* animate, ἰαίνω). 4. 17.

ἵνα where : ὅς (cf. τίνα).

ἰνδάλλομαι seem :

ἰνέω empty : εὖνις. 33. 11.

ἵνιον neck : ἴς muscle.

ἶνις son : Ags. *svān* swain Eng., υἱός. 33

ἴξ grub : ἴπος, 'harmful'.

(ἰξαλή goatskin, ἴξαλος leaper : foreign, al. ἰσάλη ἰξάνη ἰτθέλα.)

ἰξός birdlime : Lat. *viscum*, Ags. *veax* wax Eng., Lit. *wászkas*, ἴσκαι fungus, ἄσχιον. 33. 24.

ἰξύς waist : Lat. *viscera*, praeced. (cf. λαγών, λαπάρη, Eng. flank Lat. *flaccus*, NHG. *weiche* 'flank' *weich* 'soft').

ἰο-δνεφής dark : ἴον + δνόφος. 7.

ἰό-μωρος noisy : ἰά, see ἐγχεσί-μωρος.

ἴον violet : Lat. *viola* : 'fragrant', Sk. *vā* blow, breathe, ἄημι. 33. 12.

ἴονθος down :

ἰός A. arrow : Sk. *ishus*, *ish* set in motion, ἰάλλω.

ἰός B. poison, rust : Lat. *vīrus*, O Ir. *fī* poison, Sk. *vishas*, *vish* work. 33. 34.

ἰότης will : O Ir. *itu* thirst, ἵμερος. 34.

ἰοῦ Interj.

ἴουλος A. down : Sk. *vālas* hair, *var* cover εἶρος. 5.

ἴουλος B. centipede : εἰλύω. 5.

ἰόφ Interj.

(ἵπνον hippuris : ὕπνον.)

ἰπνός oven, lantern, dunghill : Got. *auhns* oven Ags. *ofen* Eng., Pruss. *umpnis* : 13. 27.

ἶπος weight, ἵπτομαι press : Lat. *ico*. 27.

ἱππο-κέλευθος driver : κέλλω.

ἵππος horse : EM. ἴκκος, Lat. *equus*, O Ir. *ech*, Ags. *eoh*, Lit. *aszwa* mare, Sk. *açvas* horse, ὠκύς. 4. 13. 27.   Hence ἱππο-φαές ἱππό-φεως euphorbia, φέως.

ἶρις lily :

ἴς muscle, strength : Lat. *vīs :* 'woven', ἰτέα. 33.

(ἰσάτις woad : Lat. *vitrum*, Got. *visdil* Ags. *vād* Eng.)

ἰσθμός isthmus : *Ϝιθ-θμός 'division', Lat. *viduus*, O Ir. *fedb* widow, Got. *viduvo* Eng., O Slav. *vĭdova*, Sk. *vidh* be empty of. 33. 20.

ἴσκε he spoke : θέ-σκελος. 5.

ἴσκω make like : *Ϝίκ-σκω, εἰκών. 31. 35.

ἴσος equal : *Ϝίσ-Ϝος, O Ir. *fiu* worthy, Sk. *vishu* on both sides. 33. 17.

ἴσσα Interj.

ἵστημι place : Lat. *sto sisto*, O Ir. *sessed* to stand, Got. *standan* Eng., Lit. *stóti*, Sk. *sthā*. 18.

ἱστίη = ἑστία. 13.

ἱστός mast, loom : ἵστημι, cf. στήμων. 5.

ἴστωρ knowing : οἶδα. 4. 20.

ἰσχάς dried fig, spurge, ἰσχνός thin : Lat. *siccus*, O Ir. *sesc* dry, O Slav. *i-secati* dry up, Zd. *hisku* dry. 33. 21.

ἰσχίον hip-joint : ἰξύς. 21.

ἰσχύς strength : ἴς + ἔχω. 31.

ἰτέα willow : Lat. *vītex*, Ags. *vīðie* withe Eng., Lit. *wytis*, Sk. *vītikā* bands : Lat. *vieo*, Welsh *gwden* withs, Got. *ga-vidan* bind, Lit. *wyti* twist. 33.

ἴτηλος fixt : = οὐκ ἐξίτηλος (ἰέναι) as δύσκηλος = οὐκ εὔ-κηλος.

(ἴτον = οὔιτον.)

ἴτρια cakes : ἐγκρίς.

ἴττυγα (Neut. Plur.) Aesch. fragm. 347 astounding :

ἴτυς rim : ἰτέα. 30.

ἰτώ note of hoopoe.

ἰύ Interj. : Hesych. ἀ-βίουκτον un-mourned, Lat. *vae*, Got. *vai* alas NHG. *wehe* Eng. *woe*. 33.

ἴφθιμος strong : ἶφι *ἶφις, ἴς (cf. Lat. *patrīmus*). 6.

(ἴφυον a plant : τίφυον, cf. ἀνθρήνη.)

ἰχθύς fish : Lit. *žuwis*, Armen. *tzwougn* : χέω, O Nor. *gjóta* to spawn. 1. 6.

ἴχνος track : Sk. *ikh* move.

ἰχώρ liquid : *ikmás*. 17. 29.

ἴψ = ἴξ. 27.

ἶψος ἰψός cork-tree : 'soft', *ἰξός*. 27.

ἰώ Interj. : Lat. *io*.

ἰωγή shelter : ἄγνυμι, 'where the force of the wind is broken'. 5. 8.

ἰωή sound : *Fι-Fω-ή, ἄημι. 5. 7.

ἰωκή ἰωχμός rout : ἰάπτω, 'swift movement'. 8. 32. 21.

(ἰῶτα I : Heb. *yod*.)

ἰωψ a fish : ἰάπτω, 'swift'?

κάβαισος glutton : foreign ?

κάγκανος dry :

καγχάζω laugh : Lat. *cachinnus*, OHG. *huoh* mockery NHG. *hohn* O Nor. *hegri* heron Eng., Sk. *kac* laugh. 29.

(κάδος jar : Heb. *kad*.)

(καδύτας dodder : Hesych. κασύτας, Syrian.)

καθαρός clean : Lat. *castus*, O Slav. *čistŭ*.

καί and : ἐκεῖ. 9.

καιάδας pit : κείω B. 9.

καικίας N.E. wind : 'dark', Lat. *caecus*, κοικύλλω. 9.

καινός new : Lat. *re-cens*, O Ir. *con* clear, O Slav. *po-činati* begin, Sk. *kanā* girl. 9.

καίνυμαι κέκασμαι excel : O Ir. *cáid* noble, Sk. *çad* distinguish oneself. 17. 19.

καίνω kill : Got. *hunsl* sacrifice Eng. *unhouseled*, Zd. *çāna* destruction. 9.

καιρόσεων Od. vii. 107 close-woven : καῖρος thrum :

καιρός proportion : κραίνω. 17.

καίω burn : Got. *heito* fever Eng. *hot heat*, Lit. *kaitra* heat.

κάκαλα walls : Ags. *hege* hedge Eng., Lit. *kinkyti* to yoke, Sk. *kanc* bind. 10.

(κακκάβη pot : Carian ἀλι-κάκαβον 'horse's head', Syrian κάκαβον pot.)

κακκαβίζω cackle : κικκαβαῦ.

κάκκη dung : Lat. *caco*, Ir. *cac*, Lit. *szikti* cacāre, Sk. *çakrt* dung. 6.

κακός bad : Got. *huhrus* hunger Eng., Lit. *kenkti* to hurt, Sk. *cakk* suffer. 10.

κάκτος cactus : foreign ?

κᾶλα logs : Lit. *kůlas* stake, Sk. *kīlas*, κλάω.

κάλαθος basket : κλώθω. 2.

καλάμη stalk, κάλαμος reed (Lat. *calamus*) : Lat. *culmus*, Ags. *healm* stalk Eng. *haulm*, O Slav. *slama*, cf. Sk. *çaras* cane.

(κάλαρις a bird : foreign.)

(καλάσιρις cloak : Egyptian *kelashir* armed with leather, Sayce.)

καλαῦροψ crook : κάλως + ῥέπω, 'thrown by a rope'. 9. 23.

καλέω call : Lat. *calāre concilium nomen-clātor clāmo*, Ir. *caileach* cock, OHG. *halon* call NHG. *holen* fetch.

καλιά hut : Lat. *cella*, Ags. *heal* hall Eng., Lit. *klḗtis* hut : Lat. *occulo cēlo clam*, Welsh *celu* to hide, Got. *huljan* to cover Eng. *hole hollow*, Lit. *klóti*.

(κάλιδρις = σκάλιδρις.)

καλινδέομαι roll : κυλίνδω. 11.

(κάλλαιον cock's comb : foreign, κάλαϊς turquoise γαλαΐζω am blue.)

(καλλαρίας cod : foreign, al. καλαρίας γαλαρίας.)

καλός beautiful : Got. *hails* sound Eng. *hale whole holy*, O Slav. *cělŭ*, Sk. *kalyas*. 17.

κάλπις pitcher : Sk. *karparas* pot :

καλύβη hut, καλύπτω cover : Lat. *clupeus*, O Slav. *po-klopŭ* cover, cf. καλιά. 2. 28.

κάλυξ seed-vessel : cf. καλιά.

καλχαίνω ponder : φύλαξ, Hesych. καχλαίνει ταράσσει, 'wakes'. 20. 5.

(κάλχη = κόχλος.)

κάλως cable : Hesych. κελλόν στρεβλόν, Lat. *cillo* move *colus*. 11.

κάμαξ vine-pole : Sk. *ksham* support, χαμαί. 32.

καμάρα covered carriage (Lat. *camera*) : Lat. *cumera camurus*, NHG. *himmel* sky Eng. *hammer-cloth* 'canopy', Zd. *kamara* vault.

καμασῆνες fish : foreign?

(κάμηλος camel : Heb. *gāmāl*.)

κάμινος furnace : O Slav. *kamina, kamenĭ* stone, ἄκμων (cf. Ir. áith 'kiln' πέτρος). 24.

(κάμμαρος crab : Macedonian, al. κάμαρος κομμάρα, NHG. *hummer*.)

(κάμμορον hemlock : OHG. *hemera* hellebore, κόμαρος.)

κάμνω work : Sk. *çam*.

κάμπη caterpillar : Lett. *kápe*, Sk. *kampanā, kamp* shake.

κάμπτω bend : Lat. *capero* wrinkle, Ir. *cam* crooked, Got. *hamfs* maimed, Lit. *kumpas* crooked.

(κάναβος wooden figure, κάναθρον carriage, κάναστρον dish, κάνειον lid, κάνεον basket, κάνης mat, κάνναι railing, κανών reed : Heb. *qāneh*.)

καναχή clang : Lat. *cano*, Ir. *canim* I sing, Got. *hana* cock Eng. *hen*, Lit. *kanklai* lyre, Sk. *kvan* sound. 32. 11.

(κάνδυλος a dish : Lydian.)

(κάνδυς = μανδύη, cf. κίνδος κράσπεδον : *κ(α)μάνδυς cf. μέλαθρον. Hence κανδύταλις clothes-press.)

(κάνθαρος A. beetle : Egyptian?)

(κάνθαρος B. = κύαθος.)

(κανθήλια pauiers, κανθήλιος pack-ass : Sk. *kandolas* basket.)

κανθός corner of the eye, κανθύλη swelling ('rounded'): Welsh *cant* rim of a circle.

(κάνναβις hemp (Eng.): Sk. *çanam*.)

καπάνη chariot (Thessalian):

κάπετος trench: σκάπτω. 32.

κάπη manger: κάπτω (cf. Eng. manger French manger 'eat').

κάπηλος huckster: Lat. *caupo cōpa* (Got. *kaupon* to traffic Eng. *cheap chapman*), Lit. *kupczus* merchant:

(καπίθη a measure: Persian, Sk. *kapatī*.)

καπνός smoke: Lat. *vapor*, ἀποκαπύω.

(κάππαρις caper: Sk. *çaparī* a plant.)

κάπρος boar: Lat. *caper* goat, Ags. *häfer*, O Slav. *veprĭ* boar: καπνός, 'rank'.

καπτήρ tube, κάπτω gulp down: 'seize', Lat. *capio*, Got. *hafts* joined, Lit. *czópti* seize, κώπη. 8.

καπυρός dry: ἀποκαπύω.

κάρ hair: κείρω. 11.

κάρα head: Lat. *cerebrum crīnis*, Sk. *çiras*: 11.

(κάραβος beetle, crayfish: Lat. *scarabēus*, Sk. *çarabhas* eight-legged monster.)

(κάρβανος foreign: Asiatic?)

(καρβάτιναι shoes (Lat. *carpatinae*): κρηπίς.)

(κάρδαμον cress: Sk. *kardamas* a plant.)

καρδία heart: Lat. *cor crē-do*, Ir. *cridhe*, Got. *hairto* Eng., Lit. *szirdis*, Sk. *çrad-dhā* believe, cf *hrd* heart. 11.

(κάρδοπος kneading-trough: χέδροπες, 'for kneading groats').

κάρηνον = κρανίον. 2.

(κᾱρίς κωρίς prawn: foreign.)

καρκαίρω ring: Sk. *karkarī* a musical instrument, κρέκω. 5. 11.

(κάρκαρον prison (Lat. *carcer*): foreign, γέργυρα.)

καρκίνος crab: Lat. *cancer*, Sk. *karkas*: 2.

κάρος torpor: Sk. *kalas* dumb.

καρπαία a dance, καρπάλιμος swift: Lat. *carpentum*, O Ir. *crip* swiftly, Lit. *krypti* to turn.

καρπός A. fruit: Lat. *carpo*, Ags. *herfest* harvest Eng., Lit. *kirpti* shave, σκορπίος. 32.

καρπός B. wrist: O Nor. *hreifi*, καρπαία, 'quick-moving' (cf. Eng. wrist writhe).

κάρτος strength: κραίνω.

(καρύκη sauce: Lydian.)

κάρυον nut: Lat. *carīna* nutshell, Sk. *karakas* cocoanut-shell.

κάρφος twig, κάρφω wither: κελεφός leper, NHG. *schrumpfen* shrivel Eng., Lit. *skrēbti* become dry. 32. 27.

καρχαλέος rough, κάρχαρος sharp: κερχαλέος. 11.

E

καρχήσιον goblet, mast-head : Καρχηδών (Sayce).

καρωτόν carrot : κάρα (cf. κεφαλωτόν).

(κασαλβάς κασαυράς κασωρίς whore, κασώριον brothel : Lat. *cāro* card, Lit. *kassyti* scratch, Sk. *kash*.)

(κάσας saddle : Persian.)

(κασία cassia : Heb. *q'tsī°āh*.)

κάσις brother : *κέμ-τις, Sk. *kam* love, κομέω. 10. 22.

(κασσίτερος tin (Sk. *kastīram*) : Assyrian *qizasaddir*, Oppert.)

κασ-σύω stitch : κατά + Lat. *suo*, Got. *siujan* sew Eng., Lit. *súti*, Sk. *siv*. 32.

(κάστανα chesnuts (Eng.) : Pontic, Lat. *corulus* hazel, Welsh *coll*, Ags. *häsel* Eng., Sk. *kashāyas* a tree.)

(κάστωρ beaver : Pers. *khaz* otter.)

κατά down : ποτί. 32. 15.

κατ-αῖτυξ helmet : ἄντυξ. 17.

κατα-πέλτης catapult : πάλλω.

κατ-άρης descending : αἰώρα.

κατα-σώχω rub : ψάω. 32. 8.

κατ-εν-ήνοθε see ἀν-ήνοθε.

κατ-έρεξε he touched : ὀρέγω.

κατ-ῆλιψ roof-beam :

κατ-ηφής downcast :

κάτ-οπιν behind : ὄπισθε.

κάτωρ Hom. Hymn. vii. 55 :

(καύηξ gull : καύης κῆυξ κήξ, Lit. *kōwa* daw, Sk. *kākas* crow, κωκύω.)

(καυκαλίς bur-parsley : καυκιάλης, foreign.)

καυλός stalk : Lat. *caulis*, Lit. *kaulas* bone.

(καννάκη rug : γαυνάκης, Persian.)

καυνός lot : Caunus in Caria.

καῦρος bad : Lat. *cavilla*, Sk. *kavāris* stingy. 23.

(καυσία hat : Macedonian, σκῦτος.)

καύχη boasting, καχάζω laugh : καγχάζω. 17. 32.

καχλάζω plash : χάλαζα. 5.

κάχληξ gravel : Lat. *calx* lime, Got. *skalja* tile Ags. *hagol* hail Eng., O Slav. *skala* stone. 5. 24. 32.

κάχρυς barley : κέγχρος. 10.

κέ in that case : ἐκεῖ.

κεάζω split : Sk. *kas*. 34.

κεάνωθος thistle : Sk. *kash* scratch κασαλβάς + ἄνθος. 34. 2.

κέαρ heart : false resolution of κῆρ on analogy of ἔαρ ἦρ.

(κεγχρηίς = κερχνήs.)

κέγχρος millet : Lat. *cicer*, Pruss. *kékirs* pea.

κεδάννυμι = σκεδάννυμι. 32.

κέδματα varicose veins :

κεδνός trusty :

(κέδρος cedar : Sk. *kadaras* mimosa.)

κεῖμαι lie : O Ir. *cae* house, Got. *heiva-frauja* οἰκοδεσπότης Eng. *hive*, Sk. *çī* lie.

κειρία cord : καιρόσεων. 9.

κείρω cut : Lat. *curtus*, Got. *hairus* sword, Lit. *kirwis* axe.

κείω A. go to bed : κεῖμαι.

κείω B. cut : Lat. *de-scisco*, Ir. *scian* knife. 32.

κεκαδών depriving :

κεκαφηότα gasping : Lat. *vapidus*, ἀποκαπύω. 29.

κεκρύφαλος = κρωβύλος. 5.

κέλαδος noise : Ags. *hrūtan* snort, Sk. *krand* roar. 25. 2.

κελαινός black : O Slav. *črŭnŭ*, Sk. *krshnas*: 25.

κελαρύζω murmur : Ags. *scral* sharp sound Eng. *shrill*. 32. 2.

κελέβη cup : κλωβός cage, καλύπτω.

κελέοντες loom-beams :

(κελεός κολιός woodpecker : foreign.)

κέλευθος path : Lat. *callis*, Lit. *kélas*, sq.

κελεύω κέλομαι A. urge, κέλης courser, κέλλω move a ship : Lit. *kélti* carry, Sk. *cal* set in motion.

κέλομαι B. = καλέω.

κέλῦφος husk : γλύφω. 32. 2.

κέλωρ son :

(κεμάς hind : κεμμάς κεμφάς, foreign.)

κέμμα lair : praeced.

κενέβρειον carrion : 'strong-smelling,' κοντλη savoury, Sk. *knūy* stink. 2.

κενεών flank, κενός empty : Sk. *çunyas*.

κεντέω prick (Ir. *cinteir* spur) : OHG. *hantag* fierce, πατάσσω.

κέπφος petrel : κόβαλος. 20. 6.

κεραΐζω plunder : κείρω.

κέραμος jar, κεράννυμι mix : Sk. *çar* cook.

κέρας horn : Lat. *cornu*, Ir. *corn*, Got. *haurn* Eng., Zd. *çrvā* :

(κέρασος cherry-tree (Eng.) : O Slav. *črěšinja*, κράνον.)

κεραυνός thunderbolt : Sk. *çarus* spear, *çar* break.

κέρδος gain : κραίνω.

κέρθιος tree-creeper : foreign ?

κερκίς A. rod for weaving : κρέκω weave. 24.

κερκίς B. aspen, κέρκος tail : Lat. *querquerus* shivering, Sk. *car* set in motion, κέλλω. 5. 25.

(κέρκουρος boat : Cyprian.)

κερτόμιος reproachful : Eng. *scold*. 32.

κερχαλέος rough, κέρχνος roughness : Welsh *cryg* hoarse.

(**κεφχνής** kestrel : foreign, κεγχρηῖs.)

κεσκίον tow :

κεστός embroidered : κεάζω.

κεύθω hide : Lat. *custōs*, Welsh *cuddiaw*, Ags. *hȳdan* Eng., σκῦτος. 32.

κεφαλή head : Got. *gibla* gable Eng., OHG. *gebal* skull : 20.

κεχλᾶδώς wantoning : χλαρός.

(**κῆβος** monkey (Eng. *ape*) : al. κῆπος κεῖπος, O Egypt. *kaf*, Birch.)

κῆδος care : κίνδυνος. 12.

(**κήθιον** box : κύαθος.)

(**κηκίβαλος** a shell-fish : foreign, popular etymology quasi κηκῑδο-βόλος.)

κηκίς juice : O Nor. *skaga* to project, Lit. *szókti* to spring, Sk. *khac* spring forth. 32.

κηλάς windy : κηλίς, ‘dark’.

κήλαστρον privet :

κηλέω charm : κωλύω. 8.

κήλη hernia : O Nor. *haull*, Lit. *kuila* :

κηλίς stain : Lat. *squālor*, O Slav. *kalŭ* clay, Sk. *kālas* black. 32.

κῆλον arrow : Sk. *çalyam* spear-point, κεραυνός. 25.

κημός muzzle : Sk. *çamyā* peg :

(**κήξ** = καύηξ.)

κῆπος garden : Lat. *campus*, Ags. *hōf* house Eng. *hovel :* 17.

κήρ death : Lit. *káras* war, κείρω.

κῆρ = καρδία, cf. παῖ(δ) ἄλλο(δ).

κηρός wax (Lat. *cēra*, Ir. *céir*) : Lit. *koris* honeycomb : Sk. *kar* pour out.

κήρυλος kingfisher :

κήρῡνος a throw of dice : foreign ?

κῆρυξ herald : Ags. *hrēd* fame, Sk. *kārus* singer, *kar* mention.

κῆτος sea-monster : Lat. *squātina* shark, Ags. *sceadd* shad Eng. : 32.

κητώεσσα full of hollows : κείω B.

κηφήν drone : κωφός. 7.

κῆχος tandem : Ion. κῆ = πῆ, cf. πολλα-χοῦ.

κηώδης fragrant : *κῆος incense, καίω. 17.

(**κίβδηλος** spurious : Heb. ?)

(**κίβισις** pouch, **κῑβωτός** box : Κιβωτὸς = Apamea in Phrygia.)

κιγκλίδες lattice (Lat. *cancelli*) : κάκαλα. 11.

κίγκλος wagtail : Lit. *kële*, κέλλω. 5.

κίδναμαι = σκίδναμαι. 32.

(**κιθάρα** lyre (Eng. *guitar*) : Semitic.)

(**κίκι** castor-oil plant : κόιξ.)

κίκιννος ringlet (Lat. *cincinnus*) : *κί-κεσ-νος, κόμη. 5. 11. 19.

κικκαβαῦ cry of screech-owl.

(**κίκκαβος** a coin : Lat. *ciccus*, Zd. *kaçu* small.)

κῖκυς strength : *κέγκυς, Lat. *cacula concinnus*, Ags. *on-hagian* to suit, Sk. *çak* be strong. 11. 17.

κιλλί-βαντες tressels (βαίνω), κίλλος ass :

κίμβιξ niggard : σκίφη. 32. 19.

κιμμερικόν gown : Κιμμέριοι.

(κινάβευμα = κάναβος.)

κινάβρα smell : κενέβρειον. 2.

κίναδος fox : κίνδυνος, 'annoying'. 2.

κινάθισμα rustling : κνάω, 'scratching'. So κίναιδος lewd (cf. κασαλβάς). 2. 17.

(κινάκη = ἀκινάκης.)

(κίνδος a herb : μίνδαξ, cf. κάνδυς.)

κίνδυνος risk : O Nor. *hitta* hit on Eng., Sk. *khidvan* oppressive, *khid* press, ὀνο-κίνδιος.

κῑνέω move, κῑνύσσομαι swing : κίω.

(κιννάβαρις τιγγάβαρι cinnabar : Pers. *zinjafr.*)

(κιννάμωμον cinnamon : Heb. *qinnāmōn.*)

κινυρός wailing : κνύος. 2.

(κιξάλλης footpad : Heb. *shālāl* steal.)

κίρκος hawk : κρίζω. 24.

κιρρός tawny : O Slav. *sěrŭ*, Sk. *çāras* variegated.

κιρσός varico-cele : κριξός :

κίς worm : Lat. *cossus*, Sk. *kash* rub κόμη. 12. So κισηρίς pumice.

(κίσθος κισθός cistus : κίστος, NHG. *heister* young stem, Zd. *çizhdra* prickly.)

κισσός ivy : *χεδ-jός, Lat. *hedera*, χανδάνω, 'clasping'. So κισσύβιον cup, 'capacious'. 24. 13. 19.

κίστη box : Lat. *quasillum quālum*, O Slav. *koš* basket.

(κίταρις tiara : Persian, Heb. *kether.*)

κίττα jay ('greedy'), craving : Hesych. κεῖσσα Laconian, *χεῖθ-ja, χατέω. 31. 20. 19.

κιχάνω κιγχάνω reach : κῖκυς. 11. 32. 29.

κιχήλᾱ κίχλη fieldfare : καχάζω, 'chirping'.

(κιχόρεια κιχώρεια chicory : foreign.)

κίω go : Lat. *cio cieo.*

(κίων pillar : Heb. *kiyūn* pedestal.)

κιών wart :

κλαγγή noise : Lat. *clango*, O Nor. *hlakka* to scream, Lit. *klegéti* laugh.

κλαδάσσομαι surge : κραδάω. 25.

κλάδος branch : κλάω, cf. κλῆμα κλών.

κλαίω weep : καλέω (cf. Eng. cry). 24.

κλάω break : Lat. *percello clādes*, Got. *halts* lame Eng. *halt*, Lit. *kálti* strike, Sk. *kar* injure.

κλείς = κληΐς. 30.

κλέος report : Lat. *inclutus*, Ir. *clú*, Lit. *szlówe* honour, Sk. *çravas* report, κλύω. 34.

κλέπτω steal : Lat. *clepo*, Got. *hlifan* Eng. *shop-lifter*, κρύπτω. 25.

κλήθρα alder :

κληΐς bar, key : Lat. *clāvis claudo*, O Ir. *clúi* nails, NHG. *schliessen* to lock Eng. *slot* bolt, O Slav. *ključi* key. 32. 34.

κλῆρος A. lot : κλάω, 'bit' of earth.

κλῆρος B. insect in beehives :

κλίβανος = κρίβανος. 25.

κλῖμαξ ladder : OHG. *hleitara* Eng., Sk. *ni-çrayanī,,* κλίνω.

(κλινό-τροχος Theophr. H. P. 3. 11. 1 maple : Macedonian, Ir. *cuileann* holly, Ags. *holegn* Eng., γλῖνος, + δρῦς.)

κλίνω incline : Lat. *in-clīno*, Ags. *hlinian* to lean Eng., Lit. *szlěti*, Sk. *çri*. Hence κλῖτύς slope, Lat. *clīvus*, Got. *hlains* hill.

κλισίη = καλιά. 24.

κλοιός collar : κλείς. 7.

κλόνις os sacrum : Lat. *clūnis*, Welsh *clun* hip, O Nor. *hlaunn* buttock, Lit. *szlaunis* hip, Sk. *çrōnis* buttock.

κλόνος throng : κέλλω. 24.

κλοτοπεύω deal subtly :

κλύζω wash : Lat. *cluo* purge *cloāca*, Got. *hlutrs* clean, Lit. *szlóti* sweep.

κλύω hear : Lat. *cluo*, Got. *hliuma* hearing Ags. *hlūd* loud Eng., *hlystan* listen Eng., O Slav. *sluti* be called, Sk. *çru* hear.

κλώζω hoot : κρώζω. 25.

κλώθω spin : κάλως. 24.

κλωμακόεις rocky : κλάω.

κνάπτω card wool : σκάπτω. 32. 24. Hence κνάφαλλον κνέφαλλον flock of wool.

κνάω scrape : Got. *hnasqus* soft, Lit. *knásyti* wallow. 34.

κνέφας darkness : *σκέμφας, cf. Lat. *crepusculum*, Sk. *kshap* night, σκέπας. 32. 24.

(κνῆκος thistle : κνηκός yellow, Sk. *kāncan* gold.)

κνήμη leg : Ir. *cnámh* bone, Ags. *hamma* ham Eng.

κνίδη nettle : Ags. *netele* Eng., κνίζω.

κνιζός exoletus : κίναιδος.

κνίζω sting : cf. κνάω.

κνίση smell, fat : *χνίθ-jη, Lat. *nīdor*, Sk. *gandhas* smell. 20. 17. 19.

κνίψ = σκνίψ. 32.

κνόος footfall : Lit. *knauti* to mew, Sk. *knū* utter a sound.

κνυζάομαι whine : Lett. *kungstét* to groan, Sk. *kunj*, cf. praeced. 24.

κνυζόω disfigure, κνύω scratch : cf. κνάω.

κνώδαλον monster, κνώδων tooth (on a spear) : Lat. *caesna cena*, Lit. *kāndu* I bite, Sk. *khād* chew, σκεδάννυμι. 32. 24.

κνώσσω sleep : *κνωγϝ-τjω, Ags. *hnāpian* Eng. *nap.*

κοάλεμος booby : Hesych. κόαλοι βάρβαροι :

κόαξ cry of frogs : Eng. *quack.*

κόβᾱλος rogue : *χόφ-ᾱλος, O Nor. *gabba* to mock Eng. *gabble gibberish gibe goblin jabber.* 20.

κόγχη mussel : Lat. *congius*, Welsh *cwch* boat (Eng. *coach*), Sk. *çankhas* cockle.

κόγχος pease-soup (Lat. *conchis*) :

κοδύ-μᾱλον quince : *κοδομό-μᾱλον, κοδομεύω roast barley, 'brown apple' : 35. 11.

κοέω perceive : Lit. *kawóti* watch, Sk. *kavis* wise, θυο-σκόος. 32. 34.

κόθορνος half-boot, κόθ-ουρος dock-tailed : Hesych. κοθώ βλάβη, Lit. *gadinti* to spoil, Sk. *gandh* injure. 20.

κοῖ cry of porker.

κοία ball :

κοικύλλω gape about : Lat. *caecus*, Ir. *caech* blind, Got. *haihs* one-eyed.

κοῖλος hollow : *κόϝιλος, κυέω. 34.

κοιμάω lull : κεῖ-μαι. 7.

κοινός common : Lat. *cum*, Ir. *con-* with. 17.

(κόιξ κόις palm : Egyptian.)

κοίρανος leader : κοέω (cf. ἀγρέω ἄγω.)

(κοκκάλια κωκάλια snails : foreign.)

κοκκο-βόας shrill, κόκκυξ cuckoo : onomatopoeic, Lat. *cucūlus*, Ir. *cuach*, Eng. *cuckoo cock*, O Slav. *kukavica*, Sk. *kōkilas.*

(κόκκος kernel of pomegranate : Lat. *cusculium*, ὕσγινον, cf. ὄγχνη.)

κόκκῡ quick : Interj.

(κοκκύ-μηλον damson : Heb.)

κολάζω punish : κόλος.

κόλαξ flatterer : Lat. *colo*, κέλλω. 7.

κολάπτω peck, κόλαφος buffet : σκαριφισμός. 32. 25. 2.

κολεόν κουλεόν sheath :

κολετράω trample on :

κολίας tunny :

κόλλα glue : Lit. *klijei* :

(κόλλαβος κόλλιξ κολλύρα cake : foreign.)

κόλλοψ A. screw of lyre :

κόλλοψ B. callus : Lat. *callus*, Sk. *çalkas* chip.

(κόλλυβος doit : Phoenician.)

(κολλυρίων κορυλλίων thrush : foreign.)

κολοβός stunted : Got. *halks* poor. 2. 27.

κολοιός daw : κορώνη A. 25.

(κολοιτέα κολουτέα κολυτέα a tree : Liparaean.)

(κολοκάσιον lotus : Egyptian.)

κολό-κῡμα swell, κολο-συρτός tumult (σύρω) : κλόνος.

κολοκύνθη gourd : 'rounded,' Lat. *culcita,* Lit. *kulka* ball, Sk. *kūrcas* cushion. 2.

κόλος stunted : κλάω. Hence κόλον great intestine, 'shorter' than the small.

κολοσσός statue : Lat. *cracens gracilis,* Ags. *hlanc* thin Eng. *lank,* Sk. *karç* grow thin. 2. 19.

κολοφών finish : κορυφή. 25.

κόλπος bosom : Ags. *hvealf* vault, Lit. *kilpa* hoop.

κολύβδαινα crab, κολυμβάω dive : κορυφή, cf. Hesych. κερανίξαι (κάρηνον) dive. 25. 32. 6.

κόλυθροι testicles : *σκόλυφροι (cf. ἐλεύθερος), ἀπο-σκολύπτω. 32.

κολώνη hill : Lat. *collis columen culmen celsus,* Ags. *hyl* Eng., Lit. *kálnas.* 2.

κολῳός brawl : κλόνος.

(κομαρίς = κάμμαρος.)

(κόμαρος arbute : Lit. *kěmerai* a plant, Sk. *kamalam,* κάμμορον.)

κομέω tend : κάσις.

κόμη hair : O Slav. *kosmŭ,* Sk. *kash* rub, shave, κασαλβάς. 35.

(κόμμι gum : Coptic *komē.*)

κομμόω decorate : κόσμος. 19.

κόμπος noise : κόπτω, 'clash'. 32.

κομψός elegant : Lit. *szwánkus* fine. 27.

κόναβος dim : καναχή.

(κόνδυ cup : Sk. *kundas* jug, see κυλίνδω.)

κόνδυλος knuckle : Sk. *kandas* lump.

κονίδες nits : Lat. *lendes* (= *cnendes), Ags. *hnitu* Eng., Bohem. *hnida:* 2.

κόνις dust : Lat. *cinis,* κνύω. 2. Hence κονί-σαλος dust, σάλος. 17.

κόνναρος privet : foreign?

κοννέω understand : κόσ-μος. 19.

κοντός pole : κεντέω. 7.

κόνυζα = σκόνυζα. 32.

κόπις babbler, κόπος toil, κόπτω strike : Lit. *kapóti* hew O Slav. *skopiti* castrate, Sk. *cap* grind. 32.

(κόππα Q : Heb. *koph.*)

κόπρος dung : O Slav. *koprŭ* dill, καπνός.

κόραξ raven : Lat. *corvus,* Ags. *hräfn* raven Eng., *hroc* rook Eng., O Slav. *krukŭ* raven, κρώζω. 2.

κόρδαξ = σκόρδαξ. 32.

κορδύλη swelling : Sk. *cūdas,* κορθύω (cf. αἰδώς).

κορδύλος = σκορδύλη. 32.

κορέω sweep : κρίνω.

κορθύω raise : κόρυς.

(κορίαννον coriander : foreign.)

κόρις bug : Sk. *cārikā* woodlouse : Lat. *curro*, Sk. *car* move, κέλλω.

(κόρκορος κόρχορος pimpernel : foreign.)

κορκορυγή tumult : κραυγή. 5. 2.

κόρος satiety : Lit. *szérti* feed.

κόρση temple : κρόταφοι. 24. 35.

κόρυζα catarrh : Ags. *hrot* mucus, Sk. *chard* pour, σκόροδον. 32. 2.

κόρυμβος κορυφή top : 'vertex', Got. *hvairban* turn about O Nor. *hvirfill* circle, top Eng. *whelm* (*whelfm) overturn *whirl*, κρωβύλος κύρβις. 2. 19. 32.

κορύνη club :

κόρυς helmet : Ags. *hreōdan* be covered, Lit. *krúva* heap.

κορώνη A. crow : Lat. *cornix*, κόραξ. 2.

κορώνη B. handle, κορωνός curved : κυρτός.

κόσκινον sieve :

κοσκυλμάτια scraps (Lat. *quisquiliae*) : σκύλλω, comic reduplication.

κόσμος order :

κοσταί a fish : foreign ?

(κόστος a spice : Sk. *kushtam.*)

(κότινος oleander : κύτισος.)

κότος wrath : O Ir. *cath* battle, Ags. *heador* fury, Sk. *çatrus* enemy, *çat* sever.

(κότταβος game of hitting the head of a puppet, κοττίς κοτίς head : foreign.)

(κόττυφος κόψιχος blackbird : O Slav. *kosŭ.*)

κοτύλη cup : Lat. *catīnus*, Got. *hethjo* chamber, Sk. *cat* hide.

κοῦ = ποῦ. 32.

(κοῦκι = κίκι.)

(κουράλιον coral : Sk. *kuruvilvas* ruby.)

κουρίδιος wedded, κοῦρος youth : κυρσάνιος. 17.

κοῦφος light : O Slav. *gybati* move. 20.

(κόφινος basket : Gallic *covīnus* wicker car.)

(κόχλος a shell-fish : κόλχος, κάλχη, foreign.)

κοχυδέω stream : Hesych. κοχύ πολύ :

κοχώνη breech : Lat. *coxa*, O Ir. *coss* foot, NHG. *hächse* inside of knee Ags. *hōh* heel Eng. *hock*, Sk. *kakshas* armpit.

(κράβυζος a shell-fish : κάραβος.)

(κράγγη = καρίς.)

κραδάω shake, κράδη branch : Welsh *cryd* ague, Lit. *sklandyti* waver, Sk. *kūrd* spring, cf. σκαίρω. 32.

κράδος blight :

κράζω I cry, κραυγή cry : Ags. *hringan* to sound Eng. *ring*, Lit. *krakti* roar. 28. 17.

κραια-ίνω κραίνω accomplish : Lat. *cerus* maker *creo*, Lit. *kurti* build, Sk. *kar* do. 24.

κραιπάλη nausea : cf. *κάρος*. 17.

κραιπνός = *καρπάλιμος*. 24. 17.

κράμβη cabbage ('with shrunken leaves'), **κράμβος** blight : *κάρφω*. 24. 19.

κρανάός rocky : cf. *κραταί-λεως*.

κρᾱνίον skull : Lat. *cernuus*, Got. *hvairnei*, *κράνος* (cf. Eng. skull O Nor. skál 'bowl').

κράνον cornel : Lat. *cornus* : 24.

κράνος helmet : *κέρνος* dish, O Slav. *čara* cup, Sk. *carus* kettle. 24.

κραπαταλός a fish : foreign ?

(**κράσπεδον** border : *μάρσιπος*, cf. *κάνδυς*.)

(**κράστις κρᾶστις** grass : al. *κράτις γράστις*, foreign.)

(**κράταιγος** thorn-tree : al. *κραταιόγονον*, foreign.)

κραταί-λεως rocky : Got. *hardus* hard Eng., + *λᾶας*. 24.

κρατενταί andirons :

κράτος = *κάρτος*, **κρατύς** strong *κρεντύς* cf. *κρείσσων* *κρέντ-jων*. 24. 10. 17.

κραῦρος rough : Lett. *krausét* thresh out. 35.

κρέας meat : Ir. *cárn* flesh, Got. *hraiv* corpse, Sk. *kravis* flesh : Lat. *crūdus*, Ags. *hreāv* raw Eng., Sk. *krūras*. 34.

κρειττόομαι have excrescences : *κροτώνη*. 17.

κρείων ruler : *κραίνω*. 9.

κρέκω make a noise by striking : *κράζω*.

κρεμάννυμι suspend : Got. *hramjan* crucify, Sk. *kram* climb.

κρέμβαλα castanets : Got. *hropjan* to cry Ags. *hearpe* harp Eng., O Slav. *skrŭstati* neigh, Sk. *kharj* creak, *σκερβόλλω*. 32. 27.

κρέξ a bird : Lit. *kurka* turkey, *κράζω*.

κρήγυος good : *κραίνω*, cf. *μεσση-γύ*.

κρήδεμνον veil : *κάρα* + *δέω*.

(**κρῆθμον** samphire : al. *κρίθμον*, foreign.)

κρημνός cliff : *κρώμαξ κλῶμαξ* heap of stones, *κλωμακόεις*. 25.

κρήνη spring : *κάρηνον* (cf. Lat. caput).

κρηπίς boot (Lat. *carpisculus*) : Welsh *crydd* shoemaker, Lit. *kurpe* shoe : *σκορπίος*, 'of cut leather'. 32. 24.

κρησέρα sieve : Lat. *cribrum*, Ags. *hriddel* Eng. riddle, *κρίνω*.

κρησφύγετον retreat :

κρίβανος oven : Got. *hlaibs* bread Eng. *loaf*, Lit. *klëpas* loaf, Sk. *çrapanā* kitchen, cf. *κεράννυμι*. 28.

κρίζω creak, laugh : Got. *hlahjan* Eng., *κράζω*. 11.

κρῑθή κρῖ (cf. *βᾶ*) barley : *χερσδή*, Lat. *hordeum*, NHG. *gerste*, *χρίω*. 24. 32.

κρίκος ring : Ags. *hring* Eng., *κυρτός*. 24. 5.

κρίμνον meal, κρίνον lily ('champion, defiant'), κρίνω separate: Lat. *cerno,* Ir. *scaraim* I separate, Got. *skeirs* clear, Lit. *skirti* to separate. 32. 24.

κρῖός A. ram : Lat. *cervus* stag, Ags. *heorot* Eng. *hart,* κέρας. 24. 34.

(κριός B. vetch : Lat. *cracca.*)

κροαίνω stamp : κρότος κείρω.

κρόκη pebble : O Ir. *cloch* stone, κάχληξ. 25.

κροκόδειλος κροκύδειλος lizard : 'yellow-necked', sq. + δειρή.

(κρόκος saffron : Heb. *karkōm.*)

(κροκόττας hyena : Indian.)

κρομβόω toast : κάρφω. 24. 19.

κρόμμυον κρόμυον onion : Ir. *creamh* wild garlic, Ags. *hramse* Eng. *ramsons,* Lit. *kermusze:* 19. 35.

κρόσσαι battlements, κρόταφοι temples : Sk. *kūtas* top, jug. 19.

κρότος noise : 'stroke', κείρω. 24.

κρότων κροτών tick, palma Christi (with seed like a tick) : κόρις. 24.

κροτώνη excrescence on trees : Lat. *crātes,* Welsh *clwyd* hurdle, Got. *haurds* door Ags. *hyrdel* hurdle Eng., O Slav. *krętati* bend, Sk. *kart* spin. 24.

κρουνός spring : κρήνη, Aeol. κράννα. 8. 17.

(κρούπαλα κρούπεζαι sabots : κρηπίς.)

κρούω strike : Ags. *hrēran* stir up Eng. *up-roar.* 34.

κρυμός frost : Ags. *hrim* Eng. *rime,* Lit. *szarma,* Sk. *çaras* cream.

κρύος frost, κρύσταλλος ice : Lat. *crusta,* Ir. *cruaidh* hard, Ags. *hrūse* earth, Lit. *krusza* hail. 34.

κρύπτω hide : Ags. *hrōf* roof Eng., καλύπτω. 25.

κρωβύλος top-knot : κορυφή. 24. 28.

κρώζω caw : Got. *hrukjan,* cf. κράζω.

κρωμακίσκος porker :

κρωπίον bill-hook : καρπός. 24.

κρωσσός pitcher : κρόσσαι. 24.

κτάομαι acquire : O Slav. *skotŭ* κτῆνος, Sk. *kshatram* dominion. 6.

κτείνω kill : Got. *skathis* harm Eng. *scathe,* Sk. *kshan* injure. 6.

κτείς comb : ξαίνω. 6.

κτίδεος of weasel-skin :

κτίζω found, κτίλος tame : O Slav. *po-čiti* to rest, Sk. *kshi* dwell, κτάομαι. 12.

κτύπος noise : κόμπος. 6. 14.

κτώ = ὀκτώ (cf. μίν σκορακίζω).

(κύαθος cup : foreign, κάνθαρος κήθιον κώθων.)

κύαμος bean, κύανος a blue metal : Lat. *caesius caeruleus caelum,* Ags. *haeven* blue *heofon* sky Eng. *heaven,* Lit. *szémas* grey, Sk. *çyāmas* dark.

κύαρ hole : κυέω.

κυβερνάω steer (Lat. *guberno*) : Lit. *kumbriti*, Sk. *kŭbaras* pole.

(**κύβηλις** axe : foreign.)

κυβιστάω tumble : E M. *κύβη* head, cf. Sk. *kumbhas* top.

κύβιτον elbow : Sicilian, Lat. *cubitum*, *κύπτω*.

κύβος die : Got. *hups* hip Eng. *hip hoop hump*, cf. *κύπτω*.

κυδάζω revile : O Slav. *kuditi*, Sk. *kud* lie. Hence **κυδοιδοπάω** (*δοῦπος*) make a noise, **κυδοιμός** uproar. 32.

(**κύδαρος** a ship : foreign.)

κῦδος renown :

κυέω conceive : Lat. *cavus cumulus inciens*, Sk. *çvi* swell. 31.

κυκάω mix : Lat. *cochlear* spoon, Ags. *sceacan* shake Eng. 32.

κυκλάμῖνος cyclamen : sq., 'with tuberous root'.

κύκλος circle : Ags. *hveogel* wheel Eng., O Slav. *kolo*, Sk. *cakras* : 14.

κύκνος swan (Lat. *cygnus*) : Sk. *çakunas* bird :

κυλίνδω roll : Sk. *kundas* (=*kulndas*) top, jug. 2.

κύλιξ bowl (Lat. *calix*) : *κάλυξ*. 11.

κύλλαρος = *σκύλλαρος*. 32.

(**κύλλαστις** spelt-bread : Egyptian.)

κυλλός = *σκολιός*. 32. 11.

κυλ-οιδιάω have swollen eyes : *κύλα* eyelids, Lat. *cilium*, *καλιά*, + *οἰδέω*. 11.

κῦμα wave, embryo : *κυέω* (cf. *οἶδμα*).

κύμβαλον cymbal, **κύμβαχος** prone, **κύμβη** pigeon ('tumbler'), boat, **κυμβίον** cup : *κυβιστάω*. 32.

κύμινδις night-jar (Ionian) :

(**κύμῖνον** cumin : Heb. *kammōn*.)

κυνέη helmet : *κυέω*.

κυνέω kiss : Sk. *cūsh* suck. 35.

κύπαιρος κύπειρος galingale : *κάπτω*, 'fodder'. 14. 9.

(**κυπάρισσος** cypress, **κύπρος** A. a tree : Heb. *kōpher*.)

(**κύπασσις** frock (Lat. *capitium*) : Persian, *κάπτω*, 'capacious'.)

κύπελλον cup, **κύπρος** B. four gallons : Lat. *cūpa* (Eng. *cup*), *κάπτω*. 14.

(**κυπρῖνος** carp (Eng.) : Sk. *çapharas*.)

κύπτω stoop, **κῦφός** stooping : Lat. *cubo incumbo*.

(**κυρβαίη** porridge : Egyptian ?)

(**κυρβασία** cap : Persian, sq.)

κύρβις pillar : *κορυφή*. 11. 28.

κυρέω meet : *κέλλω*. 11.

κυρηβάζω butt : *κρωβύλος*. So **κυρήβια** bran, 'tops' of the stalks. 2.

κυρίσσω butt : *σκυρίπτω*, cf. *σκορπίζω*. 32. 11. 2.

κυρκανάω mix : Pruss. *birga-karkis* basting-ladle.

κῦρος authority : O Ir. *caur* hero, Sk. *çūratā* fortitude, *κυέω*.

κυρσάνιος youth :

κύρτη weel : Pruss. *korto* enclosure, Sk. *katas* wickerwork, κροτώνη. 11.

κυρτός curved : Lat. *curvus cortina circus*, O Ir. *curu* gyros, Lit. *kreiwas* crooked, σκολιός. 32. 11.

κύσθος cunnus, κύσσαρος ānus, κύτταρος a hollow : Lat. *cunnus*, Sk. *çushis* a hollow.

κύστις bladder : Lat. *gutta*, Sk. *çcut* drip. 20.

(κύτινος calyx of pomegranate, κύτισος clover : foreign.)

κύτος hollow : κυέω.

(κύχραμος ortolan : foreign, al. κέχραμος κίχραμος κιγκράμας.)

κυψέλη box, κύψελος sand-martin ('building in holes') : κύμβη.

κύων dog : Lat. *canis*, Ir. *cu*, Got. *hunds* Eng. *hound*, Lit. *szŭ*, Sk. *çvan-* : κυέω, 'prolific'.

κῶας fleece : σκῦτος. 32.

(κωβιός gudgeon (Lat. *gōbio*, Eng.) : Sicilian κῶθος : 'big-headed', κύβη, cf. κέφαλος mullet.)

(κώδεια κωδύα head of a plant : al. κώδη κώδιξ, foreign.)

(κώθων = κήθιον.)

κωκύω howl : Lit. *kukti*, Sk. *ku*. 5.

κώληψ hollow of the knee, κῶλον limb : κλάω (cf. μέλος). 8.

κωλύω hinder : Lat. *calvor*, Got. *holon* deceive.

κωλώτης = ἀσκαλαβώτης.

κῶμα sleep : κάμνω, cf. οἱ καμόντες.

(κώμακον a spice : Indian ?)

κώμη village : Got. *haims* Eng. *home*, Lit. *kaimas*, κτάομαι. 8.

κῶμος revel (in honour of a god) : Got. *hazjan* to praise.

κώμυς ὁ reed-bed, ἡ sheaf :

κώνειον hemlock : Lat. *ci-cūta* :

κῶνος cone : Lat. *cuneus*, Ags. *hāne* stone Eng. *hone*, Sk. *çānas* grindstone. Hence κών-ωψ gnat (ὦπα), 'with projecting eyes'.

κώπη handle, oar : Ags. *häft* haft Eng., κάπτω.

(κώρυκος sack : Cilician.)

κωτίλος chattering : O Nor. *hád* mocking, Lit. *katillinti* to chatter, Sk. *katth* brag.

κωφός dull : κεκαφηότα (cf. τυφόομαι). 8.

κωχεύω carry : Lat. *cunctor*, Got. *hahan* perplex Eng. *hang*, Sk. *çank* doubt ('move oneself about').

κά'ψ = σκώψ. 32.

λᾱ- very : λάω B.

λᾶας stone : Ir. *ail*, Lit. *ûla* rock. 24.

λάβρος furious : Lat. *rabo*, Sk. *rabh* seize, ἀλφηστής. 28.

(λαβρώνιον cup : Pers. ?)

(λάβυζος a spice : Indian ?)

(λαβύρινθος maze : foreign.)

λάγανον cake, λαγαρός thin, λαγγάζω slacken, λάγνος lewd, λαγών flank
(cf. ἰξύς), λαγώς hare : Lat. *langueo laxus lēna*, Ir. *lag* weak (Eng. *to
lag*), Ags. *släc* slow Eng. *slack*, Sk. *lanjā* adulteress. 32.

(λάγυνος flagon (Lat. *lagēna*) : λάγηνος, foreign.)

λαγχάνω obtain : O Slav. *po-lǫčiti.*

λάζομαι seize : Ags. *läccan* Eng. *latch*, O Slav. *lŭžica* forceps, Sk. *lag*
touch. 19.

λάθυρος pulse : foreign ?

λαῖαι stones : λᾶας.

λαίθ-αργος cur :

λαικάζω = ληκάω.

λαῖλαψ whirlwind : λαιψηρός. 5.

λαῖμα throat, λαιμός throat, greedy : λαμυρός. 17.   Hence λαίμ-αργος
greedy :

λάιος thrush : λᾶας, 'breaking snail-shells on a stone'.

λαιός left : Lat. *laevus*, Got. *slavan* be quiet Eng. *slow*, O Slav. *lěvŭ* left.
32. 34.   Hence λαι-σήιον shield, 'brandished in the left hand', σείω
(cf. ζεί-δωρος).

λαισ-ποδίας bow-legged :

λαῖτμα abyss :

(λαῖφος = λῆδος.)

λαιψηρός swift : ἀρπάζω. 25. 17. 24.

(λακάρη philyrea : foreign, al. λακάθη λατάρη.)

λακέρυζα noisy : λακερός λάσκω.

λακίς rent : Lat. *lacer*, ῥάκος. 25.

λάκκος pit : Lat. *lacus*, Ir. *loch* lake, Lit. *lanka* water-meadow : λέκος,
'hollow'. 11. 6.   Hence λακκό-πεδον scrotum, πέδη.

λαλαγέω babble, λάλος babbling : Lat. *lallo*, NHG. *lallen* to babble
Eng. *lullaby*, Lit. *lalloti*, onomatopoeic.

λαμβάνω = λάζομαι. 27.

(λάμβδα L : Heb. *lamed.*)

λάμια shark, λαμυρός greedy :

λάμπη scum : ὄλπις. 32. 24.

(λαμπήνη chariot : ἀπήνη, foreign.)

λάμπω shine : Lat. *limpidus*, O Nor. *leiptr* lightning, Lit. *lĕpsna* flame,
λευκός. 11. 27.

λανθάνω escape notice : cf. Lat. *la-teo*, Sk. *rah* abandon.

λάξ with the foot : O Nor. *leggr* leg Eng., Lett. *lĕkt* to spring. 11.

λᾱός people : Ags. *leō-d*, O Slav. *lju-dŭ* :

λαπάζω plunder, λάπαθον sorrel ('aperient'), λαπαρός loose λαπάρη flank (cf. *ἰξύs*), λαπάσσω empty : Lit. *alpti* weaken, Sk. *alpas* small. 24.

λάπη phlegm : λάμπη. 32.

λαπίζω whistle : σαλπίζω. 32. 24.

λάπτω lap : Lat. *lambo labium labrum*, Ags. *lapian* to lap Eng., *lippe* lip Eng. (Lit. *lúpa*). 19.

λᾱ-ρῑνόs fat : ῥινόs, 'well covered'.

λάρκος basket, λάρναξ chest : Got. *snorjo* basket, νεῦρον, 'plaited'. 19. 11.

λάρος gull : O Nor. *liri* black tern :

λᾱρόs pleasant : λάω B. 17.

λάρυγξ throat : NHG. *slurc*. 32. 2.

λάσανα gridiron : foreign ?

λάσθη insult : O Nor. *last* blame, λάω B., 'sporting, mocking'.

λάσιος hairy : *Ϝλά-τιος, Ir. *folt* hair, O Slav. *vlasŭ*, Zd. *vareça*, εἶρος. 32. 25. 24. 22.

λάσκω cry : *λάκ-σκω, Lat. *loquor*, Got. *laian* revile (=*laihan), Lit. *rĕkti* to cry. 11. 35.

λάσταυρος lewd : λάω B.

λάταξ splash, otter ('splashing') : Lat. *latex :*

λάτος a fish : foreign ?

λάτρις hireling (Lat. *lătro*) :

λαυκανίη throat : Lit. *pa-laukys* dewlap, λύγξ B. 9.

λαύρα lane : Lat. *lūra* mouth of sack, λύω, 'opening'. 9.

λάφῡρα spoils : ἀλφάνω. 24.

λαφύσσω devour : λάπτω.

λαχαίνω dig : Lat. *ligo* rake, Ir. *laighe* spade. Hence λάχανα pot-herbs.

λάχεια low : O Nor. *lágr* Eng., λέχος. 11.

λαχμός λάχνη down : O Slav. *vlakno* hair, cf. λάσιος. 32. 21.

λάω A. devour : ἀπολαύω. 34.

λάω B. desire : Lat. *lascivus*, Ir. *air-le* counsel, O Slav. *laskati* flatter, Sk. *lash* desire. 34.

λεβηρίs skin, λέβηs kettle : Lat. *liber* bark, *labrum* vessel, λαμβάνω, 'containing'. 11.

λεβίαs λέβιον a fish :

λέγνον edge :

λέγος = λάγνος. 11.

λέγω A. lull, see λέξαι.

λέγω B. collect, detail, say : Lat. *lego*, Got. *rikan* collect Eng. *rake*. 25.

λεία ληίη booty : Sk. *lōtas*, ἀπολαύω. 30. 34.

λείβω pour : Lat. *lībo dē-lībūtus*.

λεῖμαξ λειμών meadow : Lit. *léija* valley, λιάζομαι. 31.

(λειμόδωρον λιμόδορον dodder : Semitic.)

λεῖος smooth : Lat. *lēvis :* 34.

λείπω leave : Lat. *linquo,* O Ir. *lécim* I let go, Got. *af-lifnan* remain Eng., Lit. *likti,* Sk. *ric* to empty. 27.

(λείριον lily : Lat. *līlium,* Pers. *lāla.*)

λειχήν lichen :

λείχω lick : Lat. *lingo,* Ir. *lighim* I lick, Got. *bi-laigon* lick Eng., Lit. *lëszti,* Sk. *lih.*

λέκιθος ὁ pulse : βράκανα. 32. 25.

λέκιθος ἡ yolk : λογχάδες. 32. 20.

λέκος dish : Lat. *lanx,* λέχριος.

λέκτρον bed : Got. *ligrs* Eng. *lair,* λέχος. 19.

λελιημένος eager : λιλαίομαι. 35.

(λέμβος galley : Illyrian.)

λέμνα a water-plant :

λέμφος driveling : ἀλείφω.

λέξαι to lull : Got. *ligan* lie Eng., O Slav. *ležati,* λέχος.

(λέπαδνον collar : *λάπαδνον λαμπήνη.)

λεπάζω cook, λέπας bare rock, λεπάς limpet (Eng. : 'peel, rind, shell'), λέπω peel : Lit. *lupti* to shell, ἁρπάζω. 25.

(λέσχη meeting-place : Heb. *lishkhah* assembly-room.)

λευγαλέος wretched : Lat. *lūgeo,* Lit. *luszti* burst, Sk. *ruj* break.

λευκός bright : Lat. *lūceo lūx,* Ir. *luachair* brightness, Got. *liuhath* light Eng., Lit. *laukas* pale, Sk. *ruc* shine. Hence λεύσσω see, Lit. *laukti* to watch (cf. εἶδον Welsh gwyn 'white'). 19.

λευρός smooth : λύω, 'open'. 31.

λεύω stone : λᾶας. 30.

λέχος bed : Lat. *lectus,* Ir. *lige.*

λέχριος slanting : Lat. *licinus ob-līquus,* Lit. *lenkti* bend. 21.

(λέων = λῖς.)

λέως wholly : λάω B., 'à volonté'. 30.

λήγω cease : λαγγάζω.

(λήδανον gum-mastick : Heb. *lōt,* Lat. *lentiscus.*)

(λῆδος mantle : Lat. *lōdix.*)

λήιον crop : ἀπολαύω. 34.

λήιτον town-hall : λαός.

ληκάω fornicate :

λήκυθος oil-flask :

λήμη rheum : MHG. *ulmic* rotten, Lit. *elmes* excretion, Sk. *armas* ophthalmia. 24.

ληνός trough :

λῆνος wool : Lat. *lāna,* εἶρος. 32. 25. 24.

λῆρος nonsense :

λιάζομαι retire : 'bend', Lat. *lituus*, Sk. *li* cringe. Hence λιαρός gentle, 'yielding'.

λίαν λί (cf. βᾶ) overmuch : O Slav. *lichŭ*, praeced., 'crooked, excessive'.

(λίβανος frankincense : Heb. *l'bhōnāh*.)

λιβυός a bird : Λιβύη?

λίγδην scraping, λίγδος mortar : Lat. *līma*, Sk. *likh* scratch. 19.

λιγνύς smoke : λυγαῖος. 16.

λίγξε twanged, λιγύς shrill :

λίθος stone : Ags. *leād* lead Eng., cf. λᾶας.

λικμάω winnow, λίκνον basket : Lit. *nĕkóti* winnow. 20.

λικριφίς sideways : λέχριος. 13.

λιλαίομαι = λάω B. 5.

λιμήν harbour, λίμνη lake : 'cavity', λιάζομαι (cf. λάκκος).

λῑμός hunger : Lat. *lētum*, Lit. *leilas* thin.

(λίνδος an aromatic plant : λήδανον.)

(λίνον flax : foreign, cf. λῑν-οπτάομαι, Lat. *līnum*.)

(λίνος dirge : αἴλινος, Heb. *hĕlil-nā* 'weep,' beginning of dirge for Tammuz (Sayce).)

λῑπαρής earnest : λίπος, 'sticking to it'. 17.

λιπερνής desolate : *λίπερος λείπω.

λίπος fat : Lat. *lippus*, Lit. *lipti* to stick, Sk. *lip* smear.

λίπτομαι am eager : Lat. *lubet*, Got. *liubs* dear Eng. *love lief believe*, Lit. *lúbiti* to love, Sk. *lubh* feel desire. 11. 19.

(λῖς lion : Heb. *layish*.)

λίς (cf. βᾶ) λισσός λίσπος smooth : λιτός. 19.

λισσάνιος good (Laconian) : λιτή, 'entreated.'

λίστρον hoe : Lett. *līst* to weed.

(λῖτα cloth : Lat. *linteum*, λίνον.)

λιτ-αργίζω hurry away : λιάζομαι + ?

λιτή prayer : Lat. *lito*, λιάζομαι, 'flectere deos'.

λῑτός plain : λεῖος. 31.

λιτο-υργός wicked : 'doing crooked things', λιάζομαι + ἔργον.

λίτρα pound : Sicilian, Lat. *libra* : τλῆναι, cf. τάλαντον.

(λίτρον = νίτρον.)

λίψ S.W. wind : λείβω, 'rainy'. 31.

λοβός A. pod : Lett. *lóbs* shell, λεβηρίς. 7.

λοβός B. lobe of ear : Lat. *lābor*, Ir. *lobar* weak, Got. *sliupan* slip Eng., Ags. *läppa* fringe Eng. *lappet limp*, O Slav. *slabŭ* weak, Sk. *lamb* hang down. 32.

λογγάζω = λαγγάζω. 7.

λογχάδες whites of the eyes :

(λόγχη spear-head : Celtic, Lat. *lancea*, O Ir. *laigen* spear, O Slav. *lǫšta*.

F

λοιγός ruin : Lit. *ligga* illness.

λοίδορος abusive : λάσθη (cf. αἰδώς). 17.

λοιμός plague : λύμη. 34.

λοῖσθος last : Got. *lasivs* weak, Lit. *lésas* thin.

(λόκαλος a bird : foreign.)

λοξός slanting : Lat. *luxus* dislocated, Ir. *losc* lame, λέχριος. 7.

λοπάς plate, disease of olives, oyster : λέπω.

λορδός bent : MHG. *lerz* left.

λοῦσσον pith of fir :

λούω bathe : Lat. *lavo ad-luo*, Ir. *lunae* to wash, O Nor. *laug* bath Eng. *lather lye*. 23.

λοφνία torch : λύχνος. 27.

λόφος neck : O Nor. *lypta* lift Eng., O Slav. *lŭbŭ* skull.

λόχος ambuscade : λέχος, 'lying in wait'. 7.

λῡγαῖος dark : Ags. *volcen* cloud Eng. *welkin :* Ir. *fliuch* wet, Lit. *wilgyti* to wet. 32.

λυγίζω twist, λύγος wand : Lit. *lugnas* bending.

λύγξ A. lynx : Ir. *loisi* foxes, Ags. *lox* lynx, Lit. *lúszis* :

λύγξ B. hiccough : O Ir. *slocim* I swallow, NHG. *schlucken* swallow. 32.

λυγρός = λευγαλεός. 31.

λύθρον gore : Lat. *lutum pol-luo*, λούω (cf. ῥύπος.) 31.

λυκά-βας year : λεύσσω + βαίνω, 'path of light'. 31.

λύκος wolf : Lat. *lupus* Sabine *hirpus*, Ir. *brech*, Got. *vulfs* Eng., Lit. *wilkas*, Sk. *vrkas*, ἕλκω. 32. 24.

λῦμα disgrace, λύματα dirt, λύμη outrage : λύθρον.

λύπη pain : Lat. *rumpo*, Ags. *reáfian* despoil Eng. *bereave*, Lit. *rūpét* curae esse, Sk. *lup* break, ἁρπάζω. 25.

(λύρα lute : Semitic ?)

λύσσα rage : Got. *in-rauhtjan* be angry, Lit. *rústus* angry, Sk. *ruç* be angry. 25. 19.

λυχνίς lychnis ('bright'), λύχνος lamp : λευκός. 31. 21.

λύω loosen : Lat. *re-luo so-lvo*, Got. *lausjan* Eng., Lit. *láuti* cease, Sk *lū* cut.

λώβη outrage : Lat. *lābes*, λοβός B. (cf. Lat. *cāsus*.) 30.

λωίων better : ἀπολαύω. 8.

λώπη robe : λέπω (cf. Ags. scrūd 'garment' screadian 'to cut' (Eng shroud shred), O Slav. rabŭ 'rag' rabiti 'to cut'.) 7.

λωτός clover : λήιον. 8.

λωφάω relieve : ἐλαχύς, 'lighten'. 27.

μά by : μέν.

μᾶ = μαῖα (cf. βᾶ).

(μάγαδις harp, flute : Lydian.)

(μαγγανεύω juggle : μάγγανον engine (Eng. *mangonel mangle*), Italian μαγγάνα wine-cask.)

μάγειρος cook : μάσσω, 'confectioner'. 28.

(μάγος wizard : Persian.)

(μαγύδαρις seed of silphium : foreign.)

μαδάω lose hair : Lat. *madeo māno mamma* breast *mulier*, O Slav. *mǫdo* testicle. Hence

μαδωνία water-lily : Sk. *madanas* a plant.

μαζός cod, breast : Ir. *mas* buttock. 19.

μᾶζα barley-bread : μάσσω. 19.

μαῖα mother : onomatopoeic. Hence μαιεύομαι deliver.

μαιμάω rage : μένος. 5. 17.

μαινίς sprat :

μαίνομαι rage : μένος. 9.

μαίομαι = μαστεύω. 34.

μάκαρ rich, μακρός long : Lat. *macte macto* honour, Zd. *maçita* great, cf. μέγας μῆχος.

μά-κελλα pick-axe : μόνος + κέλλω, cf. δί-κελλα.

μακκοάω moon : onomatopoeic, Lat. *maccus*, Eng. *mock mope*.

μάλα very : Lat. *multus*, Lett. *milns* much. 11.

μαλακός soft : Lat. *mulceo mulco*, Sk. *març* to smooth, cf. ἁμαλός. 11. 2.

μαλάχη μολόχη mallow : Lat. *malva* (Eng.) : μαλάσσω, praeced., 'emollient'.

μάλευρον flour : μύλη A. 11.

μάλη = μασχάλη. 35.

(μάλθα wax : Heb. *melet* mortar.)

μαλθακός soft : Got. *milditha* mildness Eng., Sk. *mardh* neglect, cf. ἁμαλός.

(μαλινα-θάλλη (θαλλός) a plant : Egyptian.)

μαλλός wool : Lit. *millas* woollen stuff :

μάμμη mother : Lat. *mamma* mother, Welsh *mam*, Eng. *mamma*, Lit. *mama*, μαῖα.

μάνδαλος bolt ('hindrance'), μάνδρα stall ('stopping-place': Eng. *madrigal* 'shepherd's song') : Lat. *menda mendīcus*, Got. *ga-motjan* meet Eng., O Slav. *mŭdlŭ* slow, Sk. *mand* linger, cf. μένω. 11.

(μανδραγόρας mandrake (Eng.) : μαδωνία, quasi ἀνδρ-αγόρας, ἀγείρω.)

(μανδύη cloak : κάνδυς, Persian.)

(μάνης statuette : Got. *manna* man Eng., Sk. *manus*, μένος.)

μανθάνω learn : Lat. *meditor medeor*, Welsh *meddwl* mind, Got. *mundon* consider, Zd. *madha* wisdom, cf. μένος. 11.

(μάννα a gum : Heb. *man*.)

μανός loose : *μαν-Ϝός cf. μάνο-στήμων, Lat. *mancus*, Sk. *manāk* a little. 17.

μαντίλη pot (Lat. *matula*) : Lit. *menturre* whisk, ἄμοτον μάτη ματτύη, cf. μόθος.

μάντις prophet : μένος, 'thoughtful'. 11.

μαπέειν seize : μάρπτω. 10.

μάραγνα whip : Hesych. σμάραγνα, σμαραγέω. 32.

μάραθον μάραθρον fennel :

μαραίνω destroy : Lat. *morior morbus*, Ir. *marbh* dead, Got. *maurthr* murder Eng., Lit. *mirti* die, Sk. *mar* crush, die, μύλη. 11. Hence μαρ-αυγία loss of sight, αὐγή.

(μαργαρίτης pearl : Sk. *manjarī*.)

μάργος mad : cf. μάρπτω, 'greedy.'

μάρη hand, μάρις a measure : cf. μάρπτω.

μαριεύς inflammable stone, μαρίλη embers, μαρμαίρω flash, μάρμαρος crystal (Lat. *marmor* Eng. *marble*), μαρμαρυγή flashing : Lat. *merus*, Sk. *marīcis* ray. 11. 5.

(μαρῖνος = σμαρίς.)

μάρναμαι fight : O Nor. *merja* crush Eng. *mar*, μαραίνω.

μάρον sage :

μάρπτω seize : Hesych. βράξαι συλλαβεῖν, cf. μαλακός. 27.

(μάρσιπος pouch (Lat. *marsupium*) : κράσπεδον, Persian.)

μάρτυς witness : μέριμνα. 11.

μασάομαι chew : Lat. *mando* chew, Got. *mats* food Eng. *meat* : μαδάω, 'moisten'. 35.

μάσθλη = μάστιξ.

(μάσπετον leaf of silphium : μεσπίλη.)

μάσσω knead : Lat. *mācero*, Ags. *mengian* mingle Eng., Lit. *minksztas* soft. 10.

μάσταξ mouth, locust, μασταρύζω mumble, μαστιχάω gnash the teeth, μαστίχη mastich (for chewing) : μασάομαι.

μαστεύω seek :

μάστιξ whip : *σμάστιξ, cf. ἱμάς. 32.

μαστός = μαζός.

(μαστροπός leno : Lat. *masturbor*, Heb. *misht°ārib* strongly mingling.)

μασχάλη arm-pit : μόσχος, 'mesh' of muscles. 11.

ματεύω seek : Lit. *matyti* see.

ματέω tread on : Welsh *mathru* to tread, Lit. *minti*, Sk. *carma-mnas* tanner ('hide-treader').

μάτη folly : O Ir. *madae* vain, Got. *missa-deds* misdeed Eng. *miss*, O Slav. *mętą* I confuse.

μάτιον measure : μέτρον. 11.

(μᾱτρυλεῖον fornix : μαστροπός.)

(ματτύη hash : Macedonian, μαντίλη.)

(μαυλιστήριον fee : Hesych. μαῦλις leno, Lydian.)

μαυρόω obscure : μῶλυς. 25.

μάχαιρα knife, μάχη battle : Lat. *macellum dī-mico macto* kill *mucro*, Ir. *mactadh* slaughter, O Slav. *mĭčĭ* knife (Got. *meki* sword.) 29.

μάχλος lewd : Pruss. *manga* meretrix, Sk. *makhas* lively.

μάψ idly : ἐμ-μαπέως.

μὲ = ἐμέ.

μεγα-κήτης huge : χανδάνω, as though from κῆτος.

(μέγαρον hall : Μέγαρα, Phoen. *māgūr* habitation (Lat. *māgālia*), Sayce.)

μέγας great : Lat. *magnus*, O Ir. *do-for-maig* auget, Got. *mikils* much Eng., Ags. *macian* make Eng., Lit. *magóti* to help, cf. μακρός.

μέδιμνος a measure : Lat. *modius modus*, Got. *mitan* to measure Eng. *mete.*

μέδομαι think of, μέδω rule : μήδεα A. 30.

μέζεα = μήδεα B. 6.

μέθη strong drink, μέθυ wine : O Ir. *med*, Ags. *medu* mead Eng., Lit. *middus*, Sk. *madhu.*

μειδάω smile : Lat. *mīrus*, OHG. *smielan* smile Eng., Lett. *smĭt* to laugh, Sk. *smi* smile. 32.

μείλια gifts : O Slav. *milo* dowry, sq.

μείλιχος gentle : Lat. *mollis*, Lit. *mylěti* to love. 17.

μείραξ girl : Lit. *marti* bride, Sk. *mānavas* boy : 17.

μείων less : Sk. *mi* diminish.

μελάγ-χιμος black : μέλας, on analogy of δύσ-χιμος.

μέλαθρον rafter : EM. κμέλεθρον, Zd. *kameredha* head, καμάρα. 32. 25.

μέλας black : Lett. *mels*, Sk. *malam* dirt, μολύνω. 7.

μέλδομαι melt : NHG. *schmelzen* Eng. *smelt.* 32.

μέλε friend : μείλιχος.

μέλεος useless, wretched : Lat. *molestus*, O Slav. *milŭ*, μῶλυς. 7.

μέλη cup : μέτρον (cf. δέπας).

μέλι honey : Lat. *mel mulsum*, Ir. *mil*, Got. *milith*, μείλιχος. Hence μελίνη millet, Lat. *milium* (Eng.), 'honey-fruit'.

μελίη ash :

μέλλω intend, μέλω am' a care : Lat. *mora*, O Ir. *maraim* I remain, μέριμνα. 25.

μέλος limb, song ('piece'), μέλπω sing : *λέμος, Ags. *lam* lame Eng., *lim* limb Eng., O Slav. *lomiti* break. 24.

(μεμβράς = βεμβράς.)

μέμονα strive, μένος force : Lat. *mens*, O Ir. *menme* mind, Got. *muns* thought Ags. *mynde* Eng. 'mind, Lit. *miněti* think, Sk. *manas* mind *man* think.

μέμφομαι blame : O Ir. *mebul* shame.

μέν = μήν B.

μένω remain : Lat. *maneo*, Zd. *upa-man* ὑπο-μένειν : μένος (cf. μέλλω μέριμνα).

μέριμνα μέρμηρα care, μέρμερα baleful : Lat. *memor*, Got. *merjan* proclaim, Sk. *smar* remember. 32. 5. 30.

μερμίς = μήρινθος. 5.

μέρος part : Lat. *mereo* 'take a part'.

μέροψ bee-eater, μέροπες men : μάρπτω, 'greedy'. 2.

(μέσαβον strap : Heb. °*asab* bind).

(μεσπίλη medlar (Eng.) : foreign.)

μέσσος middle : *μέθ-jos, Lat. *medius*, O Ir. *medón*, Got. *midjis* Eng., O Slav. *meždinu*. 19.

μεστός full : μαδάω. 11. 20.

μέσφα till, μετά with : Got. *mith* Eng. *mid-wife*, Sk. *mithas* together, ἅμα. 19. 32.

μεταλλάω inquire : ματεύω. 11.

(μέταλλον mine : Phoenician ?)

μετ-αμώνιος idle : *ἆμος wind, ἀμουργός, Hesych. ἀμῶνας ἀνεμώνας Aeolic.

μετα-ξύ between : cf. δι-ξός.

μετα-χρόνιος high up : false formation as though sq. were from ὥρη.

μετ-έωρος high up : ἐώρα.

μέτρον measure : Lat. *mēto mētior*, Ir. *medh* balance, Lit. *matóti* to measure, Sk. *mā*. 30.

μέχρι up to : μακρός. 11. 21.

μή not : Sk. *mā*, μήν B. (cf. οὐ οὖν).

μήδεα A. plans : O Ir. *mess* judgment, Got. *miton* think, μέδιμνος.

μήδεα B. genitals : μαδάω.

μηκάομαι cry : onomatopoeic, NHG. *meckern* bleat, Lit. *mekénti*, Sk. *makakas* bleating, μακκάω.

μῆκος length : μακρός. 30.

μήκων poppy : OHG. *māgo* Eng. *maw-seed*, O Slav. *makŭ* : μάσσω, the seeds being chewed.

μήλη probe :

μῆλις a distemper : μῶλυς. 7.

μηλ-ολόνθη cockchafer :

μῆλον A. sheep : O Nor. *smali* : Got. *smals* small Eng., cf. σμικρός. 32.

μῆλον B. apple, μηλ-ωψ bright : Lat. *mālum*, μαρμαίρω. 25.

μήν A. month : Lat. *mensis*, Ir. *mi*, Got. *menoths* Eng., Lit. *menesis*, Sk. *mās*, μέτρον. So μήνη moon : Got. *mena* Eng., Lit. *menesis*, Sk. *mās*.

μήν B. indeed : μοῦνος, 'altogether'. 8.

μῆνιγξ membrane : μηρός. 17.

μῆνις wrath : Sk. *manyus*, μένος. 30.

μηνύω report : Lat. *mentio moneo*, Welsh *mynegu* tell, Ags. *manian* warn Eng. *mean*, Sk. *ā-mnā* mention.

μήρινθος = σμήρινθος. 32.

μηρός ham : *μεμσ-ρός, Lat. *membrum*, Got. *mimz* flesh, O Slav. *męzdra* rind, Sk. *mąsam* flesh. 17.

μηρυκάζω ruminate, μηρύομαι draw up : μήρινθος.

μήτηρ mother : Lat. *māter*, Ir. *mathair*, Ags. *mōdor* Eng., Lit. *motere*, Sk. *mātar-* : Sk. *mātar-* Masc. measurer, μέτρον, 'house-wife' (cf. ταμίη). Hence μήτρα womb, pith, queen-bee.

μῆτις counsel : μένος. 17.

μῆχος means : Ir. *cu-mhang* power, Got. *magan* be able Eng. *may*, O Slav. *mogą* am able, Sk. *mahas* great, cf. μακρός μέγας.

μία one : ἅμα. 32.

μιαίνω stain, μιαί-φονος bloody : O Slav. *myti* wash, Sk. *minv* swell. 34.

μίγνυμι mix : Lit. *maiszyti*, Sk. *miçras* mixt, cf. μάσσω. 28.

μικκός μῖκρός small : σμικρός. 32. 19.

μῖλαξ ὁ boy : μέλλαξ, μεῖραξ. 17. 25.

μῖλαξ ἡ convolvulus, μῖλος yew : σμῖλαξ. 32.

μίλτος ruddle : Lat. *mulleus*, Lit. *mulwas* red, μολύνω. 11.

(μιμαίκυλον μεμαίκυλον arbute-fruit : foreign.)

(μίμαρκυς hare-soup : al. μίμαρκις, foreign.)

μῖμος imitator : ἀμεύομαι. 5.

μίν him : Lat. *imim*, ἕ (cf. κτώ.) 5.

(μίνδαξ incense : κίνδος, Persian.)

μίνθα mint : μόθος, 'with flowers in whorls'. 11. So μίνθος ordure (cf. σφυράδες).

μινύθω lessen : Lat. *minuo minor*, Ir. *min* little, Got. *mins* less Eng. *mince*, O Slav. *minij*, μανός. 11.

μινυρός moaning : Lat. *minūrio mintro*, Sk. *man* utter a sound. 11.

μίσγω mix : Lat. *misceo*, Ir. *cu-mascc* mixture, OHG. *miskan* mix Eng. *mix mess mash*, Sk. *miksh*, μίγνυμι. 32. 19.

μισθός hire : Lat. *miles*, Got. *mizdo* Eng. *meed*, O Slav. *mizda*, Zd. *mizhda* :

μῖσος hatred : Lat. *miser*, Sk. *mith* altercate. 17.

μιστύλλω cut up : Lat. *mutilus muticus*, μυστίλη. 16.

(μίσυ vitriol, truffle : Egyptian.)

μίσχος stalk, spade : μόσχος. 11.

μίτος thread : Lat. *mitto*, Gallic *mataris* pike, Lit. *metu* I throw (cf. Eng. shuttle shoot, thread throw, warp Got. vairpan 'throw').

(μίτρα girdle : Phrygian, Lit. *muturas* cap.)

(μίτυς wax : μύτις.)

(μνᾶ pound : Heb. *māněh*.)

μνάομαι woo, μνεία μνήμη memory, μνώομαι remember : Lat. *memini reminiscor*, O Ir. *do-muiniur* I think, Got. *ga-minthi* memory, Lit. *at-mintis*, μηνύω. 24.

μναρός Cratin. incert. 79 soft : μνόος.

(μνάσιον μναύσιον a plant : Egyptian.)

μνοία serfs (Cretan) : μένω.

μνόος down : μνίον sea-weed μνιός soft, Lit. *minnawa* felt-grass. 34.

μόγος toil : ἐπι-σμυγερός. 32. Hence μογοσ-τόκος delivering, *μόγοσι Loc. Plur. (cf. θεοσ-δοτος).

μόδιος = μέδιμνος. 7.

μόδος = μαδωνία.

μόθος din, μόθων impudent : Ir. *moth* penis, O Nor. *möndull* mill-handle, Sk. *manth* stir : 'whirling', cf. μαντίλη.

μοῖρα = μέρος. 7. 17. Hence μοιρο-λογχέω receive a portion, λαγχάνω.

μοῖτος thanks : Sicilian, Lat. *mūtuus*, ἀμεύομαι.

μοιχός paramour : μάχλος. 17.

μοκλός Anacreon 88 = μοχλός (cf. μύκλος πλαδδιάω).

μολγός hide : OHG. *malha* wallet Eng. *mail*, ὀμόργνυμι.

μολεῖν see βλώσκω.

μόλις scarcely : μῶλυς. 30.

μολοβρίτης wild porker, μολοβρός beggar : 'wandering', ἀμορβέω. 25. 2.

(μόλυβδος μόλιβδος μόλιβος lead : Lat. *plumbum*, NHG. *blei* : sq., cf. Sk. *bahu-malas* 'very black' = lead.)

μολύνω stain : μορύσσω. 25.

(μόναπος, wild ox : μόνωψ μόνωτος, βόνασος, Paeonian.)

μονθυλεύω stuff with forced meat : μίνθος. 11.

(μόρμυρος μόρμυλος μύρμης a fish : Gallic *mirmillo*.)

μορμύρω roar : Lat. *murmur*, Got. *maurnan* mourn Eng., Lit. *murmēti* grumble, Sk. *marmaras* rustling. 5.

μορμώ bugbear : Lat. *formido* (cf. μύρμηξ) :

μορόεντα bright : μαρμαίρω.

(μόρον mulberry (Lat. *mōrum*, Ir. *merenn*, Eng. *mulberry*, Lit. *móras*) : Semitic.)

μόρος fate : μοῖρα.

μορύσσω stain, μόρφνος dark : *μόρχϜ-jω, Lit. *murksztinti* befoul. 2. 27. 29.

μορφή shape : μάρπτω (cf. O Slav. tvorŭ ἔξις Lit. twérti 'seize'). 29.

(μόσσῡν wooden tower : Pontic.)

μόσχος sprout, calf : Ags. *max* mesh Eng., Lit. *mázgas* knot.

μοτός lint : μίτος.

μοῦνος alone : *σμῶνος, Sk. *samānas* like, ἅμα. 32.

μόχθος = μόγος.

μοχλός lever : μῆχος. 30.

μῦ A. Interj.

(μῦ B. M : Heb. *mem*.)

μύα a plant : Lat. *muscus*, Ags. *mōs* moss Eng., O Slav. *mŭchŭ*. 34.

μυάω compress the lips, μυέω initiate ('bind to silence') : μύω.

μυδάω am damp, μύδρος molten iron : μαδάω.

μῠελός marrow : μιαίνω, 'greasy.' 17.

μύζω A. groan : Lat. *mūgio*, NHG. *mucken* grumble, Sk. *muj* utter a sound, cf. μῦθος.

μύζω B. suck : μυδάω.

μῦθος word : Lat. *mūtio musso*, MHG. *māwen* roar Eng. *to mew* Ags. *maev* sea-mew Eng., Lett. *maut* bellow.

μυῖα fly : Lat. *musca*, Lit. *musse* : Sk. *mush* steal, 'greedy of blood'. 34.

μῡκάομαι roar : cf. μύζω A.

μύκης mushroom, μυκτήρ nose : ἀπομύττω.

μύκλος lewd : Phocaean (cf. μοκλός), μυχλός stallion-ass, Lat. *mūlus*, μάχλος.

μύλη A. mill : Lat. *mola* (Eng.) *molo*, O Ir. *melim* I grind, Ags. *melo* meal Eng., Lit. *málti* grind, μαραίνω. So μύλη B. abortion, Lit. *milliti* fail. 11. 25.

[μύλλος μύλος a fish : foreign.)

μυνδός dumb : μύω.

μύνη excuse : Sk. *mīv* move. 31.

μύξα phlegm (Eng. *match*) : ἀπομύττω. So μύξων = σμύξων. 32.

μύραινα μύρινος = σμῦρος. 32.

[μυρίκη μυρῐκη tamarisk : foreign.)

μῡρίος countless : Zd. *baēvare* 10,000, *būiri* plenty ?

μύρμηξ ant : Lat. *formīca*, Ir. *moirbh*, O Nor. *maurr* Eng. *pis-mire*, O Slav. *mravij*, Zd. *maoiri* :

μύρον oil : σμυρίζω. 32.

[μύρρα myrrh : σμύρνα, Heb. *mōr*.)

[μυρσίνη μύρτος myrtle : Pers. *mūrd*.)

μύρω weep : μορμύρω (cf. κλαίω).

μῦς mouse, mussel, whale, muscle : Lat. *mūs*, Ags. *mūs* mouse Eng., O Slav. *myšĭ*, Sk. *mūsh*, Hesych. σμῦς : Sk. *mush* steal, μυῖα. 32.

μύσος defilement : μυδάω. 35.

μύσσομαι = ἀπομύττω.

μύσταξ upper lip (French *moustache*) : μάσταξ. 11.

μυστίλη sop, μύστριον spoon, μυττωτός salad : ματτύη. 11. 20.

[μύτις μύστις liver of mollusc : μίτυς, foreign.)

μυχθίζω snort, μυχμός groaning : μύζω A. 6. 21.

μυχός corner : Ags. *smūgan* creep Eng. *smuggle*, 'bend'. 32.

μύω shut my eyes : Lat. *mūtus*, Sk. *mūkas* dumb, *mū* bind.

μυών muscle : Lat. *musculus*, Ags. *mūsle*, O Slav. *myšĭca* arm, Sk. *mushkas* testicle, μῦς. 34.

μύωψ gadfly, goad ('stinging') : μυῖα + ὦπα. 34.

μωκός mocker : μακκοάω.

μῶλος struggle : μάρναμαι. So μῶλυς feeble, Got. *ga-malvjan* crush. 25.

[μῶλυ mandrake, garlic : Cappadocian name for wild rue ἅρμαλα.)

μώλ-ωψ weal : μέλας + ὦπα. 7.

μῶμαι seek : μάομαι, μένος. 17.

μῶμος blame : Sicilian *momar* foolish, O Slav. *mamŭ*, μνάω. 17.

μῶνυξ strong-hoofed : *μουν-όνυξ, μοῦνος, 'with undivided hoof'. 35.

μωρός stupid : Sk. *mūras*, μῶλυς.

(νάβλα harp : Heb. *nebhel* flute.)

ναί = νή.

(ναῖρον a spice : Indian.)

ναίω A. dwell : Lat. *nidus*, O Ir. *net* nest, Ags. Eng. *nest*, Sk. *nĭdas*, νέομαι (cf. οἶκος.) 34.

ναίω B. am full : νέω B.

νάκη fleece : νάσσω.

νᾶνος dwarf : Hesych. ἀννίς grandmother, Lat. *anus*, Welsh *nain*, OHG. *ana*, Lit. *anyta* mother-in-law, Sk. *nanā* mother.

νᾶός temple : Aeol. ναῦος : 17.

νάπη dell : Hesych. νενώπηται τεταπείνωται :

(νᾶπυ = σίναπι.)

(νάρδος spikenard : Heb. *nerd*.)

νάρθηξ wand : Hesych. νάθραξ, Lit. *néndre* reed, Sk. *nadas*. 24. 21.

νάρκη numbness : OHG. *snarahha* noose, νεῦρον. 11. Hence νάρκισσος daffodil, 'narcotic'.

(νάρτη = ναῖρον.)

νάσσω stuff : Lat. *nacca* fuller :

ναύ-κληρος captain, ναύ-κρᾱρος householder : κραίνω. 25.

ναῦς νηῦς ship : Lat. *nāvis*, Ir. *nau*, Ags. *naca*, Sk. *naus*, νέω A.

νάω flow : νέω A.

νε-ᾱλής fresh : νέος + ἀλής.

νεβρός fawn :

νείατος lowest, νειόθεν from the bottom : Ags. *niðer* down Eng. *nether beneath*, O Slav. *nizu*, Sk. *ni*. Hence νειός 'deep' fallow land, O Slav. *niva* field.

νεῖκος strife : Lett. *nizinát* revile.

νέκταρ nectar : νώγαλα. 7. 19.

νέκυς corpse : Lat. *neco noceo*, Ir. *ecc* death, Got. *naus* corpse, O Slav. *navĭ* dead, Sk. *naç* perish.

νέμεσις wrath ('imputatio'), νέμω distribute, νέμομαι feed, νέμος pasture : Lat. *numerus nemus*, Got. *niman* take Eng. *nimble*, Lit. *nûmas* gain.

νεο-γῑλός young : *νεο-γεν-λός γένος. 17.

νέομαι go : Sk. *nas* join some one. 34.

νέος new : Lat. *novus*, Ir. *nua*, Got. *niujis* Eng., Lit. *naujas*, Sk. *navas* : *σ-νέ-Fος, see υἱός. 32. 34.

νέποδες children : popular etymology (as if *νή-ποδες footless) for *νέποτες, Lat. *nepōs*, O Ir. *necht* niece, Got. *nithjis* kinsman Ags. *nefa* nephew Eng., O Slav. *netij*, Sk. *napāt* son :

νέρθε νέρτερος below : ἀριστερός.

νέρτος hawk : foreign ?

νέτωπον oil of almonds : Heb. *nātāph* drop.)

νεῦρον sinew : Lat. *nervus*, NHG. *schnurfen* contract Ags. *snear* noose Eng. *snare narrow*, Lit. *nerti* draw in. 32. 17.

νεύω incline : Lat. *nuo*, Sk. *nu* remove.

νεφέλη νέφος cloud : Lat. *nebula nimbus nūbes*, Welsh *niwl*, NHG. *nebel* mist, O Slav. *nebo* sky, Sk. *nabhas* mist.

νεφρός kidney : Lat. *nefrōnes* testes, O Ir. *áru* kidney, NHG. *niere* Eng. *kid-ney*, Sk. *nīv* grow fat.

νέω A. swim : Lat. *no nato*, Ir. *snuadh* river. Sk. *snu* let flow, *sna* bathe. 32.

νέω B. spin, heap up ('bind together') : Lat. *neo*, Ir. *snath* thread, Got. *nethla* needle Eng., OHG. *nāwan* spin NHG. *nähen* sew, Lit. *nytis* loom-beam. 32.

νέωτα next year : *νεό-Fετα, ἔτος. 17.

νή yea : Lat. *nē* indeed *nam*, Zd. *kem-nā* quem-nam.

νή- un- : Lat. *ne-fas ni-si nī-mirum*, Ir. *ni* not, Got. *ni* Eng. *nay no naught not*, Lit. *ne*, Sk. *nā* : ἀν-, praeced. (cf. μή οὐ).

ν-ηγάτεος beautiful : ν wrongly prefixt from preceding word cf. sq. (cf. Eng. newt nickname nonce nugget) : ἄγαμαι, 'admirable'.

ν-ήδυμος sweet : ἥδυμος ἡδύς (cf. praeced.).

ηδύς belly : Got. *niutan* enjoy, Sk. *nand* enjoy oneself (cf. Lat. alvus alo, Eng. maw might).

νηέω νηνέω heap up : νέω B. 30.

νηλίπους unshod : νη- + ἦλιψ shoe :

νηνίατον dirge : Lat. *nēnia*, Phrygian.)

νή-πιος νη-πύτιος child : πινυτός.

νηρείτης νηρίτης periwinkle : ἀναρίτης, foreign).

νή-ριτος huge : ἀριθμός.

νῆσος island : *ἄνασος (cf. sq.), Lat. *insula*, Ir. *inis* :

νῆσσα duck : Lat. *anas*, Ags. *äned*, Lit. *ántis* :

νήφω am sober : NHG. *nüchtern* fasting : 27.

νίγλαρος fife : foreign).

νίζω νίπτω wash : O Ir. *ne-naig* lāvit, Sk. *nij* to clean. 27.

νίκη victory : *Fίγκη, Lat. *vinco*, Got. *veihan* to fight, Lit. *weikti* do. 32. 24.

νίν = μίν. 19.

νίσσομαι go : νέομαι. 13. 19.

νίτρον natron : Heb. *nether*.)

νίφα snow : Lat. *nix ninguit*, Welsh *nyf*, Got. *snaivs* Eng., Lit. *snégas*, Zd. *çnizh* to snow. 32. 27.

νόθος bastard : Hesych. νυθός dark, Lat. *umbra*, Lit. *júdas* black, Sk. *andhas* blind. 24.

νόος mind : Lat. *nota*, Got. *snutrs* wise. 32.

νορύη pulse : foreign ?

νόστος return : νέομαι. 7.

νόσφι apart : ἄνευ. 32.

νοτία rain, **νότος** S. wind : νέω νάω. 7.

νοῦμμος a coin : Sicilian, Lat. *nummus*, νέμω.

νοῦσος disease : *νῶσος, νέομαι, ' visitation '. 7.

νυκτάλ-ωψ dim-sighted : νύξ νυκταλός nocturnus (cf. αἰγίλωψ.)

νύμφη bride : Lat. *nūbo* : Νύμφαι ' cloud-maidens ', νέφος, Lydian.

νῦν now : Lat. *num nunc*, Ir. *nu* until, Got. *nu* now Eng., Lit. Sk. *nu, νή.*

νύξ night : Lat. *nox*, O Ir. *in-noct* to-night, Got. *nahts* night Eng., Lit. Sk. *naktis :* 11.

νυός daughter-in-law : Lat. *nurus*, Ags. *snoru̅*, O Slav. *snŭcha*, Sk. *snushā :* *συνυσός, see υἱός. 32. 34.

νύσσα turning-post (' sharp stake '), **νύσσω** prick : Lit. *nĕszti* to itch. 19.

νυστάζω = νεύω. 31.

νύχιος nightly : νύξ (cf. ἀνακῶς). 29.

νώγαλα dainties : Eng. *snack snatch snap.* 32.

νωθής sluggish : νη- + ὄθομαι.

νῶι we two : Lat. *nōs*, O Slav. *na* Acc., Sk. *nau.*

νῶκαρ sleep : νέκυς, ' lifelessness '. 7.

νωλεμές continually : νη- + *ὄλεμές ' broken ', μέλος. 1.

νώροπι flashing : O Nor. *snarpr* sharp : νάρκη, ' dazzling '. 32. 2. 27.

νῶτον back : Welsh *nant* valley, Sk. *natas* bent *nam* bend.

νωχελής sluggish : νῶκαρ (cf. τημ-ελέω.) 29.

ξαίνω scratch, **ξανάω** stiffen (as with carding wool) : O Nor. *skinn* skin Eng., Sk. *khan* dig. 24.

ξανθός ξουθός yellow : Lat. *candeo accendo*, Welsh *can* white, Ags. *hādor* clear, Lit. *skaidrus*, σπινθήρ. 24. 11. 17.

ξεῖνος stranger : Sk. *kshēmas* stopping, κτίζω. 24.

ξερός ξηρός dry : Sk. *kshāmas* singed. 24. 30.

ξέω ξύω polish : Lit. *skusti* shave. 24. 34.

(**ξιρίς ξυρίς** iris : foreign.)

ξίφος sword : σκάπτω. 24. 12.

ξύλον wood : σκύλλω (cf. δρῦς). 24.

ξύν with, **ξυνός** common : Sk. *sacā* together, ἕπομαι. 24.

ξυρόν razor : Sk. *kshuras*, σκύλλω. 24.

ὅ ὄ Interj.

ὀ- copulative : Sk. *sa-.* 33.

ὁ he : Lat. *sum sam sīc*, Welsh *hwy* they, Got. *sa* he Eng. *she*, Sk. *sa.* 18.

(ὄα A. service-tree : al. οἴη οὔα, foreign.)

ὄα B. fringe : ὦα. 30.

(ὀά alas : Pers.)

ὄαρ wife : ὁ- + εἴρω A. 11.

ὄαρος discourse : ὁ- + εἴρω B. 11.

ὀβελός ὀδελός spit, ὀβολός penny : Sk. *agram* point. 27. 26. 2. 25.

ὄβρια young animals : νεβρός. 10.

ὄβριμος ὄμβριμος mighty : Got. *abrs* strong, Sk. *ambhrnas.* 32. 19.

ὄγδοος eight : ὀκτώ, weakened on analogy of ἕβδομος.

ὀγκάομαι bray : Lat. *onco,* Got. *auhjon* to clamour, O Slav. *jęčati* groan, Sk. *ac* murmur, ἐνοπή.

ὀγκία ounce : Sicilian, al. οὐγκία οὐγγία, Lat. *uncia,* ὄγκος bulk.

ὄγκιον chest, ὄγκος barb, bulk ('roundness') : ἀγκάλη. 11.

ὄγμος swathe : ὁ- + γέντο. 31.

(ὄγχνη pear : Hesych. κόγχνη (cf. κόκκος).)

ὀδάξ with the teeth : ὁ- + δάκνω. Hence ὀδάξω feel irritation.

ὀδάω sell (cf. Eng. trade tread), ὁδός way : οὖδας. 18.

ὀδμή smell : Lat. *odor oleo,* Lit. *ůdziu* I smell.

ὀδούς tooth : Armen. *atamn,* ὁ- + Lat. *dens,* Welsh *dant,* Got. *tunthus* Eng., Lit. *dantis,* Sk. *dantas:* (Aeol. ἔδοντες popular etymology.)

ὀδύνη pain : ἔδω. 7.

ὀδύρομαι lament : ὁ- + δύρομαι (cf. ὄμαδος).

ὀδύσσομαι am angry : Lat. *odium ōdi,* Ags. *atol* horrible, Armen. *adyel* to hate.

ὄζος shoot : Lit. *ůgis,* ὑγιής. 6.

ὀθνεῖος foreign : *ὀνθ-νεῖος νόθος. 35.

ὄθομαι regard :

(ὀθόνη linen : Heb. 'ĕṭūn.)

οἴ Interj.

οἴαξ οἰήιον rudder : Lit. *waira,* οἴσω.

οἴγω open : Sk. *vij* put in motion. 33.

οἶδα know : O Ir. *ro-fessur* sciam, Got. *vait* I know Eng. *wit, un-veis* un-wise Eng., O Slav. *věděti* know, Sk. *veda* I know : 'I see', εἶδον.

οἰδέω swell : Lat. *aemidus* swollen, Ags. *ātā* oats Eng., O Slav. *jadro* fold.

(οἶδνον ὕδνον truffle : foreign.)

οἰετής aequalis : ὁ- + ἔτος, diphthong metri gratia.

ὀϊζύς distress :

οἶκος house : Lat. *vicus,* Ir. *fich* village, Got. *veihs,* O Slav. *vĭsĭ* farm, Sk *vēças* house : 'meeting-place', ἵκω (cf. ναός). 33.

οἶκτος pity : Lat. *aeger,* O Slav. *jęza* disease : ἐπ-είγω, 'oppression'. 7. 19.

οἶμα rush, οἴμη song, οἶμος path : Zd. *aēshma* wrath, Sk. *ish* set in motion, ἰάλλω. 31. 35.

(οἴνη vine, οἶνος wine (Lat. *vīnum*, Got. *vein* Eng.) : Heb. *yāyin*.)

οἰνό-φλυξ drunken : φλύκταινα.

οἶος alone : Lat. *oi-nos ūnus*, ἴα. 31.

ὄις sheep : Lat. *ovis*, Ir. *oi*, Got. *avi-str* sheepfold Eng. *ewe*, Lit. *awìs* sheep, Sk. *avis* : ἀύω B., 'bleating'. 34.

οἶσος osier : ἰτέα. 33.

οἰσο-φάγος gullet :

(οἴσπη οἰσύπη οἰσπώτη sheep-dirt : foreign, al. οἴστη.)

ὀιστός arrow : *ὀσ-ισ-τός, Sk. *as* throw, ὀστέον. 34. 5. 16.

οἶστρος gadfly : αἴθω. 20.

οἴσω feram : Lat. *vēnor*, Ags. *vaedian* hunt, Lit. *wyti*, Sk. *vi* set in motion. 33.

οἶτος doom : αἶσα.

οἴχομαι am gone : ἴχνος. 31.

ὀίω think : ἀίω B. 9.

οἰωνός bird : Lat. *avis*. 34.

ὀκέλλω move a ship : ὀ- + κέλλω.

ὀκλάζω crouch, ὄκνος A. hesitation : Lat. *vacillo*, Sk. *vak* roll. 33.

ὄκνος B. heron : ὀγκάομαι. 32.

ὀκρι-βας platform, ὄκρις point : O Lat. *ocris* cliff, ἄκρος. 8.

ὀκρυόεις horrible : false reading for κρυόεις.

ὀκτά-βλωμος in eight pieces : βλωμός piece, βλῆρ.

ὀκτώ eight : Lat. *octo*, Ir. *ocht*, Got. *ahtan* Eng., Lit. *asztoni*, Sk. *ashtan* :

ὄλβος wealth : ἀλφάνω. 11. 28.

ὀλέκρᾱνον elbow : Lat. *arcus*, Lit. *alkunė*. 2.

ὀλέκω kill : cf. ὄλλυμι. 2.

ὀλίγος little :

ὄλισβος penis coriaceus :

ὀλισθάνω slip : *ὀ-σλιθ-θάνω, Ags. *slide* fall Eng. *slide*, Lit. *slidau* I slip. 1. 35. 20.

ὀλκός furrow : Lat. *sulcus*, Ags. *sulh* plough, ὀρύσσω. 18. 25.

ὄλλυμι destroy : Lat. *ab-oleo ex-olesco*, Sk. *ārtas* injured, *ar* reach. 19.

ὄλμος mortar : εἰλέω. 18.

ὀλολύζω cry, ὄλολυς effeminate ('baby') : Lat. *ululo*, Sk. *ulūlus* owl, ὑλάω. 5. 16.

ὀλοί-τροχος boulder : εἰλύω. 7. 2.

ὀλοό-φρων wise : Lat. *salvus*, Got. *sels* good Eng. *silly*, O Slav. *sulěj* better. 33. 2.

ὀλός sepia :

ὅλος = οὖλος A. 18. 35.

ὀλοφυδνός lamenting, ὀλοφύρομαι lament : Lit. *ulbauti* moan, cf. ὀλολύζω. 2.

ὀλο-φυκτίς pimple : ὅλος + φλύκταινα. 35.

ὁλοφώιος destructive : ὁλοός ὄλλυμι + φύω.   17.

ὄλπις oil-flask : Sk. *sarpis* grease, cf. ἀλείφω.   33.

(ὄλυνθος winter fig : ἐρινεός, foreign.)

(ὄλυρα spelt : Zd. *urvara* plant, Sk. *urvarā* tilth.)

ὀμ Interj. Aesch. Suppl. 827.

ὄμαδος din : ὁμός, 'joint cry'.

ὀμάμαιτα urine Aesch. fragm. 389 :

ὄμβρος rain : Lat. *imber*, O Ir. *imrim* storm, Sk. *abhram* cloud.   19.

ὀμῑχέω mingo : Lat. *mingo* *mējo*, Got. *maihstus* dung, Lit. *myszti* mingere, Sk. *mih.*   1.

ὀμίχλη mist : Ags. *mist* Eng., Lit. *migla*, Sk. *mēghas*.   1. 32.

ὄμμα eye : ὄπωπα.   19.

ὄμνυμι swear :

ὀμόργνυμι wipe off : ἀμέργω.   1. 7.

ὁμός in common : ἅμα.   7.

ὄμπνιος big : Lat. *opes*, Lit. *apstas* abundance, Sk. *apnas* revenue.

ὀμφαλός navel : Lat. *umbilīcus*, O Ir. *imbliu*, Ags. *nafela* Eng., Sk. *nābhīlas* cunnus : Lat. *umbo amnis*, Welsh *afon* river, Ags. *nafu* nave of a wheel Eng., Lett. *naba* navel, Sk. *nābhis*, *nabh* burst.   24.   So ὄμφαξ unripe grapes, 'swelling'.

ὀμφή voice : Lit. *ambiti* chide.

ὄναρ dream : *ὀνθ-ρ νόθος.   32. 2.

ὄνειαρ refreshment, ὄνησις advantage, ὀνίνημι profit : Sk. *van* love, ἄναξ.   33. 2.

ὄνειδος reproach : Got. *ga-naitjan* revile, Lett. *náids* hatred, Sk. *nind* mock.   1.

ὄνθος = μίνθος, ὀνθυλεύω = μονθυλεύω.   10.

ὀνο-κίνδιος ass-driver : κίνδυνος.

ὄνομα name : Lat. *nun-cupo*, Ir. *ainm*, Got. *namo* Eng., O Slav. *imę*, Sk. *nāman* : 2.

ὄνομαι blame : ὀνοστός blameable, ὄνειδος.   35. 20.

(ὄνος ass : Lat. *asinus* (Ir. *asal*, Got. *asilus* Eng., Lit. *ásilas*) : Heb. *'āthōn*.)

ὄνυξ nail : Lat. *unguis*, O Ir. *inga*, Got. *ga-nagljan* nail to Eng., Lit. *nágas* nail, Sk. *nakhas* : 2.

(ὄνωνις rest-harrow : ἄνωνις ὄνοσμα, see ἄνηθον.)

ὀξύα beech : Ags. *äsc* ash Eng., Lit. *ûsis* :

ὀξυ-ρεγμία heartburn : ἐρεύγομαι.   16.

ὀξύς sharp : Sk. *aksh* reach.

ὄπ Ar. Ran. 208. Interj.

ὄπα voice : ἔπος.   7.

ὀπᾱδός ὀπάων attendant, ὀπάζω make to follow : ἔπομαι.   33. 7.

ὄπεας awl, ὀπή hole : ὄπωπα, 'spy-hole'.   Hence ὀπ-ίουρος peg, ἰωρός keeper ὥρα.   5.

ὀπιπτεύω watch, ὄπις vengeance ('observation') : ὄπωπα.   5. 16.

ὄπισθεν ὀπίσσω behind : ἐπί, Lat. ob. 7.

ὁπλή hoof, ὅπλον instrument : ἕπω. 7.

ὁπλότερος younger : ἀπαλός. 2.

ὀπός juice : Lat. opimus ad-eps, ἄπιος.

ὅππως that : ὅς + πῶς, see ποῦ. 27. 19.

ὀπτάω roast : ἕψω. 7.

ὀπυίω marry : Lat. opus, Sk. apas active.

ὄπωπα have seen : ὄσσε.

ὀπώρα August : ὀπτάω (cf. θαλπ-ωρή), 'ripening'.

ὀράω see : Welsh gweled, Lett. wáirit to watch, ὥρα, Sk. var cover εὐρύς. 18.

ὀργάζω knead : ἔργον. 7.

ὀργάς meadow, ὀργάω swell : Lat. virga, Sk. ūrj sap. Hence ὀργή anger, O Ir. ferg. 33.

ὀργεών priest, ὄργια worship : ἔργον.

ὄργυια ὀρόγυια fathom, ὀρέγω stretch : Lat. rego, O Ir. rigim I stretch, Got. uf-rakjan lift up Eng. reach, Lit. ražyti stretch, Sk. arj. 2. 24.

ὀρεσ-κῷος wild : κεῖμαι. 7.

ὀρεύς mule : ὄρος.

ὀρεχθέω bellow : ὀ- + ῥόχθος. 7.

(ὄρθαπτον cloth : foreign).

ὀρθό-κραιρος straight-horned : κέρας. 24.

ὀρθός straight : Dor. βορθός, NHG. wald wood, O Slav. vladi hair, Sk. ūrdhvas upright, vardh strengthen. 33.

ὄρθρος dawn : ἀλθαίνω. 11.

(ὀρίγανον ὀρείγανον marjoram : foreign.)

(ὀρίνδης of rice : ὄρυζον.)

ὀρίνω = ὄρνυμι. 2.

ὀρκάνη enclosure, ὅρκος sanction : ἕρκος. 7.

(ὄρκῡς tunny : foreign.)

ὁρμή attack : ἅλλομαι. 18. 11.

ὄρμῑνον clary :

ὅρμος A. collar : εἴρω A. 18.

ὅρμος B. anchorage : O Nor. vörr landing-place Eng. weir : ἐρύω, 'place for dragging ships ashore'. 18.

ὄρνις bird : Welsh eryr eagle, Got. ara, Lit. erélis :

ὄρνυμι ὀροθύνω stir : Lat. orior, Got. rinnan run Eng., Sk. ar rise, ἔρχομαι. 7. 2.

(ὀροβάγχη ὀροβάκχη dodder : foreign.)

(ὄροβος vetch : Lat. ervum, OHG. araweiz pea NHG. erbse, Sk. aravindam lotus.)

ὀρόδαμνος bough : Lat. verbēna verber, ὀρθός (cf. αἰδώς). 2.

ὄρομαι attend : οὖρος ὁ B. 35.

δρος = οὖρος τό. 35.

δρος = οὖρος ὁ C. 4. 35.

ὀρός whey : Lat. *serum*, Sk. *saras* fluid, *sar* run, ἅλλομαι. So ὀρρός
whey, *ὀρ-σός. 33. 19.

ὀρούω rush : ὄρνυμι. 2.

ὄρπηξ sapling : ῥῶπες. 33.

ὄρρος rump : Ags. *ears* Eng., Eng. *wheat-ear* (λευκόπυγος). 19.

ὀρρωδέω dread :

ὀρσο-δάκνη an insect : *ὀρσός bud, οὖρος τό, + δάκνω.

ὀρσο-θύρη back door : 'raised', οὖρος τό.

ὀρσο-λοπεύω provoke :

ὀρτάλιχος chick, ὄρτυξ quail : 'dancing', Lat. *verto*, Welsh *gwerthyd*
spindle, Ags. *vridan* bind Eng. *writhe wrest wrestle*, Lit. *wersti* turn,
Sk. *vartakas* quail, *vart* roll. 33. 28.

(ὀρύα ὀροῦα sausage : ἀλλᾶς, foreign.)

(ὄρυζον rice : Sk. *vrihis*.)

ὀρυμαγδός din : Hesych. ὀρυγμάδες θόρυβοι, Lat. *rugio*, OHG. *rohjan*
bellow NHG. *röcheln* breathe hard, cf. ὠρύομαι. 1. 24.

(ὄρυς gazelle : Libyan.)

ὀρύσσω dig : Lat. *runco*, Sk. *lunc* pluck, ὁλκός. 1. 35. 24.

ὀρφανός bereft : Lat. *orbus*, O Ir. *erpim* I surrender, Armen. *worp*
orphan.

ὀρφνη darkness, ὀρφώς sea-perch : μόρφνος. 10.

ὄρχαμος leader : ἔρχομαι. 7.

ὀρχάς enclosing, ὄρχατος ὄρχος row of trees : εἴργω. 7. 29.

ὀρχέομαι dance, ὄρχιλος gold-crest (cf. ὄρτυξ τροχίλος) : Sk. *rghāy* shake.

ὄρχις testicle, ὀρχί-πεδα (cf. λακκό-πεδον) testicles : Ir. *uirge* penis, Lit.
erzilas stallion, Armen. *wortz* male.

ὅς he, who : ἕ.

ὅσιος hallowed :

ὀσκαλσις digging : ὀ- + σκάλλω.

(ὄσπριον pulse : ὄσπρεον, foreign.)

ὄσσα rumour : *Fόκ-ja, ἔπος. 33. 19.

ὄσσε eyes : *ὄκ-je, Lat. *oculus*, O Ir. *agaid* face, Got. *augo* eye Eng. *eye
ogle*, O Nor. *vind-auga* window Eng., Lit. *akis* eye, Sk. *akshi*. Hence
ὄσσομαι forebode, Got. *ahjan* think. 19.

ὄστακος lobster, ὀστέον bone : Sk. *asthan* bone, *as* throw, 'refuse'.

ὀσταφίς = ἀσταφίς. 1.

ὀστλιγξ tendril : ὀ- + στλεγγίς. 11.

ὄστρακον potsherd, ὄστρειον oyster (Lat. *ostrum*) : στερεός. 1. 24.

ὄστριμον cattle-pen :

(ὀστρύα hornbeam : foreign, ἄσπρις.)

ὀσφραίνομαι smell : ὀδμή + φρήν, 'perceive a smell'. 19.

ὀσφύς loin : ὀ- + ψόα. 24.

ὄσχη scrotum, ὄσχος vine-branch : μόσχος. 10.

ὄτλος disturbance : ὀ- + τλῆναι.

ὄτοβος noise :

ὀτρηρός busy : ὀ-, Hesych. τρηρὸν ἐλαφρόν, τρέω.

ὀτρυγη-φάγος corn-eating : ὀ- + τρύγη.

ὀτρύνω rouse : ὀ- + τρύω.

οὐ not : αὖ.

οὖδας ground, οὖδός threshold : Lat. *solum*, O Slav. *choditi* go, Sk. *ā-sad*
     reach. 33. 17.

οὖθαρ udder : Lat. *über* Subst., Ags. *üder* Eng., Lit. *udróti* get milk,
     Sk. *ūdhar* udder :

(οὔιγγον οὔιπον οὔιτον a plant : ἴτον, Egyptian.)

οὖλα gums : 'covering the teeth', Sk. *var* cover εἶρος. 17. 25.

οὐλαί groats : ἀλέω. 3.

οὐλαμός throng : εἰλέω. 3.

οὖλε hail : Lat. *salve*, ὀλοό-φρων. 17.

οὐλή scar : Lat. *volnus*, Welsh *gweli* wound, Sk. *vranam*, ἀπαυράω. 25.

οὔλιος destructive : ὄλλυμι. 3.

οὖλος A. whole : Lat. *solidus* Oscan *sollo*, Sk. *sarvas*. 33. 17.

οὖλος B. woolly : εἶρος. 17.

οὖν certainly : αὖ.

οὐρά tail, οὔραξ grouse, οὐρίαχος butt-end : Lat. *urruncum* beard of
     corn *ad-ūlor*, Ir. *err* tail :

οὐράνη pot, οὖρον A. urine : Lat. *ūrina*, Ir. *fual*, O Nor. *ver* sea, Sk.
     vāris water. So οὐρανός sky, 'rainy'. 33.

οὖρος ὁ A. fair wind :

οὖρος ὁ B. warder : ὁράω. 33. 17.

οὖρος ὁ C. οὖρον B. boundary, οὐρός trench : ἀραιός. 17.

οὖρος τό mountain : *Ϝόρσος, Lat. *verrūca*, O Nor. *varta* wart Eng., Lit.
     wirszus point, Sk. *varshman* height, ῥίον. 33. 17.

οὖς ear : *οὖσ-ας, Lat. *ausculto auris audio*, Got. *auso* ear Eng., Lit.
     ausis, ἀΐω B.

οὐτάω wound : O Ir. *futhu* stigmata, Got. *vunds* wounded Eng., Zd. *van*
     strike. 33. 17.

οὖτος this : ὁ, ἡ-ἑ, τό. 23.

ὀφείλω owe, ὄφελος advantage : ὠφελέω. 30.

ὀφθαλμός eye : ὄπωπα *ὄπαλος (cf. σχινδαλμός). 6.

ὄφις snake : ἔχις. 7. 27.

ὄφ-ρα while : *ὄφι Instrum., ὅς. 33.

ὀφρύς eyebrow : Lat. *frons*, O Ir. *brúad* Gen. Dual., Ags. *bräv* Eng.,
     O Slav. *brŭvĭ*, Sk. *bhrū, bhur* move quickly, πορφύρω. 1. 24.

ὄχα by far : = ἐξ-οχα, ἔχω.

ὀχετός water-pipe, ὀχέω bear, ὄχος chariot: Lat. *veho*, Ir. *fén* wagon, Got. *ga-vigan* move Eng. *wagon wag wing weigh*, Lit. *weszti* travel, Sk. *vah* carry. 33. So

ὀχθέω am angry: Lat. *vehe-mens*.

ὀχλέω disturb, ὀχλίζω heave up, ὄχλος trouble, crowd: Lat. *vexo vectis*, Sk. *vāhinī* army.

ὀχεύς strap, bolt: ἔχω. 7. So

ὀχμάζω grip: ἔχμα support.

ὀχυρός firm: ἐχυρός.

ὄχθη bank:

(ὄχθοιβος purple stripe: foreign.)

ὀψέ late: ὀπίσσω.

ὄψις sight, ὄψομαι shall see: ὄπωπα.

ὄψον meat: ὀπτάω.

πάγη trap, πάγος rock, frost: πήγνυμι. 30.

(πάγουρος = φάγρος.)

πάγχυ quite: Hesych. πάμφι, πᾶς (cf. πολλα-χοῦ).

(πάδος pine: Gallic *padus*.)

πάθος = πένθος. 10.

παιάν hymn: O Slav. *pěti* sing.

παιπάλη = πάλη B. 5.

παιπαλοείς rocky:

πάις boy: Lat. *paulus*, παῦρος. 34.

παιφάσσω rush: cf. φαίνω, 'glance'. 5. 19.

παίω strike, eat: Lat. *pavio*, Lit. *pjauti* cut, Sk. *pavīrus* spear. 34.

παλάθη = πέλανος. 11.

πάλαι long ago: τῆλε. 27. 30.

παλάμη hand: Lat. *palma*, O Ir. *lám*, Ags. *folme*, cf. πλάξ. 2. So παλαστή palm.

παλάσσω A. draw lots, πάλος lot, πάλλω shake: σπαίρω. 32. 25. Hence

παλάσσω B. παλύνω sprinkle.

παλεύω attract by movements.

πάλη A. wrestling, παλέω am disabled.

πάλη B. flour: Lat. *palea pollen pulvis*, O Slav. *plěva* chaff, Sk. *palāvas*.

πάλιν back: τῆλε, 'from far'. 27.

παλίουρος thorn-tree:

(πάλλαγμα Aesch. Suppl. 296 concubinage, παλλακή concubine (Lat. *pellex*): Sk. *pallavas* lecher, πτελέη.)

(πάλμυς king: Lydian.)

παμφαίνω = φαίνω. 5.

παμφαλάω look round : φαλακρός (cf. λεύσσω λευκός). 5.

(πάνθηρ leopard : Sk. *pundarīkas* tiger.)

πανία satiety : Lat. *penus*, Lit. *pénas* food, Sk. *panasas* breadfruit-tree.

πᾱνός torch : Got. *fon* fire, Pruss. *páno*.

πάξ Interj. : Lat. *pax*.

πάομαι acquire : Lat. *patro*, κτάομαι. 27.

παπαῖ Interj. : Lat. *papae*.

πάππας father, πάππος grandfather, thistle-down ('hoar') : onomato-poeic, Lat. *pa* father, Eng. *papa*.

παππαίνω peer :

(πάπῡρος papyrus : Egyptian).

παρά beside : Lat. *per*, O Ir. *ar* for, Got. *fram* from Eng., Lit. *pér* through, Sk. *parā* away, περί. 15.

(παραβίας a drink : Paeonian, πράμνειος).

(παράδεισος park : Pers. *firdos*, Babylonian (Delitzsch).)

(παρασάγγης mile : Pers. *farsang*, O Pers. *āthangaina* of stone (Spiegel).)

παρδακός damp : Lat. *prātum*, Zd. *frith* rotten, πλάδη.

(πάρδαλις πόρδαλις panther : Sk. *prdākus*.)

πάρδαλος a bird : πέρδιξ.

παρειά παρήιον cheek : Aeol. παρ-αύα, οὖς, cf. ἄ-ανθα. 30. 34.

(παρείας παρώας brown : foreign.)

πάρθενος maiden : Got. *bruths* bride Eng., Ags. *berstan* burst Eng., Lit. *brendu* I swell, βρενθύομαι. 20. 11.

πάρνοψ locust : κόρνοψ : 27. 11.

πάρος = πρόσθε.

πᾶς all : *πὄγκϜ-s, Lat. *cunctus*, see πέντε. 11. 26

πασπάλη grain : NHG. *spreu* chaff, σπαίρω. 5.

πάσσαλος peg : see πήγνυμι. 19.

πάσσω sprinkle : Zd. *path* fill up. 19. Hence παστή porridge (Eng. *paste*), 'salted'.

παστάς porch, chamber : Lat. *postis*, Sk. *pastyam* dwelling.

πάσχω suffer : *πάθ-σκω πάθος. 35. 19.

πάταγος clash, πατάξ Ar. Av. 1258 striking, πατάσσω strike : κεντέω. 27. 10.

πατάνη dish (Lat. *patina*) : πέταχνον. 14.

πατέομαι eat : Got. *fodjan* feed Eng., O Slav. *pitati* : Lat. *potior*, Sk. *pat* potiri.

πατήρ father : Lat. *pater*, Ir. *athair*, Got. *fadar* Eng., Sk. *pitar-*, *pā* protect. Hence πάτρως uncle : Lat. *patruus*, Ags. *fädera*, Sk. *pitrvyas*.

πάτος path : Lat. *pons*, Ir. *ath* ford, O Slav. *pǫti* path, Sk. *path* go.

παῦρος little : Lat. *paucus pauper*, Got. *favai* few Eng. .

παύω stop : Welsh *powys* rest.

παφλάζω boil : φλέω. 5.

πάχνη frost : πάγος. 21.

παχύς thick : Lat. *pinguis*, Eng. *big*, Sk. *bahus* strong. 20. 10.

πεδά with : πούς, cf. Lat. *ad pedem*. 7. So

πέδη fetter : Ags. *fetor* Eng.

πέδον ground : Sk. *padam* step, place.

πέζα foot. 19.

πείθω persuade : Lat. *fides feido foedus* Subst. *offendix*, O Ir. *band* law, Got. *bindan* bind Eng., Lit. *bendras* partner, Sk. *bandh* bind, πεῖσμα πενθερός. 20. 12.

πείκω comb, shear : Lat. *pecto pecten*, Ags. *feax* hair Eng. *Fair-fax*, Lit. *pészti* pluck. 17.

πείνα hunger : Lat. *pēnūria*, πένομαι. 17.

πεῖρα trial : Lat. *experior perītus perīculum*, Ags. *faer* danger Eng. *fear*, περάω. 17.

πεῖραρ πέρας end : Lat. *paries* (cf. Lit. *sena* 'boundary, wall'), πέρα. 3.

πείρινθα basket : περί, 'enclosing' the load on a wagon. 3.

πείρω pierce : O Slav. *prati* split.

πεῖσμα cable : Lat. *fūnis*, πείθω. 17. 19.

πέλαγος sea : *φέλχος, O Nor. *bylgja* billow Eng., O Slav. *brŭžaj* current, φλύκταινα. 20. 2.

πέλανος mess :

πελ-αργός stork : πελός, 'black and white'.

πέλας near : πλήσσω (cf. ἴκταρ Lat. *ico*).

πέλεθος = σπέλεθος. 32.

πέλεθρον = πλέθρον. 2.

πέλεια ringdove : Lat. *palumbes*, πελός.

πέλεκυς axe : O Ir. *lec* stone, Sk. *paraçus parçus* axe, πλήσσω. 2.

πελεμίζω shake : Got. *us-filma* frightened, πάλλω. 2.

πελίχνη πέλλη bowl : Lot. *pelvis*, Sk. *pālavī* vessel :

πέλλυτρα bandage, πέλμα sole of shoe : Ags. *filmen* skin Eng. *film*, ἐπίπλοον.

πελός dark : Lat. *pullus* dark *palleo*, Ags. *fealo* yellow Eng. *fallow*, Lit. *palwas*, Sk. *palitas* grey.

πέλτη shield, pole : πάλλω.

(πέλτης salted perch : Egyptian.)

πέλω go, be : κέλλω. 27. Hence πέλωρ monster, 'creature'.

πέμπω send :

πέμφιξ bubble : Lat. *papula pampinus*, Lit. *pampti* swell. 29.

πενθερός father-in-law : 'connexion', πείθω.

πένθος grief : Lat. *defendo offendo*, Lit. *bĕda* pain, Sk. *bādh* oppress. 20.

πένομαι toil :

πέντε πέμπε five : Lat. *quinque,* Ir. *cóig,* Got. *fimf* Eng., Lit. *penki,* Sk. *pancan : *πέμ-πεμ,* Lat. *quid-que,* 'all' the five fingers. 27. 26. 5.

πέος penis : Lat. *pēnis,* O Ir. *ál* proles, Ags. *fäsel* seed, Lit. *pisti* coire, Sk. *pasas* penis, *pish* grind πίσος. 34.

πεπαρεῖν display : Lat. *ap-pāreo,* πορεῖν. 11.

(πέπερι pepper : Sk. *pippalā.*)

πέπλος robe : στολάς. 5. 32.

πέπων A. ripe : πέσσω. 27.

πέπων B. gentle : Lat. *cicur cōmis,* κῖκυς. 27. 32.

πέρ altogether : περί.

πέρα beyond : Lat. *peregre peren-die,* O Ir. *ire* further, Got. *fairra* far Eng., Sk. *paras* yonder, παρά περί. Hence

περάω pass through, sell (cf. ὁδάω) : Lat. *porto,* Got. *faran* go Eng. *fare ferry ford,* Sk. *par* carry over.

πέρδιξ partridge (French *perdrix,* Eng.) : sq., from the sound it makes (cf. O Nor. rjúpa 'ptarmigan', ropa 'belch').

πέρδομαι pedo : Lat. *pēdo,* Ags. *feortan* Eng., Lit. *pérdziu* pedo, Sk. *pard* pedere.

πέρθω destroy : Sk. *spardh* contend, Ags. *spildan* destroy Eng. *spill.* 32.

περί around : Lat. *per-magnus,* Ir. *er-* very, Sk. *pari* around, παρά.

περι-γογγύζω murmur : O Slav. *gǫgnati,* Sk. *gunj.*

περι-ημεκτέω am angry :

περί-νεος breech : νείατος. 34.

περι-ρρηδής reeling : ῥαδινός. 19.

(περιστερά dove : Thracian.)

περίστια lustration : περί + ἱστίη (cf. ἀπέρωπος).

περι-φλεύω περι-φλύω scorch : φλοιός. 31.

περιχαμπτά Aesch. Suppl. 878, R. Ellis conj. περί, χάμψα, βρυάζεις 'un-measured is thy wantonness, O crocodile.'

περι-ώσιος immense : περί, on analogy of Perf. Part.

περκνός dark : Lat. *spurcus,* O Nor. *frecknur* freckles Eng., Lit. *prészas* spot, Sk. *pṛçnis* speckled, *sparç* touch. 32. Hence

πέρκη perch : Ir. *earc* spotted, salmon, OHG. *forhana* trout NHG. *forelle* (cf. Ir. *breac* 'spotted, trout').

(περσέα a tree : Egyptian.)

πέρυσι last year : O Ir. *in-uraid,* Sk. *parut,* πέρα + ἔτος. 23. 22.

(πεσσός draughtsman : Aramaic *pīsā* stone.)

πέσσω cook : Lat. *coquo,* Welsh *pobi* bake, Lit. *képti.* 27. 19.

πέταλον leaf, πετάννυμι spread, πέταχνον saucer : Lat. *pateo,* O Ir. *etem* fathom, Ags. *fädm* Eng., Zd. *pathana* broad.

πέτευρον perch, πέτομαι fly : Lat. *penna praepes accipiter impetus peto,* O Ir. *aith* wing, Ags. *feðer* Eng. *feather,* O Slav. *pŭtica* bird, Sk. *pat* fly, fall, πίπτω.

πέτρος stone : Ir. *aith* kiln : 27.

πεύθομαι = πυνθάνομαι. 31. 32.

πευκάλιμος wise, πευκεδανός sharp, πευκέδανον hog's fennel ('bitter') : πικρός. So πεύκη fir : 'sharp-leaved', NHG. *fichte*, Lit. *puszis*. 12.

πέφνον slew : φόνος. 31.

πήγανον rue, πηγός firm : Sk. *pajras* strong.

πηγή fountain :

πήγνυμι fasten : Lat. *pango pignus*, cf. Lat. *paciscor pāx*, Ir. *aicc* bond, Got. *fahan* seize Eng. *fang finger*, Bohem. *pásati* gird, Zd. *paç* bind. Hence πηκτίς harp, 'compact'.

πηδάω leap, πηδόν oar : σφαδάζω. 32.

πήκασμα Hipp. 55. 30 :

πήληξ helmet : πέλλη. 17.

πηλός clay : Lat. *palus*, Lit. *pelkë* swamp, Sk. *palvalam* pool : πελός (cf. Hom. μέλαν ὕδωρ). 17.

πῆμα woe, πηρός disabled : πένομαι. 17.

πήνη thread : Lat. *pannus*, Got. *fana* cloth Eng. *gon-fanon vane* 'flag'. Hence πηνέλ-οψ duck, *πηνέλη (cf. αἰγίλωψ), 'braided-looking, streaked'.

πηός kinsman : πάομαι (cf. 'one's belongings').

πήρα pouch : πῶμα. 8.

πῆχυς fore-arm : Sk. *bāhus* arm. 20.

πῖδαξ fountain : πίων, 'swelling'.

πιέζω press : O Ir. *tadaim* I shut. 19.

πίθηκος ape : 'cringing', πείθομαι. 31.

πίθος jar : Lat. *fidēlia*, Ags. *byde* tub : 20.

(πικέριον butter : παχύς, Phrygian.)

πικρός sharp : Ir. *oech* foe, Got. *fijan* hate Eng. *fiend*, Ags. *fāh* foe Eng., O Slav. *pisati* scratch.

πῖλος felt : Lat. *pilleus*, Eng. *felt*, Bohem. *plst* : Lat. *pīlātus* dense, Lett. *spilēt* squeeze. 32.

πίμπλημι fill : πλεῖος. 5.

πίμπρημι burn : πρήθω. 5.

πίναξ plank : O Slav. *pinĭ* trunk, Sk. *pinākas* staff :

(πίννα a shell-fish : πίνα πῖνα, σπῖνα.)

(πῖνον beer : Lit. *pywas*, πίνω.)

πῖνος dirt : σπῖλος. 32.

πινυτός wise : Lat. *pius*, Ir. *ciall* sense, τίω. 27.

πίνω drink : Lat. *bibo*, Ir. *ibhim* I drink, O Slav. *piti* to drink, Sk. *pi* : cf. πέπωκα, Lat. *pōto*, Lit. *póta* drinking-bout, Sk. *pā* drink. 12.

πιππίζω chirp : onomatopoeic, Lat. *pipo pīpulum*, Ags. *pipe* pipe Eng., Lit. *pépala* quail, Sk. *pippakā* a bird.

πίπτω fall : πέτομαι. 5. 31.

πίσεα meadows : πίων.

πίσος pea : Lat. *pīsum pinso*, NHG. *fese* husk, Lit. *paisyti* thresh, Sk. *pish* grind.

πίσσα pitch : Lat. *pix*, Lit. *pikkis*, Sk. *picchā* gum. 19.

(πίσυγγος shoemaker : Lydian ?)

πίσυρες = τέσσαρες. 27. 13. 22. 11.

πιττάκιον tablet : Πίττακος.

πίτυλος plash : πτύω. 2.

πίτῡρον bran : πτύον. 2.

πίτυς pine : Lat. *pīnus*, Sk. *pītu-dārus* a tree, πίων. 30.

πιφαύσκω shew : φάος. 5. 23.

(πίφιγξ lark : foreign, πίφηξ πίφαλλος.)

πίων fat Adj. : Lat. *pītuīta*, Ir. *ith*, Ags. *fät* Eng., Sk. *pīvan*, *pī* swell.

πλάγιος slanting, πλάζω make to wander : O Slav. *plŭzěti* creep, cf. πάλλω. 24. 19.

πλαδδιάω prate (Laconian) : φλέδων.

πλάδη moisture : παρδακός. 24. 25.

πλάθω approach : πέλας. 24.

πλαισίον brick : πλάσσω. 17. 22.

πλάνη wandering : πάλλω. 24.

πλάξ plain : Lat. *plānus*, NHG. *flach* flat, Lit. *ploksztas* : πλήσσω, 'beaten down' (cf. Got. *slaihts* 'smooth' *slahan* 'smite', ταπεινός). 30.

πλάσσω mould : *πλάθ-jω, Got. *falthan* fold Eng. 19.

πλάστιγξ πλήστιγξ scale of a balance :

πλαταγή rattle, πλατύς A. broad : O Ir. *lethan*, Lit. *platus*, Sk. *prthus*, *prath* stretch.

πλατύς B. brackish : Sk. *patus* : 24.

πλέθρον rood, πλεῖος full : Lat. *plēnus amplus compleo*, Ir. *lán*, Got. *fulls* Eng., Lit. *pilnas*, Sk. *par* fill. 30. Hence

πλείων more : Lat. *plūs*, Ir. *lia*, O Nor. *fleiri*, Zd. *frāyāo*. Hence πλήν except.

πλῆθος crowd : Lat. *plēbes populus*, Ags. *folc* Eng. *folk*, O Slav. *plemę* tribe.

πλήμνη nave of wheel, πλημυρίς flood-tide.

πλέκω weave : Lat. *plecto plico*, Got. *flahta* plaiting Eng. *flax*, O Slav. *plesti* weave, Sk. *praçnas* basket.

πλεύμων lung : Lat. *pulmo*, Lit. *plauczei* lungs : sq., 'floating' (cf. Ags. *lunge* 'lungs' *lungre* 'lightly', Eng. *lights*). So πλευρά rib. 23.

πλέω sail : Lat. *pluit*, Ir. *luam* yacht, Got. *flodus* flood Eng., Eng. *flow float*, Sk. *plu* swim. 34.

πλησίος near : πέλας. 24.

πλήσσω strike : Lat. *plecto* punish, Lit. *plákti* strike, cf. πόλεμος.

πλίνθος = πλαισίον. 11.

πλίσσομαι trot, πλιχάς interfeminium ('rubbed in walking'): πλίξ step:

πλοῦτος wealth: πλεῖος. 7.

πλύνω wash clothes: Lit. *pláuti*: πλέω, 'let float'. 31.

πνέω blow: Ags. *fnaest* panting. 34.

πνίγω choke: σφίγγω. 32. 21. 24.

πνύξ ecclesia: πυκνός, 'crowded'. 24.

ποδο-κάκκη stocks: κιγκλίδες. 10. 6.

πόθος longing: Got. *bidjan* beg Eng. *bid* pray. 20.

ποιέω make: Lat. *puer pŭsus*, Sk. *putras* son. 34.

ποίη grass: παίω (cf. Eng. hay hew). 9.

ποικίλος variegated: Lat. *pingo*, Got. *filu-faihs* manifold, Sk. *piç* adorn: πικρός, 'carved' (cf. κεστός). 31.

ποιμήν herdsman, ποίμνη flock: Lit. *pĕmŭ* herdsman, πῶυ.

ποινή fine: Lat. *poena pŭnio paenitet*, Zd. *kaēna* punishment, τίω. 27.

ποιπνύω bustle: πνέω. 5. 31.

ποιφύσσω breathe: cf. πτύω. 5. 32.

πόλεμος war: Zd. *paiti-par* fight. 25.

πολέω range, πόλος axis: πέλω. 7.

πολιός grey: πελός. 7.

πόλις city: Lit. *pillis* castle, Sk. *puris* city, πλεῖος. 24.

(πόλτος porridge, πολφός macaroni: Lat. *puls*, πάλη B.)

πολυ-δευκής Od. xix. 521 changeful: δοκέω. 31.

πολύ-ρρηνος rich in sheep: ἄρνα. 19.

πολύς many: Lat. *plērīque*, Ir. *il*, Got. *filu*, Sk. *purus*, πλεῖος. 24.

πομφόλυξ bubble: φλύκταινα. 5. 2.

πομφός blister: πέμφιξ. 7.

πόνος labour: πένομαι. 7.

πόντος sea: O Slav. *pạcina*:

πόπαξ πόποι Interj. Hence ποππύζω whistle.

πορεῖν supply, πορθμός ferry, πόρος ferry, means, πορσύνω prepare: Lat. *paro porta portus*, O Ir. *ernais* dedit, περάω. 7. Hence πόρις πόρτις calf: Lat. *pario*, Ags. *fear* ox Eng *hei-fer*, Lit. *perĕti* to brood.

πόρκης ring, πόρκος net: πλέκω. 25. 24.

πόρνη meretrix: Sk. *panyastrī*: 'venal'; πέρνημι περάω. 7.

πόρπη pin: πείρω. 7.

πορφύρα murex (Lat. *purpura*), πορφύρεος purple, πορφύρω darken: φύρω. 5.

πόσθη = πέος. 7.

πόσις husband: Lat. *potis potior* Adj. *compŏs*, Got. *bruth-faths* bridegroom, Lit. *patis* husband, Sk. *patis* lord. 22. Hence πότνια lady, Sk. *patnĭ*.

ποταίνιος fresh : *ποτι-ταίνιος, καινός. 35. 26.

ποταμός river : foreign ?

ποτί to : ποῦ + τό.

πότμος fate : τέτμον τύχη. 27.

ποῦ where ? : Lat. *ubi*, Got. *hvar* Eng., Lit. *kur*, Sk. *kva* : Lat. *quis*, Got. *hvas* who Eng., Lit. Sk. *kas*. 27.

πούς foot : Lat. *pēs*, Got. *fotus* Eng., Lit. *pádas* sole, Sk. *pād* foot.

(πράμνειος a wine : παραβίας.)

πράμος = πρόμος. 11.

πρᾶος gentle : Got. *frijon* to love *frijonds* friend Eng., *freis* free Eng., O Slav. *prijati* care for, Sk. *pri* delight.

πραπίδες midriff : Ags. *hrif* belly Eng. *mid-riff*, Sk. *krpītam*. 27.

(πράσον leek, πρασιά garden-plot : Lat. *porrum*, Aramaic *karrat* leek.)

πράσσω pass, do : περάω. 24.

πρέμνον stem : O Slav. *prążalĭ* stumbling-block. 19. 27.

πρέπω appear :

πρέσβυς old : Cretan πρεῖγυς, Hesych. σπέργυς : 32. 27.

πρευ-μενής πρηΰς friendly : πρᾶος. 30.

πρηγορεών crop : πρό + γαργαρεών.

πρήθω blow out : NHG. *sprühen* splutter, σπαίρω. 32. 24.

(πρημάς πριμαδίας tunny : foreign.)

πρηνής prone : πρό + ἀπ-ηνής.

πρηών πρών headland : πρό.

πρίασθαι to buy : Sk. *krī*. 27.

πρίν before : Lat. *prius*, πρό.

πρῖνος ilex : Lat. *quercus*, O Nor. *fura* fir Eng. 27. 24.

(πρίστις πρῆστις whale : Lat. *pistrix*, foreign.)

πρίω saw : cf. πείρω. 24. 34.

πρό before : Lat. *prō prae*, O Ir. *ro*, Got. *faur* Eng., Lit. *pirm*, Sk. *pra-*, παρά.

πρό-βατον sheep : βόσκω. 14.

προ-ΐκτης beggar, προ-ΐσσομαι beg, προΐξ gift : *προ-ΐσκτης, Ags. *āscian* ask Eng., Lit. *jëskóti* seek, cf. ἴστης. 32.

πρόκα straightway : πρό.

προ-κώνια groats : κῶνος, 'pointed'.

πρόμαλος willow :

πρόμος chief : Lat. *prīmus*, Ir. *rem-* before, Got. *fruma* first, πρό. Hence *προμνέω *προμνηστής (cf. ὀρχηστής) προμνηστῖνοι one by one.

προ-νωπής falling forward : see νάπη.

πρόξ deer : περκνός. 24.

προ-πρεών = πρηΰς. 30.

πρός from, at, to : παρά. 24.

προσ-αυρίζω meet with : ἐπ-αυρίσκω.

προσ-ηνής kind : ἀπ-ηνής.

πρόσθεν before, πρόσσω forward : πρό. 19.

πρό-σφατος fresh : φθάνω.

προ-ταινί in front of : τείνω. 9.

προτί to : O Ir. *leth-u* apud eos, O Slav. *proti* to, Sk. *prati*, πρό + τό.

(προύμνη plum-tree (Eng.) : foreign.)

προυσελέω insult : *προ-σϝελέω, σαλάκων. 17.

πρό-χνυ kneeling : γόνυ. 21.

πρύλεες champions, πρύλις war-dance, πρύτανις lord : πρό. 11.

πρυμνός hindmost : πέρας. 24.

πρώην lately, πρωΐ early : πρό. So πρώϊ-ζα lately, cf. χθι-ζός. 19.

πρωκτός ānus :

πρώρα prow : πρό.

πταίω cause to stumble : παίω (cf. σφάλλω Sk. sphal 'strike'). 6.

πτάξ hare : πτήσσω. 30.

πτάρνυμαι sneeze : Lat. *sternuo*, σπαίρω. 6.

πτελέη elm : OHG. *felawa* willow NHG. *felber*, Sk. *pallavas* shoot. 6.

πτέρνη heel, πτέρνις hawk ('long-heeled') : Lat. *perna*, Got. *fairzna*, O Slav. *plesna* sole of foot, Sk. *pārshnis* heel. 6. 32.

πτερόν feather : Lit. *sparnas* wing, σπαίρω. 6. Hence πτερίς fern, Ags. *fearn* Eng.

πτηνός winged : πέτομαι. 31.

πτήσσω scare : Lat. *conquinisco* cower. 27. 6. 19.

πτίλον feather : Lat. *pilus* hair, Lett. *spilwa* down, σπαίρω. 6. 25.

πτίσσω winnow : πίσος. 6. 19.

πτοέω excite : κατα-πτήτην, Lat. *paveo*, παίω. 6. 9.

πτόλεμος πτόλις = πόλεμος πόλις. 6.

πτόρθος sapling : Ags. *spreót* sprout Eng., cf. σπαργάω. 6.

(πτύγξ eagle-owl : φῶυξ.)

πτύον winnowing-fan : Lat. *putus* clean *pūrus*, OHG. *fowjan* winnow, Sk. *pavanam* sieve, *pū* cleanse. 6.

πτύρομαι am scared : Lat. *consternāre*, σπαίρω. 6. 11.

πτύσσω fold : Got. *biugan* bend Eng. *to bow*, Sk. *bhuj*, φεύγω. 20. 6. 19.

πτύω spit : Lat. *spuo*, Got. *speivan* Eng. *spue*, Lit. *spjauti*. 6.

πτῶμα fall : πίπτω. 31.

πτώσσω crouch : πτήσσω. 8.

πύανος = κύαμος. 27.

πῡγή rump, πῡγών length of the bent arm : πτύσσω. 20.

πυγμή fist : Lat. *pugnus pugil*, Eng. *fist*, O Slav. *pęsti* : πήγνυμι, 'compact'. 12.

πυδαρίζω see ἀποπυδαρίζω.

πύελος tub : πλύνω. 35.

πυθμήν bottom : Lat. *fundus*, Ir. *bonn*, Ags. *botm* Eng., Sk. *budhnas.* 20.

πύθω make to rot : Lat. *puter pūteo*, Ir. *úr* mould, Got. *fuls* rotten Eng. *foul* O Nor. *fúi* rottenness, Lit. *púti* to rot.

πύκα firmly, πυκνός solid : see πήγνυμι. 14.

(πυκτίς πικτίς beaver : foreign.)

πύλη gate : πόλις, 'city gate' (cf. Zd. *dvara* 'door, palace'). 11.

πύματος last : Lat. *post pōne*, O Ir. *ossar* posterus. 11. 35.

πύνδαξ = πυθμήν. 32. 20.

πυνθάνομαι learn : Got. *faur-biudan* forbid Eng., Lit. *budéti* watch, Sk. *budh* wake, perceive. 20.

πύξ with the fist : πυγμή.

(πύξος box (Lat. *buxus*, Eng.) : Asiatic.)

πύον pus : Lat. *pūs*, Sk. *pūyas*, πύθω. So πυός beestings.

πύππαξ Interj.

πῦρ πύιρ fire : Lat. *prūna* Umbrian *pir*, O Ir. *úr*, Ags. *fyr-* Eng., Bohem. *pyr* embers, Armen. *hhwour* fire.

πυραμίς wheaten cake, pyramid (from its shape) : πυρός.

πύργος tower : Hesych. φύρκος wall, Got. *baurgs* town Eng. *borough*, φράσσω. 20. 24.

πυρήν stone of fruit, πύρνον bread, πῡρός wheat : Lit. *púrai* winterwheat, EM. σπυρός : 32. Hence πῡρ-αύστης a moth, αὔω.

πυριάτη milk-pudding :

πυρσός Adj. red, Subst. beacon : πῦρ.

πυτίζω see ἀποπυτίζω.

πῡτίνη flask covered with osier :

πώγων beard : πηγός. 7.

πωλέομαι range, πωλέω sell : πολέω. 30.

πῶλος foal : Lat. *pullus* young, O Ir. *haue* nepos, Got. *fula* foal Eng., ποιέω.

πῶμα lid : Sk. *pā* protect, πατήρ. 8.

πωρητύς distress : πηρός. 7.

πῶρος tufa : Lit. *puriti* loosen.

πῶυ flock : Sk. *pā* protect, πατήρ. 8.

ῥάβδος wand : Lat. *verber*, Lit. *wirbas*. 18. 24. 6.

ῥαδινός slender : Sk. *vrad* become soft. 18.

ῥάδιος ῥήιδιος ῥᾳ (cf. βᾶ) easy : Sk. *vrthā* merrily, *var* choose, ἔλδομαι. 18. 24.

ῥάζω = ῥύζω. 11.

ῥαθάμιγξ drop, ῥαίνω sprinkle : νεο-αρδής Il. xxi. 346, Welsh *gwlith* dew, O Swedish *vriða* sprinkle (Johannes Schmidt), cf. ἄρδω. 18. 17.

ῥαθα-πυγίζω slap : ῥόθος + πυγή. 11.

ῥαιβός bent : Lat. *valgus urvus*, Got. *vraiqs* Eng. *wrick* twist *wriggle wry*, εἴργω. 18. 24. 17. 27.

ῥαίω break :

ῥάκος rag : ἕλκω. 18. 24.

ῥάμνος thorn-tree : ῥαχός. 19. 27.

ῥάμφος beak : ῥύγχος. 11. 27.

ῥάξ grape (Lat. *racēmus*) :

ῥαπίζω beat : ῥέπω. 11.

ῥάπτω connect : Lat. *sarcio*, cf. οὖλος A.. 18. 24. 27.

(ῥάπυς turnip, ῥάφανος cabbage : Lat. *rāpum*, NHG. *rübe* turnip, Lit. *rópe*.)

ῥάσσω push : ῥήσσω.

ῥᾱχία surge, shore : ῥήγνυμι. 29.

ῥάχις back :

ῥᾱχός hedge, bush :

ῥέγκω ῥέγχω snore, snort : Welsh *rhwnc* a snore, snort. 29.

ῥέγος ῥῆγος rug, ῥέζω A. dye : Ir. *lig* colour, dye, Sk. *raj* be coloured, ἀργός. 24. 30. 19.

ῥέζω B. = ἔρδω. 24. 19.

ῥέθος limb, face : ἀραρίσκω. 24.

ῥέπω incline : Lit. *wirpēti* shake, ῥίπτω. 18. 24.

ῥέω flow : Lat. *rumis* breast, Ags. *streám* Eng., Lit. *srawéti* flow, Sk. *sru*, cf. ἅλλομαι. 18. 34.

ῥηγμίς breakers, ῥήγνυμι break : Ir. *blogh* fragment (Eng. *block*). 18.

ῥῆμα word, ῥήτωρ speaker : Ir. *briathar* word, εἴρω B. 18. 24.

ῥῆνιξ sheepskin : ἄρνα. 18. 24.

ῥήσσω stamp :

(ῥητίνη resin : Lat. *rēsīna*.)

ῥῖγος frost : Lat. *frīgus*, Lit. *strégti* freeze. 18.

ῥίζα root : Lat. *rādīx*, Welsh *gwraidd* roots, Got. *vaurts* root Eng., cf. ὀρθός. 18. 24. 19.

ῥικνός shrunken : ῥοικός. 31.

ῥίμφα quickly : NHG. *ge-ring* light, Lit. *rengtis* to hurry, ἐλαφρός ὀρχέομαι. 11.

ῥίνη file : Lat. *serra*: 18. 24.

ῥῑνός skin : Sk. *var* cover εἶρος. 18. 24.

ῥίον peak : *Fρισον, οὖρος τό. 18. 24. 34.

ῥῑπή swing, ῥίπτω throw : Lit. *werpti* spin (cf. μίτος). 18. 24. Hence ῥίψ mat, ῥιπίς fan ('plaited work').

ῥίς nose : Welsh *rhyn* cape.

(ῥίσκος = ἄρριχος.)

(ῥόγος barn : Italian, Lat. *rogus*, λέγω B.)

ῥοδάνη woof, ῥοδανός waving : ῥαδινός.

(ῥόδον rose : Lat. *rosa*, Armen. *vart*.)

ῥόθος noise : ῥέω.

(ῥοιά pomegranate, ῥοιάς poppy, ῥοῦς sumach : Sk. *sravā* a plant.)

ῥοῖβδος ῥοῖζος whizzing : ῥύζω.   17. 27. 5.

ῥοικός crooked : Got. *vruggo* snare, Ags. *vringan* wring out Eng., cf. ῥαιβός.   18. 17.

ῥόμβος wheel : ῥαιβός.

ῥοφέω swallow : Lat. *sorbeo*, Ir. *srubh* snout, Lit. *srĕbti* swallow.   18.

ῥοχθέω roar, ῥυάχετος mob (Laconian), ῥύβδην noisily, ῥύζω snarl : cf. O Slav. *vrŭkati* cry.   18. 27.

ῥύγχος snout : ὀρύσσω.   18. 29.

ῥυθμός movement, ῥύμη impetus : ῥέω.   31.

ῥῦμα drawing, ῥῦμός pole : ἐρύω.   18.

(ῥυνδάκη a bird : ῥυντάκης, Indian.)

ῥύομαι rescue : ἐρύομαι.   18.

ῥύπος dirt, ῥύπτω cleanse :

ῥυππαπαί cry of rowers.

ῥύσιον booty, ῥυσός wrinkled, ῥυτίς wrinkle, ῥυστάζω drag : ἐρύω.   18.

ῥυτόν rue, ῥύτρος echinops :

ῥωδιός heron : Lat. *ardea*, O Nor. *arta* teal : 24.

ῥώμη strength, ῥώννυμι strengthen, ῥώομαι rush : ῥέω.   17.

ῥώξ A. Od. xxii. 143 entrance : ῥήγνυμι.   8.

ῥώξ B. Archil. 191 = ῥάξ.   8.

ῥῶπες brushwood, ῥῶπος frippery : Lat. *sarpo* prune.   18. 24.

σά what ? : τίς.   19.

σαβακός putrid (Chian), σαβάκτης shatterer : Hesych. σαυχμόν σαθρόν, Lat. *saucius*.

(σαβαρίχη cunnus : σαμαρίχη μαρίχη σαμβρίχη, foreign.)

(σάγαρις axe : Persian.)

(σάγδας = ψάγδαν.)

σάγη harness : σάττω.

σαγηνεύω sweep clean : Ags. *svāpan* Eng.   32.

(σαθέριον = σαπείριον.)

σάθη penis :

σαθρός rotten :

σαικωνίζω move : σείω.   9.

σαίνω fawn : NHG. *schwanz* tail, cf. σείω.   32. 9.

σαίρω sweep : Lat. *sarrio*, σύρω.

(σάκκος σάκος ὁ bag : Heb. *saq*, Coptic *sok*.)

σάκος τό shield : Sk. *tvac* skin.   19.

σάκτας physician : σάττω.

σαλάκων swaggerer, σάλος tossing : Lat. *salum*, Ags. *svellan* swell Eng., ἀείρω. 32. 11. 25.

(σαλαμάνδρα lizard : Pers. *samandar*.)

(σαλάμβη σαλάβη chimney : foreign.)

(σαλητόν σαρητόν tunic : foreign.)

(σάλπη σάρπη a fish : foreign.)

σάλπιγξ trumpet : Lit. *szwilpti* to pipe, cf. σῦριγξ. 32.

σάμαξ mat : foreign ?

(σαμβύκη harp : Aramaic *sabb'kā*.)

(σάν a letter : Heb. *shin*.)

(σάνδαλον σάμβαλον shoe : Pers. *sandal* boat.)

(σανδαράκη σανδαράχη realgar : Sk. *sindūram*.)

(σανίς board : foreign (cf. δέλτος).)

(σαννάκιον σαννάκρα cup : Persian.)

σάννας buffoon (Lat. *sannio, sanna* mockery) : Lat. *sonus persōna*, Ir. *son* word, Ags. *svin* song, Sk. *svan* tingle. 32. 11.

σάος safe : Lat. *sānus sospes*.

(σαπείριον beaver : foreign.)

(σᾱπέρδης salt perch : Pontic.)

(σάπφειρος sapphire : Heb. *sappīr*.)

(σαράβαρα trowsers : Heb. *sar'bol*, Pers. *shalwār*.)

(σάρᾱπις robe : Persian.)

(σάρβιτος Sappho 154 lyre : foreign.)

σαργάνη band, basket : Hesych. ταργάναι πλοκαί : 19.

(σαργῖνος sardine, σαργός a fish : Egyptian.)

σάρδα a fish : Σαρδώ Sardinia.

σαρδάνιον grimly : σεσηρώς.

σαρδών edge of net :

(σάρι a plant : Egyptian.)

(σάρισσα pike : Macedonian, *σϜάριθja, Ags. *sveord* sword Eng.)

σάρξ σύρξ flesh :

σατίνη chariot : Hesych. σάσαι sit (Paphian), θαάσσω.

(σατράπης ἐξατράπης viceroy : O Pers. *khshatra-pāvā* (Spiegel), see κτάομαι and πῶυ.)

σάττω load : Lat. *sagina*, Lit. *segti* to buckle, Sk. *svaj* embrace. 32. 19.

σαῦλος mincing : σάλος. 17.

(σαύνιον spear : foreign.)

σαύρα lizard : foreign ?

σαυρωτήρ spike : Lat. *surculus*, MHG. *swir* stake, Sk. *svaras*. 32.

σαυσαρισμός dryness : dialectic, Lat. *sūdus*, OHG. *sorēn* dry up Eng. *sere*, Lit. *sausas* dry, Zd. *hush* to dry.

σαφής clear : Lat. *sapio*, Ags. *sefan* teach. 29.

σάω sift : Lat. *sero* sow, Got. *saian* Eng., Lit. *sijóti* sift.　32.

σβέννυμι quench : Got. *qistjan* spoil, Lit. *gessyti* quench, Sk. *jas* be exhausted.　27.

σέβω worship : Got. *svikns* clean, innocent.　32. 27.

σεῖν Interj.

σειρά cord : Lat. *sero* join, Got. *sarva* armour, Lit. *séris* thread, Sk. *sarat.*

σειρινός aestivus : Ags. *svelan* glow Eng. *swelter sultry,* Lit. *swelti.*　32. 3.

(σείστρος vetch : Lydian.)

σείω shake : σεύω.　34.

σέλας light, σελήνη moon : Lat. *serēnus sōl,* O Ir. *selam* sky, Got. *sauil* sun, Lit. *sáule,* Sk. *svar.*　32.

(σέλαχος shark : Ags. *seolh* seal Eng.)

σέλινον parsley (Eng. *celery,* πετρο-σέλινον *parsley*) : σέρις.　25.

σέλμα deck : Lit. *szalma* rafter, σαυρωτήρ.　25.

(σεμίδᾱλις flour : Lat. *simila.*)

σεμνός holy : σέβω.　19.

σέρις endive :

(σέρφος gnat : σέριφος συρφός στέρφος, foreign.)

(σέσελις a shrub : Egyptian.)

σεσερῖνος a fish :

σεσηρώς grinning : σῆραγξ, 'opening'.

(σέσῑλος snail : σέσηλος, foreign.)

σεῦτλον τεῦτλον beet : 19.

σεύω move : Lat. *sucula* windlass, Sk. *su* set in motion.

σήθω = σάω.

σηκός pen : Lat. *saepes,* OHG. *sweiga* cow-house, O Slav. *o-sĕkŭ* sheepfold.　32.　Hence σήκωμα weight, 'enclosure' in the scale.

σῆμα sign :

σήμερον τήμερον today : τ-Fός(τό) + ἡμέρα.　19.

(σημύδα birch : foreign.)

(σηπία cuttle-fish, σήψ snake : Heb. *tsabh.*)

σήπω corrupt : Lit. *su-szuppęs* rotten :

σῆραγξ cave :

(σής moth : Heb. *sās.*)

(σήσαμον sesame : foreign.)

σητάνιος this year's : ἔτος, cf. σήμερον.

σθένος strength : ἵστημι.　21.

σιᾱγών jawbone : ὑαγών :

σίαλον saliva, σίαλος A. grease : Hesych. σίαι πτύσαι (MSS. πτῆσαι) Paphian :

σίαλος B. hog : *σF-ίαλος σῦς.　32.

(σιβύνη σίγυνον spear : Macedonian.)

σῑγαλόεις glossy : Ags. *svegle* sky. 32. 17. 28.

σῑγή silence : Ags. *svīg-dåg* day of silence. 32. 28.

(σίγλος a coin : Heb. *sheqel*.)

(σίδη pomegranate, water-lily : σίβδα, Pers. *sīb* apple.)

σίδηρος iron : Lit. *swidus* bright, Sk. *svēdanī* iron pan. 32.

σίζω hiss : Got. *sviglon* to pipe. 32. 28.

(σίκιννις a dance : Phrygian, Ags. *svingan* swing Eng., O Slav. *sukati* spin.)

σικύα gourd :

σικχός squeamish :

σιλη-πορδέω insult (πέρδομαι) : 7.

(σιλλι-κύπριον a plant : Egyptian.)

σιλλόω mock : σίλλος lampoon :

σίλουρος shad :

(σίλφη cockroach (Eng. *sylph*) : τίλφη τίφη, σέρφος.)

(σίλφιον asafoetida (Lat. *sirpe*) : foreign.)

σῖμβλος hive : σμῆνος.

σῖμός snub-nosed : σιγή, 'compressed'. 32.

(σίναπι mustard : Egyptian.)

(σινδών muslin : Babylonian *sindhu* (Sayce) : 'Indian', Sk. *Sindhus* Indus.)

σίνομαι injure : OHG. *swīnan* pine NHG. *schwinden* vanish Eng. *swindle*. 32.

(σιπταχόρας a tree : Indian.)

(σιπύη vessel : σίββα σιφνίς ἰπύα, Lat. *simpuvium*.)

σίραιον defrutum :

(σιρός pit : Cappadocian.)

(σίσαρον a plant (Lat. *siser*) : Egyptian.)

σισύμβριον = θύμβρα, dialectic. 5.

(σισύρα rug : σίσυρνα σίσυς, foreign.)

(σισυρίγχιον gladiolus : foreign.)

(σῖτος corn : Thracian, O Slav. *žito*, βίος.)

σίττη nuthatch : σίζω, 'whistler'.

(σίττυβος pot : foreign.)

σιφλόω cripple : σιφλός empty :

σίφων pipe : O Slav. *soplĭ*:

σιώ-κολλος sacristan : σιός (Laconian) θεός + βού-κολος.

σιωπή silence : σωπάω. 5. 34.

σκάζω limp : O Nor. *skakkr* wry, Sk. *khanj* limp.

σκαιός left : Lat. *scaevus obscaenus*, O Nor. *skeifr* oblique Eng. *skew*. 34.

σκαίρω skip : O Nor. *skrída* creep, Zd. *çkar* spring.

σκαλαθύρω dig, **σκάλλω** hoe : O Ir. *scailt* a cleft, Ags. *sceran* cut Eng. *shear share*, Lit. *skélti* split. 11. 2.

σκαληνός = σκολιός. 11.

σκαλίας head of artichoke, **σκαλμός** thole : σκῶλος, 'pointed'.

(**σκάλιδρις** redshank : foreign.)

(**σκαλμή** sword : Thracian, O Nor. *skálm*, σκάλλω.)

σκάλοψ mole : Lat. *talpa*, σκορπίζω. 11. 25. 2.

(**σκαμωνία σκαμμωνία** bindweed : κάμων, Mysian.)

σκανδάληθρον springe : Lat. *scando*, O Ir. *ro-sescaind* prosiluit, Ags. *scotian* shoot Eng. *shoot scud*, Sk. *skand* spring.

σκάνδιξ chervil :

σκαπερδεύω abuse : σκαπέρδα rope used in a game (cf. διασύρω) :

σκάπτω dig : Lat. *scabo*, Got. *skaban* shave Eng. 19.

σκαρδαμύσσω wink : *σκάρδαμος 'dazzling', O Nor. *skart* finery.

σκαρίζω = σκαίρω.

σκαρῑφισμός scratching up : Lat. *scrobs*, Welsh *crafu* scratch, Lett. *skrabt* scrape, cf. σκάλλω. 2.

σκάρος a fish (Lat. *scārus*) : σκαίρω.

σκάφη tub, **σκάφος** hull : σκάπτω, 'dug out'.

σκεδάννυμι scatter : Eng. *scatter*, Sk. *kshad* cut up.

σκεθρός exact : ἐχυρός ἔχω. 20.

σκελιφρός = σκληφρός. 2.

σκέλλω parch : σκάλλω 'penetrate,' of the sun's rays (cf. parch pierce).

σκέλος leg : σκῶλος (cf. O Nor. *leggr* 'leg, shaft'). 7.

σκέπαρνος adze :

σκέπας shelter : cf. κνέφας.

σκέπτομαι = σκοπέω. 7.

σκερβόλλω scold : Lit. *skélbti* denounce, κρέμβαλα.

σκεῦος implement : Got. *skevjan* go, O Slav. *skytati* wander, Sk. *cyu* moliri.

σκηνή tent : σκιά (cf. Eng. shed shade).

σκηπτός storm, **σκήπτω** hurl : Sk. *kshap*.

σκήπτομαι lean, **σκῆπτρον** staff : Lat. *scāpus scamnum*, Ags. *sceaft* shaft Eng., cf. Sk. *skambh* support.

σκηρίπτομαι support oneself : σκαριφισμός, 'clutch'. 2. 19.

σκιά shade : Ir. *sciath* shield, Sk. *chāyā* shade. 31.

σκίδναμαι spread : σκεδάννυμι. 13.

(**σκίλλα** = σχῖνος B., Lat. *squilla*.)

σκιμᾱλίζω handle :

σκιμβάζω = σκάζω. 11. 27.

σκίμπους couch : *σκιμπό-πους, σκήπτομαι. 11. 35. So **σκίμπων σκῑπων** staff, Lat. *scipio*. 17.

σκίμπτω overthrow : σκήπτω. 11.

σκινδάριον a fish, σκινθός diving : Lit. *skendau* I sink, σκανδάληθρον. 11.
(σκινδαψός harp : foreign.)

σκίραφος dice-box :

σκῖρος callus : ξηρός. 11.

σκιρτάω = σκαίρω. 11.

σκίφη stinginess : σκάπτω, 'scraping'. 17.

σκληρός hard : σκέλλω. 24.

σκληφρός lean : σκαριφισμός (cf. λεπτός).

σκνιπός purblind : *σκεμπός, σκέπας, cf. κνέφας. 24.

σκνίψ ant : NHG. *schabe* moth, Sk. *kipyas* worm : 24.

(σκοῖδος lord : Macedonian.)

σκολιός crooked : O Nor. *skjálgr* Eng. *shelving shallow*.

(σκολόπαξ woodcock : σκολῶπαξ ἀσκαλώπας, foreign.)

σκολοπένδρα milleped : σκορπίος. 25. 2.

σκόλοψ stake : σκορπίζω, 'cut up.' 25. 2.

σκόλυθρος stool : 'cut short', κόλυθροι ἀπο-σκολύπτω.

σκόλυμος = σκαλίας.

σκολύπτω see ἀποσκολύπτω.

σκόμβρος mackerel : Hesych. σκομβρίσαι γογγύσαι, Lit. *skambĕti* to ring (cf. Eng. gurnard, 'grunter').

σκόννυζα elecampane : foreign ?

σκοπέω look out : Lat. *specio*, NHG. *spähen* Eng. *spy*, O Slav. *pasti* feed ('provide for,') Sk. *spaç* see. 24.

σκορακίζω insult : 'ἐς κόρακας' (cf. κτώ).

σκόρδαξ cancan, σκορδύλη tunny : O Ir. *ceird* going, NHG. *scherzen* play, Sk. *kürd* spring, cf. σκαίρω.

σκορδινάομαι yawn, σκόρδον σκόροδον garlic : O Slav. *skarędŭ* disgusting, Sk. *chard* vomit. 2.

σκορπίζω scatter, σκορπίος scorpion ('multifidus') : O Ir. *cerp* cutting, Lit. *kirpti* shear, Sk. *krpānas* sword, cf. σκάλλω.

σκότος darkness : Ir. *scáth* shade, Got. *skadus* Eng., cf. σκιά.

σκύβαλον refuse :

σκυδμαίνω σκύζομαι am angry, σκυθρός angry : Lit. *skaudus* painful.

σκυζάω prurio : Lat. *cauda*, Sk. *khud* pene percutere.

σκύλαξ puppy, σκύλια dog-fish :

σκύλλαρος hermit-crab :

σκύλλω tear : σκάλλω. 11.   Hence σκῦλον spoil, Lat. *spolium*.

σκύμνος whelp :

σκυτάλη staff, σκύτον neck ('support' of the head) :

σκῦτος hide : Lat. *scūtum obscūrus*, Lit. *skura* skin, Sk. *sku* cover, cf. σκιά.

σκύφος cup : σκάφος. 14.

σκώληξ worm : σκάλλω.

σκῶλος stake, thorn : σκάλλω, 'digger, pricker'.　30.

σκώπτω mock : O Nor. *skaup* mockery Eng. *scoff*, Sk. *kshapanyus*, *kshap*
hurl σκήπτω (cf. Eng. slang sling).　8.　Hence **σκώψ** owl (cf. NHG.
hohu 'mockery', heher 'magpie').

σκώρ dung : Lat. *stercus su-cerda*, Welsh *ysgarth* offscourings, Ags.
scearn dung, O Slav. *skvara* dirt, Sk. *ava-skaras* excrement, κρίνω.

σκωρνυφία snare Epicharmus μησί :

(σμάραγδος emerald : Sk. *marakatam* (cf. σμύρνα).)

σμαραγέω roar :

(σμάρις σμαρίς picarel : foreign.)

σμάω rub : Lat. *macula*.

σμερδαλέος terrible : Lat. *mordeo*, Eng. *to smart*.

σμῆνος hive, swarm : ἐσμός.

σμηρέα ivy ('winding'), **σμήρινθος** cord :

σμῖκρός small : Lat. *macer*, Ir. *bec*, cf. Ags. *smeā* small Got. *smals* Eng. :
17.

σμῖλαξ oak, yew, convolvulus : σμηρέα.　25.

σμίλη chisel, **σμίνθος** vole : σμάω.

σμινύη mattock : Welsh *mynawyd* awl :

σμύξων a fish : Lat. *mūgil*, ἀπομύττω.

σμύραινα lamprey, **σμύρος** eel :

σμυρίζω anoint : Got. *smairthr* fat Eng. *smear*, Lit. *smársas*, μύρον.

(σμύρνα = μύρρα (cf. σμάραγδος).)

σμύχω burn :

σμῶδιξ weal : σμάω.　8.

σοβέω scare, shake, strut : σαγηνεύω.　27.

(σόγκος σόγχος sow-thistle : foreign.)

(σόλοικος clumsy : foreign.)

σόλος quoit : σάλος, 'swung'.

σομφός spongy : Got. *svamms* sponge *svumfsl* pond Eng. *swamp*.　32.

σόος rush : σεύω.　7. 34.

(σορός urn : σιρός).

σοῦ Interj.

(σούσινος liliaceus : Heb. *shūshan* lily.)

σοφός skilful : σαφής.

σπάθη blade : σπάω.

σπαίρω shake : Lat. *sperno*, Ags. *speornan* spurn Eng., Lit. *spirti* kick,
Sk. *sphur* shake.　9.

σπάλαξ = σκάλοψ.　24.

σπάνις want :

σπαράσσω tear : *σπαργ-τjω : 2.

σπαργάω swell : Lat. *turgeo*, O Nor. *sprökla* sprawl Eng., Lit. *sprogti*
break out, Sk. *sphurj*.　11.

σπάργω swathe : σπαράσσω (cf. λώπη).

σπαρνός scanty : Lat. *parcus parvus*, Ags. *spär* sparing Eng.

σπάρος bream : σπαίρω.

σπάρτον rope, σπάρτος esparto : Lat. *sporta* basket, Lit. *spartas* band.

(σπατάγγης sea-urchin : foreign.)

σπατίλη dung : σκώρ Gen. σκατός. 27. 10.

σπάω draw, tear : Lat. *spatium*.

σπεῖρα roll : σπάρτον.

σπείρω sow : σπαίρω.

σπέλεθος dung :

σπένδω offer : Lat. *spondeo*, Sk. *chand*.

σπέος cave : 'spiraculum', Lat. *spīro*, O Slav. *pachati* to fan. 34.

σπέρχω hasten : Sk. *sparh* be jealous.

σπεύδω urge on : Lat. *studeo*, cf. Ags. *spōvan* succeed Eng. *speed*.

σπήλαιον σπῆλυγξ cave : O Slav. *puchlŭ* hollow, σπέος. 17.

σπιδής broad : στάδιον. 14.

σπίζω chirp : Ags. *fine* finch Eng. :

σπιθαμή span : Lat. *pando*, O Slav. *pędĭ*, σπιδής.

σπιλάς σπίνος A. rock, σπῖλος stain (as from porous rock) : στῖον. 19.

(σπῖνα a fish : πίννα.)

σπινθήρ spark : Lit. *spindĕti* shine, ξανθός : cf. Lat. *scintilla*, O Ir. *cáin* clear, Got. *skeinan* shine Eng.

σπίνος B. finch : σπίγγος, Eng. *spink*, σπίζω.

σπλάγχνα lungs, σπλήν spleen : Lat. *lien rēnes*, O Ir. *selg*, O Slav. *slezena*, Sk. *plihan :* Hence σπληνίον bandage, 'laid on the spleen'. 35.

(σπλεκόω σπεκλόω coeo : foreign.)

(σπόγγος sponge (Lat. *fungus*) : foreign.)

σποδέω strike, devour (cf. παίω) :

σποδός ashes : Lett. *spódrs* bright.

σπολάς coat : στολή στέλλω. 19.

σπονδύλη σφονδύλη beetle, σπόνδυλος σφόνδυλος vertebra : σφαδάζω. 21.

σποργίλος Ar. Av. 300 a bird : Hesych. σπέργουλος, Got. *sparva* sparrow Eng., Pruss. *spurglis :* σπαργάω, 'wanton'.

σπύραθος dung, σπυράς pill : σφαῖρα. 11.

σπυρθίζω dance : σκόρδαξ. 27. 11.

σπυρίς basket : σπάρτον. 11.

στάδιον race-course : Dor. σπάδιον, σπάω. 19.

στάζω drop : *στέγγ-jω, Lat. *stagnum* Lit. *stingti* coagulate. 10. 19.

σταθεύω roast, 'set before the fire', στάθμη line σταφύλη plummet (see θήρ), σταθμός dwelling, στάμνος jar : ἵστημι.

σταίς dough, στέαρ fat : 'stiff', ἵστημι.

σταλάσσω drop : *στλέγγ-τjω στράγξ. 2. 25. 10.

σταλίς prop : στέλλω. 11.

σταυρός stake : O Nor. *staurr*, Sk. *sthāvaras* firm, ἵστημι.

σταφίς raisin, σταφυλή grape : στέμφυλον, 'thick'. 10.

στάχυς ear of corn : O Nor. *stanga* to prick, Lit. *steyerys* stalk. 10.

στέγω shelter : Lit. *stégti* to thatch, Sk. *sthag* cause to disappear, τέγος.

στείβω press : στάζω, 'coagulate'. 12. 27.

στειλειόν handle : Eng. *stalk stilt*, σταλίς.

στεινός narrow : Sk. *styānas* thick : 17.

στείρα cutwater : Ags. *steōran* to steer Eng., Lit. *styras* rudder : 'strengthener', στερεός. So στεῖρος barren : Lat. *sterilis*, Got. *stairo*, Sk. *starī* barren cow ('hard, unfruitful').

στείχω walk : O Ir. *tiagaim* I walk, Got. *steigan* ascend Eng. *stair stile*, Lit. *staigus* hasty.

στέλεχος trunk : σταλίς.

(στελίς mistletoe : ἀστυλίς, foreign.)

στέλλω place : Ags. *stäl* a place Eng. *stall*, Lit. *stellóti* to order, cf. ἵστημι. Hence στελμονίαι belts, Hesych. στέλμα belt.

στέμβω shake, στέμφυλον oil-cake ('compressed') : στέφω. 19. 32.

στένω groan : Ags. *stȳnan* Eng. *stun*, Lit. *stenĕti*, Sk. *stan* roar.

στέργω love : Ir. *serc* love.

στερεός solid : Ir. *seirt* strength, Lit. *styrĕti* stiffen, Sk. *sthiras* firm, cf. ἵστημι. So στέριφος firm, barren (cf. στεῖρος) : O Slav. *strabiti* refresh.

στερέω deprive : O Ir. *serb* theft, Got. *stilan* steal Eng.

στέρνον chest : NHG. *stirn* forehead : στορέννυμι, 'extended'. 7.

στεροπή lightning, στέροψ bright :

στεῦμαι purpose : στύω. 31.

στέφω put round : Lit. *stebyti* stop, Sk. *stambh* support.

στῆθος chest : ἵστημι, 'prominent'.

στήλη pillar : Aeol. στάλλᾱ, σταλίς.

στήμων web : Lat. *stāmen*, Sk. *sthavis* weaver, ἵστημι.

στηρίζω set fast : στερεός. 30.

στίβη rime : στείβω. 31.

στίζω prick : Lat. *distinguo instīgo stilus stimulus*, Got. *stiks* point Eng. *to stick*, Sk. *tij* be sharp.

στίλβω shine, στιλπνός shining : Lit. *stelgti* to look. 11. 27. 19.

στίλη drop : Lat. *stīria stilla*.

(στίμμις pigment : Coptic *stēm*.)

στίον pebble : Got. *stains* stone Eng., O Slav. *stĕna* wall :

στῖφος mass, στιφρός firm : στέφω. 17.

στίχος στοῖχος row : στείχω, 'procession'. 31. 7.

στλεγγίς flesh-brush : Lat. *strigilis*, στραγγαλίς. 25.

στοά στοιά portico : στύω. 34.

στόμα mouth : Zd. *çtaman:* Hence στόμ-αργος noisy, cf. λαιθ-αργος.

στόμβος στόμφαξ bombast : στέφω, 'padding.' 7. 19.

στορέννυμι spread : Lat. *sterno struo*, O Ir. *srethi* sternendum, Got. *straujan* strew Eng., Sk. *star.*

στόρθυγξ = στύραξ A.

στοχάζομαι aim at : στάχυς, 'aim at a point'.

στραβαλο-κόμας curly-haired, στράβηλος snail, olive : Lit. *straige* snail, στρεβλός. 11.

στραγγαλίς knot (Lat. *strangulo*) : 'pressed, turned', Lat. *stringo striga* row, Got. *striks* line Eng. *stretch.* 11. Hence

    στραγγεύομαι loiter, 'turn to and fro', στρεύγομαι am worn out. 17.

    στράγξ drop, 'pressed out'.

στράπτω lighten : στεροπή. 24. 2.

στρατός army : στορέννυμι, 'spreading out, encampment'. 24.

στρεβλός crooked : στραγγαλίς. 27.

στρέφω turn : Ags. *strengan* stretch *streng* string Eng., cf. στραγγαλίς. 32. 27.

στρηνιάω wanton : στρηνής loud, Lat. *strēnuus*, στερεός.

στριβι-λικίγξ Ar. Ach. 1035 a whit : στρίβος whisper + λικίγξ chirp :

στριφνός = στέριφος. 24.

στρόβος whirling : στρεβλός.

στρόμβος top : στρέφω. 7. 19.

στρογγύλος round : Lit. *stulgus* oval, στραγγαλίς. 7.

στροῦθος sparrow : *σπρόγγ-θος, σπογγίλος. 19. 24. 17. 32.

στρυφνός harsh, stiff : στριφνός. 11.

στρύχνος nightshade :

στρώννυμι = στορέννυμι. 24.

στυγέω hate :

στῦλος pillar : Lit. *stůlys* stump, Sk. *sthūnā* pillar, στύω.

στύπειον tow (Lat. *stūpa*) :

στύραξ A. spike : Ags. *steort* tail Eng. *red-start:* στερεός, 'stiff'. 11.

(στύραξ B. a gum : Heb. *tsorē* balsam.)

στυφελίζω buffet, στυφελός στυφλός hard, στύφω dry up : στέμβω. 14. 32.

στύω erigo : Sk. *sthūlas* big, cf. ἵστημι.

στωμύλος noisy : στόμα. 3.

σύ τύνη thou : Lit. *tū*, Ir. *tu*, Got. *thu* Eng., Lit. *tu*, Sk. *tvam.* 22. 30.

(συβήνη flute-case : σιβύνη.)

(σῦκάμῖνον mulberry : Heb. *sheqmāh.*)

(σῦκον τῦκον fig: Lat. *ficus*, O Slav. *smoky* (Got. *smakka*), Armen. *thwouz.*)

σῦλάω despoil: σύρω. 25.

σύν = ξύν. 32.

συο-βαύβαλος of a sty: βαυβάω.

συρβηνεύς noisy: τύρβη. 22.

σῦριγξ pipe: Dor. τυρίσδω I pipe, Lat. *susurrus absurdus*, Got. *svaran* swear Eng., Lit. *surma* pipe, Sk. *svar* sound. 32.

(σύριχος = ἄρριχος.)

σύρφαξ συρφετός rubbish: Got. *af-svairban* wipe off. 32.

σύρω drag: see τορύνη. 22. Hence συρμαία purgative, συρμός vomiting.

σῦς pig: Got. *svein* Eng. *swine*, O Slav. *svinija*, ῦς. 32. Hence συ-φεός sty, φωλεός. 34.

σῦφαρ slough: Lat. *suber:*

συχνός numerous: σάττω (cf. Lat. frequens farcio). 14. 21.

σφαδάζω struggle: Lat. *pendo* 'let swing', Sk. *spand* move quickly. 21. 10.

σφάζω kill: σφίγγω. 10. 19.

σφαῖρα ball: Lit. *spirra:* σπαίρω, 'thrown about'. 21.

σφάκελος gangrene, convulsion:

(σφάκος sage: σφάγνος, foreign.)

σφάλλω overthrow: Welsh *pall* failure (Eng. *to pall*), Ags. *feallan* fall Eng., Lit. *pulti*, Sk. *sphal* strike (cf. πταίω παίω). 21.

σφαραγέομαι burst: σπαργάω. 21. 2.

σφέ him: Pruss. *subs* self, ἒ + φή.

σφεδανός σφοδρός vehement: σφαδάζω. 7. Hence
    σφένδαμνος maple, 'luxuriant'. 32.
    σφενδόνη sling (Lat. *funda*), 'jerked'.

σφέλας footstool: Hesych. σφαλλός stocks:

σφηκόομαι am bound, σφήξ wasp (Lat. *fucus*), 'tight-waisted': Ags. *spange* clasp, Zd. ςρας press. 21.

σφήν wedge, σφίγγω bind: 35. 11.

(σφρᾱγίς seal: foreign.)

σφριγάω = σπαργάω. 21. 24.

σφυδόομαι am vigorous, σφύζω throb: σφαδάζω. 14.

σφῦρα hammer, σφυρόν ankle, σφυρόομαι penem erigo: σπαίρω, Welsh *ffer* ankle. 21. 11.

σφυράδες dung: σφαῖρα (cf. βόλιτον βολβός). 11.

σφῶι ye two: σύ + φή.

σχαδών larva of bee, honeycomb: 'hiding, hiding-place', Lat. *squama*, Sk. *chad* cover. 21. 32.

σχάζω A. σχάω (on analogy of βιάζω βιάω) cut: σκεδάννυμι. 21. 10. 19.

σχάζω B. drop: σκανδάληθρον. 21. 32. 19.

σχαλίς forked stick, σχελίς rib : σκέλος σκῶλος. 21.

σχέδην gently : σκεθρός.

σχεδία raft of laths, σχίζω split : Lat. *scindo,* Sk. *chid* divide, σκεδάννυμι. 21. 12. So σχινδαλαμός σχινδαλμός splinter, Lat. *scandula.* 2.

σχεδόν near, σχερῷ row, σχέτλιος pertinacious : ἔχομαι cling to, ἔχω.

σχῆμα form : ἔχω (cf. Lat. *habitus*).

σχῖνος A. mastich-tree : foreign ?

(σχῖνος B. squill : foreign.)

σχοῖνος rush :

σχολή leisure : ἔχω, 'holding, stopping'.

(σωδάριον napkin : Lat. *sūdārium*).

σῶκος strong, σῶς safe : σάος.

σωλήν pipe : Lat. *sīlānus :*

σῶμα body : σῆμα, 'mark, object'. 8.

σωπάω am silent : Got. *sveiban* cease. 32.

(σωρακός box : σορός.)

σωρός heap : Ags. *thruma,* σύρω.

(ταβαίτας bowl : Persian.)

ταγγή putrescence : Ags. *stincan* to smell Eng. *stink :* τεταγών, cf. Lat. *con-tāges.* 32.

(τάγηνον = τήγανον.)

τᾱγός ruler :

ταγυρί morsel : 'drop', σταγών στάζω. 32.

ταινία fillet : τείνω. 9.

(τάκων τακών sausage : foreign.)

ταλαι-πώρος (πωρητύς) ταλαός τάλας wretched, τάλαντον balance, τάλαρος basket ταλασία spinning (cf. Lat. *pensum*) : τλῆναι. 24. So ταλα-ύρινος stout : ῥινός, 'raising the shield'. 23.

τᾶλις bride : Lit. *talokas* adult :

ταμίας distributor : τέμνω. 11.

τάμισος rennet : Lat. *tēmētum,* Sk. *tam* suffocate, 'coagulating'. 11.

τᾶν sir : ἔτης, Aphaeresis after ὦ.

τανεῖαι beams : τείνω. 11.

ταν-ηλεγής laying low : τείνω + λέχος (as though δυσ-ηλεγής were from λέχος).

τανθαρυστός shaking : O Slav. *drŭgati* tremble. 5. 2.

τανταλόομαι swing : τλῆναι, cf. τάλαντον. 5.

τανύω = τείνω. 11.

ταπεινός low : τύπτω, 'struck down' (cf. πλάξ). 14.

(τάπης rug : Persian.)

(τάρανδος elk : foreign.)

ταράσσω stir up : τραχύς. 2. 19.

τάρβος terror : Hesych. ταργαίνειν ταράσσειν, Lat. *torvus*, Ags. *thrācian* loathe, Sk. *tarj* threaten. 27.

τάργανον vinegar : τρύξ. 24.

τάρες = τέτταρες, cf. ταρτη-μόριον quarter. 35.

τάρῑχος dried fish : τρύγη. 2. 24. So ταρχύω bury, 'dry, burn'.

ταρσός crate : τέρσομαι, for drying cheeses. 11.

ταρφύς thick : τρέφω. 11.

τάσσω arrange : τέκτων. 10. 19.

(ταῦ T : Heb. *tav*.)

ταῦρος bull : Lat. *taurus*, Got. *stiur* Eng. *steer*, O Slav. *turŭ*, Sk. *sthūras* solid, ἵστημι. 32.

τάφος A. burial : θάπτω. 20.

τάφος B. wonder : θάμβος. 32.

τάφρος trench : τράφος, Ags. *delfan* dig Eng. *delve*, O Slav. *dlŭbokŭ* deep. 20. 24.

ταχύς quick : τρέχω. 10.

(ταῶς peacock : Lat. *pāvo* (Eng.), Pers. *tāwūs*.)

τὲ and : Lat. *-que*, Got. *-uh*, Sk. *ca*, τίς. 26.

τέγγω moisten : Lat. *tinguo*, NHG. *tunken* dip.

τέγος roof : Lat. *tegò*, O Ir. *teg* house, Ags. *theccan* to cover Eng. *thatch deck tight*, στέγω. 32.

τέθηπα am astonished : θάμβος. 24.

τεθμός law : θέμις. 20.

τείνω stretch : Lat. *tendo tenuis*, Ir. *tana* thin, Got. *uf-thanjan* stretch Eng. *thin*, Sk. *tan*. 17.

τείρεα stars : τρανής, 'conspicuous'.

τείρω distress : Lat. *tero*, Got. *thaurnus* thorn Eng., Lit. *trinti* rub. 17.

τεῖχος wall : Ags. *dīc* ditch Eng. *dyke dig*, Sk. *dēhī* dam : θιγγάνω, 'moulded' (cf. Lat. *māceria mācero*). 20.

τέκμαρ end : Lat. *texo*, Ags. *thicgan* obtain, Ags. Eng. *thing*, Lit. *tikkyti* to aim, Sk. *taksh* to shape. So

　　τέκνον child : Ags. *thegn* squire Eng. *thane*, Sk. *takman* child.

　　τέκτων carpenter : Lat. *tignum*, OHG. *dehsa* hatchet NHG. *deichsel* pole, Sk. *takshan* carpenter.

τελαμών belt : στελμονίαι. 32. 2.

τελέθω be, τέλλω rise, τέλος A. end : πέλω. 26.

τελλίνη a shell-fish :

τέλμα swamp : 'coagulated', στέλλω contract. 32.

τέλος B. tax : Ir. *taille* wages, τλῆναι.

τέλσον boundary-furrow : Sk. *kārshman* bounds, *karsh* draw, plough. 26.

τέμαχος slice, τέμενος precinct, τέμνω cut : O Slav. *tęti*. So τένδω gnaw, τένθης gourmand : Lat. *tondeo*. 19.

τέναγος shallow:

(τενθρηδών wasp: θρέομαι, ἀνθρήνη.)

τέραμνα τέρεμνα chambers: Lat. *trabs* (cf. μέλαθρον roof-beam, hall), O Nor. *thref* granary, Lit. *tróba* a building: 2. 11. 19.

τεράμων τέρην delicate: Sk. *tarunas:* τείρω, 'worn'.

τέρας marvel: τρανής, 'striking'. 24.

τερετίζω whistle: τορός. 7.

τέρετρον gimlet, τερηδών woodworm: τείρω 'rub, bore'.

τερθρεία jugglery: τέρθρον yard-arm, 'high-flying'.

τέρθρον τέρμα end: Lat. *terminus trans,* Ir. *tar* through, Got. *thairh* Eng., Eng. *thrum* end of thread, Sk. *tar* carry over, complete.

(τέρμινθος turpentine-tree: τερέβινθος (Eng.), Persian.)

τερπι-κέραυνος hurling thunderbolts: τρέπω. 24.

τέρπω satisfy: Got. *thrafstjan* to comfort, Lit. *tarpti* thrive, Sk. *tarp* be satisfied, τρέφω.

τέρσομαι dry up: Lat. *torreo,* Got. *thaursjan* to thirst Eng., Sk. *tarsh.*

τέσσαρες four: Dor. τέτορες Aeol. πέσσυρες, Lat. *quattuor,* O Ir. *cethir,* Got. *fidvor* Eng., Lit. *kéturi,* Sk. *catvāras:* 26. 19. 11.

τεταγών seizing: Lat. *tango,* Got. *tekan* touch Eng. *take tickle,* Sk. *tājat* snddenly.

τέτανος tension: τείνω. 5. 11.

τετίημαι mourn: Sk. *tvish* be excited. 32. 34.

τέτμον found: τυγχάνω. 26.

(τετράδων τέτραξ grouse, τέτριξ whinchat: O Nor. *thidurr* partridge, Sk. *tittiris.*)

τετραίνω pierce: τείρω. 5. 24.

τετρ-ακίνη lettuce: ἀκίς, cf. θριδ-ακίνη θρίδαξ.

τετρα-φάληρος with four plumes: φαληριάω.

τετρεμαίνω = τρέμω. 5.

τέττα father; Lat. *tata,* Welsh *tad* (Eng. *dad*), NHG. *tate,* Lit. *tétis,* Sk. *tātas,* ἄττα. Hence τέττιξ grasshopper.

τευθίς cuttle-fish: θύω A. 5.

τευμάομαι prepare: Zd. *skyaoma* progress. 32. 26. So τευτάζω am busied.

τεύχω make, τέχνη art: τέκμαρ. 12. 29. 21.

τέφρα ashes: Lat. *favilla,* Ags. *thäcan* burn, Lit. *degti,* Sk. *dah.* 20. 27.

τέως so long: Sk. *tāvat,* τό.

τῆ take: τείνω. 17.

(τήγανον saucepan: Asiatic (cf. ἀνθρήνη).)

τήθη grandmother: Lit. *dëde,* θεῖος. 5.

τῆθος mollusc: θῆσθαι, 'cleaving to the rock'. 20.

τήκω dissolve: cf. Lat. *tābes,* O Nor. *theyja* thaw Eng., O Slav. *talŭ* liquid.

τῆλε far off: Aeol. πῆλυι, Lat. *pro-cul,* Sk. *ciras* long, κέλλω. 26.

τηλεθάων = θάλλων. 20.

τηλέφιον a plant : Τήλεφος.

τηλία board : Ion. σηλία, σέλμα. 19.

τῆλις fenugreek :

τηλύγετος stripling : *τῆλυς (cf. ἀτρύγετος), Sk. *cārus* dear. 26. 25.

τημελέω take care : Lat. *timeo*, Sk. *tam* be perplexed, τάμισος.

τῆμος then : Sk. *tasmāt* therefore, τό. 35.

τήνελλα sound of lyre.

τηρέω watch : τρανής, 'look piercingly'.

τητάομαι want : O Ir. *táid* thief.

τῆτες this year : σητάνιος.

τηΰσιος idle : *τη-Fέτιος, Lat. *tantum* only, τό (cf. Eng. so-so). 23. 22.

(τίγρις tiger : Zd. *tighri* arrow, στίζω.)

(τιήρης turban : Persian.)

τιθαιβώσσω build honey-combs : Hesych. θαιμός honse (cf. ἁμάμαξυς), τίθημι. 5.

τιθασός tame : Lat. *familiaris*, sq. 5.

τίθημι place : Lat. *famulus facio*, O Ir. *dénim* I do, Got. *ga-deds* action Eng. *do*, Lit. *děti* to place, Sk. *dhā*. 5.

τιθήνη nurse : θῆσθαι. 5.

τιθύμᾱλος spurge :

τίκτω beget : Got. *theihan* thrive, τέκνον. 13.

τῑλάω discharge : Welsh *tail* dung.

τίλλω tear :

τινάσσω shake : EM. ἀκινάγματα τινάγματα : 26.

τιό note of hoopoe.

τίς who? : Lat. *quis*, Sk. *kim* Neut., ποῦ. So τὶς any : Lat. *quis*, Sk. *na-kis* no one. 26.

τιταίνω = τείνω. 5. 9.

(τίτανος gypsum : Hesych. κίτανος, foreign.)

τιτήνη queen : τίω.

τίτθη nurse, τιτθός breast : θῆσθαι. 5. 6.

τιτρώσκω wound : τρώω. 5.

τιττυβίζω chirp : onomatopoeic, Sk. *tittibhas* a bird.

τιτύσκομαι prepare, aim : τεύχω. 5. 31. 32.

τίφη A. spelt :

(τίφη B. water-spider (Lat. *tippūla*) : al. τῑφη, σίλφη.)

(τίφυον = ἴφυον.)

τίω honour : Lat. *quaero*, Lit. *skaityti* count, Sk. *ci* observe, ποινή. 31. 26.

τλῆναι endure : Lat. *tollo tetuli tolero*, O Welsh *dluith* lever (Stokes), Got. *thulan* endure Scotch *thole*, O Slav. *tulŭ* quiver, Sk. *tul* raise.

τμήγω = τέμνω. 24.

τό this : Lat. *tum tam tot tălis tantus*, Got. *thata* that Eng. *this that the*, Lit. *tas* the, Sk. *tat* that.

τοί indeed : Sk. Dat. *tē* (enclitic), σύ.

τοῖχος = τεῖχος. 7.

τόλμα daring : τλῆναι.

τολύπη ball of wool : τρέπω 'spin', cf. ἄτρακτος. 25. 2.

τονθορύζω mutter : τανθαρυστός. 5. 2.

τόξον bow : 'shaped wood,' Lat. *tēlum*, τέκτων. 7.

τοπάζω guess, τόπος B. commonplace : τέκμαρ (cf. Eng. guess get). 7. 27.

τοπεῖον rope : στυπεῖον. 32.

τόπος A. place : τύπτω (cf. Lat. plăga πληγή, NHG. fleck 'spot, place ').

τορέω bore, τόρμος hole, τόρνος pin, chisel : τείρω. So τορός clear, 'penetrating', Lit. *tarti* say ; whence τορο-λιλίξ τορο-τίξ note of hoopoe.

τορύνη ladle : Lat. *trua*, O Nor. *thvara* Eng. *twirl*, Sk. *tvar* hurry. 16.

τόσσαις happening : *τόκσ-σαις, Sk. *taksh* shape, τέκτων. 32.

τόσσος so much, τότε then : τό. 19.

τοτο-βρίξ note of hoopoe, τοτοῖ Interj.

(τράγος goat : Cilician *tarkus* (Sayce).)

τράμις perineum : Ags. *thearm* gut, τόρμος. 24.

τρᾱνής = τορός.

τρά-πεζα table : τέσσαρες. 35.

τραπέω tread grapes (Lat. *trapētum*) : Lit. *trépti* stamp. 11.

τρασιά = ταρσός. 24.

τραυλός lisping, τραῦμα wound : τρώω. 9.

τραύξανα chips : dialectic, Hesych. τραύσανον φρύγανον, τέρσομαι.

τράχηλος neck :

τρᾱχύς rough : θράσσω.

τρεῖς three : Lat. *trēs*, Ir. *trí*, Got. *threis* Eng., Lit. *trys*, Sk. *trayas*: τέρμα Lat. *trans*, 'over' two.

τρέμω tremble : Lat. *tremo*, Got. *thram-stei* grasshopper, Lit. *trimti* tremble.

τρέπω turn : Lat. *torqueo trepidus*, Welsh *treiglaw*, Got. *threihan* press Eng. *throng*, O Slav. *traků* band. 24. 27.

τρέφω solidify, nourish : Lat. *torpeo*, Lit. *tirpti* stiffen, τέρπω. 24. 29.

τρέχω run : Ir. *traigh* track, Got. *thragjan* run Ags. *thrael* servant Eng. *thrall*.

τρέω flee : Lat. *terreo*, Ir. *tarrach* timid, Lit. *triszěti* tremble, Sk. *tras*. 34.

τρῆμα = τόρμος.

τριάκοντα thirty : Lat. *trīgintā*, Sk. *trimçat* : *τρία Neut. of τρεῖς + δέκα, cf. εἴκοσι.

τρίβω rub : Got. *thriskan* thresh Eng. :* τέρσγϜω, cf. τείρω. 24. 32. 27.

τριβωλετήρ Alcaeus 38 thistle-eater : *τριβολ-ολετήρ, τρί-βολος + ὄλλυμι.* 35.

(**τρίγλη** mullet, **τριγόλας** a fish : foreign.)

τρίζω squeak : Lat. *strix* owl, *τρύζω.* 32.

τρι-ήρης trireme : *ἀραρίσκω,* cf. *δι-ήρης.*

τριοτό note of hoopoe.

τριχά-ϊκες threefold : *οἶκος.* 34.

τροπᾱλίς bunch ('thick'), **τροφᾱλίς** cheese : *τρέφω.* 29.

τρόπις keel : *τρέπω,* 'turning the ship'. 7.

τρόχμαλος pebble : *τρέχω,* cf. *ὀλοοί-τροχος.*

τρύβλιον cup : *τύρβη* (cf. *δῖνος).* 24.

(**τρύγγας** sandpiper : foreign.)

τρύγη ripe fruit : Θαργήλια harvest-home, Ags. *drig* dry Eng., Sk. *dhrākh* become dry. 20.

τρῡγών turtle-dove, roach (cf. *σκόμβρος),* **τρύζω** mutter : *στρύζω, τρίζω.* 32. 11.

τρύξ must, lees : O Nor. *dregg* dregs Eng., Ags. *drähnian* drain Eng., O Slav. *droždiję* dregs. 20.

τρῡπάω bore : Lit. *trupĕti* crumble, Sk. *trup* injure, cf. *τρύω.*

τρῡτάνη tongue of a balance : *τορύνη,* 'mobile'. 24.

τρυ-φάλεια helmet : *τέσσαρες + φάλος.* 35. 11.

τρυφή luxury, **τρύφος** piece : cf. *τρύω.*

τρύχνος = *στρύχνος.* 32.

τρύχω consume, **τρύω** wear out, **τρώω** injure : Ags. *throvian* suffer Eng. *throe, τείρω.* 17.

τρώγλη hole, **τρώγω** gnaw : Lat. *trāgula* spear, Got. *thairko* hole, cf. *τραχύς.*

τρώκτης knave : Lat. *trīcae* tricks, Sk. *trkvan* thief, *τρέπω.*

τρώξανον twig : *τραύξανα.*

τυγχάνω hit : *τέκμαρ.* So **τύκος** hammer. 12.

τύλη pad, **τύλος** knot : Lat. *tumeo tūber,* Ir. *túithlae* hump, Ags. *theoh* thigh Eng., *thūma* thumb Eng., Eng. *thews,* Lit. *twinti* swell, Sk. *tu* be strong.

τύμβος cairn : *τάφος* A. 11. 19.

τύμπανον kettle-drum, **τύπτω** strike : O Slav. *tepą* I strike, Sk. *tump tup* injure, *ἀπο-στυπάζω.* 32.

τυννοῦτος so small : Dor. *τυννός, τό,* cf. *τηὔσιος.* 11.

τύντλος mud : *σϜόντλος, σομφός.* 19.

(**τύραννος** lord : Asiatic, Lit. *turrĕti* possess, Sk. *turvanis* victorious, *τρύω.*)

τύρβη trouble : *στυρβάζω,* Lat. *turba turbo* Subst. Verb *turma,* O Ir. *treb* hamlet, Got. *thaurp* Eng. *thorp.* 32.

τῡρός cheese : 'curdled', *τορύνη.*

τύρσις tower : Lat. *turris,* Ags. *thrydlīc* strong, Lit. *twirtas, twérti* seize, enclose.

τυτθός little : τό, cf. τυννοῦτος. 6.

τύφη cát's-tail : Lat. *tōmentum*, τύλη.

τύφω smoke, τοφώς whirlwind : Lit. *dumpti* blow the fire, Sk. *dhūpas* fumigation, cf. θύω A. 20. Hence τυφλός blind, τῦφος stupor : Got. *daubs* deaf Eng., *dumbs* dumb Eng.

τύχη chance : τυγχάνω. 32.

τωθάζω mock :

ὕ ὗ Interj.

ὑάκινθος iris : *ὕαξ, ὗς.

(ὕαλος glass : Egyptian.)

ὑβός hump-backed : ἄγνυμι. 18. 15. 27.

ὕβρις insolence ὕβρίς owl (cf. σκώψ), ὑγιής sound : Lat. *vigeo vegetus vigil*, Got. *vakan* watch Eng. *wake watch*, ἀέξω. 18. 15. 27.

ὑγρός wet ; Lat. *ūveo ūmor ūligo*, Ir. *úr* fresh, O Nor. *vökr* wet Ags. *vaxan vascan* wash Eng., Sk. *uksh* sprinkle. 18. 15.

ὕδωρ water : Lat. *unda pal-ūs*, Ir. *uisce* (Eng. *whisky*), Got. *vato* Eng. *water wet winter*, Lit. *wandů*, Sk. *ud* to wet. 18. 15. Hence ὕδρος water-snake : Ags. *oter* otter Eng., Lit. *udra*, Sk. *udan*.

ὕει it rains : Ir. *súth* juice, Got. *saivs* sea, Sk. *savam* water. 18.

ὕθλος babble :

υἱός son : O Ir. *suth* offspring, Got. *sunus* son Eng., Lit. Sk. *sūnus*, Sk. *su* generate. 18.

(ὕκης mullet : Cyrenaic.)

ὑλάω bark : O Ir. *yla* howl, Lit. *uloti*. 4. 25.

ὕλη wood : Lat. *silva :* 18. 17.

ὑλίζω cleanse :

ὑμεῖς ye : Aeol. ὕμμες, *jú-σμες, Sk. *yushmē :* Got. *jus* Eng., Lit. *jus*. 18. 17.

ὑμήν membrane, ὕμνος song ('connected') : Sk. *syūman* band, cf. ἱμάς. 18.

ὕπαρ reality : Sk. *vapus* a marvel. 18. 15.

ὑπέρ over : O Ir. *for*, Got. *ufar* Eng., Sk. *upari*, cf. Lat. *s-uper*, ὑπό. 4. Hence ὕπερον pestle, 'above the mortar'.

ὕπερα spider :

ὑπερ-ικταίνομαι hurry : ὠκύς. 13.

ὑπέρ-κοπος extravagant : κόπτω.

ὑπέρ-φευ overmuch : φύω. 31. So ὑπερ-φίαλος overbearing (cf. σίαλος σῦς). 32.

ὑπερ-ώη palate : 'above the mouth', ἠόεις. 8.

ὑπερ-ώιον bower : ἄστυ. 30. 34.

ὑπήνη moustache : Sk. *vap* shear. 18. 15.

(ὕπνον moss : ἱπνον, foreign.)

ὕπνος sleep : Lat. *somnus sopor sōpio*, Ir. *suan*, Ags. *svefn* dream, Lit. *sápnas*, Sk. *svapnas* sleep. 32. 18. 15.

ὑπό under : O Ir. *fo*, Got. *uf*, Lit. *po*, Sk. *upa*, cf. Lat. *s-ub*.   4.

ὑπό-βρυχα under water : βρέχω.   11.

ὑπό-δρα fiercely : δενδίλλω.

ὑπο-λᾱῑs wheatear : λᾶας, 'hiding behind stones'.

ὕπτιος supine : ὑπό, cf. Lat. *supīnus*.

(ὑρισός = ἄρριχος.)

(ὕρχα jar : Spanish, Lat. *orca urceus*.)

ὗs pig : Lat. *sūs*, Eng. *sow*, Zd. *hu :* υἱός, 'prolific'.

(ὕσγῑνον kermes : Galatian ὕσγη ilex, κόκκος.)

ὑσμίνη contest : Ir. *idna* arms, Sk. *yudh* fight.   18. 19.

ὕσ-πληξ rope at starting-point of race : ὕστερος + πλήσσω.

(ὕσσακος cunnus : σάκας, foreign.)

ὕστερος later : Got. *ut* out Eng., Sk. *ud*.   4. 20.   Hence ὑστέρα womb, Lat. *uterus*, 'lower'.

(ὕστριξ porcupine : Libyan, ὕστριγξ ὕσθριξ, quasi ὗs + θρίξ.)

ὑφαίνω weave : Ags. *vefan* Eng., *veb* web Eng., Sk. *ūrna-vābhis* spider.   18. 15.

ὕφεαρ misletoe (Arcadian) : σῦφαρ.

ὕψος height : *ὕψ (cf. ἄψ ἐξ), ὕπατος highest, Lat. *summus :* ὑπό, 'at the other end'.

φαγεῖν to eat : Sk. *bhaj* divide.

(φάγρος bream : φάγωρος φαγρώριος πάγριος πάγουρος, foreign.)

φαείνω shine : φάος.

φαίδιμος φαιδρός bright : Lit. *gaidrus* clear.   27.

φαίνω shine : Lat. *fenestra*, Ir. *bán* bright, Got. *bandva* sign, cf. φάος.

φαιός dusky : Lit. *gaisas* reflected light.   27. 34.

(φάκελος bundle : φάσκωλος.)

(φακός lentil : ἀφάκη, foreign.)

φάλαγξ rank : βαλβίς.   2.

φαλ-ακρός bald : Lat. *fullo*, Ags. *bael* pyre Eng. *bald* ('shiny'), Lit. *balti* grow white, Sk. *bhālas* brightness.   So φαλαρίς coot, Lat. *fulica*, φαληριάω whiten.

(φάλλαινα whale (Lat. *bālaena*) : Ags. *hväl* Eng.)

φαλλός penis : O Ir. *ball* membrum, φλέω.   11.

φάλος boss : O Nor. *böllr* ball Eng.

φᾱνός torch : σφήν.   32.

φάος light : Aeol. φαῦος : cf. Sk. *bhā* shine.   34.

φάραγξ ravine : Lat. *frango*, Ags. *brecan* break Eng.   2.

φαρέτρα quiver : φέρω (see τλῆναι).   11.

φαρκίς wrinkle : φρίκη φρίσσω, 'roughness'.   24.

φάρμακον drug : Lat. *fermentum*, Ags. *beorma* barm Eng., φύρω. 11.

φάρος plough, φάρσος part: 'divider, division', Lit. *báras* allotment :

φᾶρος cloth : Hesych. *φάραι ὑφαίνειν*, Lett. *buras* sail.

φάρυγξ throat : *βρόγχος*. 2. 11.

φάσγανον knife (Lat. *fuscina*) : *βόθρος*, 'digger'. 14. 19.

(φάσηλος bean : *φασήολος φασίολος*, Egyptian.)

(φάσκον lichen : *σφάκος*, foreign.)

(φάσκωλος wallet : Lat. *fiscus*, Gallic *bascauda* basket Welsh *basged* (Eng.).)

(φάσσα ringdove, φάψ dove : Oriental.)

φάτνη manger : *βόθρος*. 14. 20.

φαῦλος slight : *φηλόω*. 17.

φαῦσιγξ blister : *φυσάω*. 9.

φάω shine : *φάος*.

φέβομαι flee : Ags. *bifian* shake, Lit. *bĕgti* flee. 27.

φέγγος light : Lett. *spógalas* gloss. 32.

φείδομαι spare : 'take only a bit of', Lat. *findo*, Got. *beitan* bite Eng., Sk. *bhid* split.

φέλλια stony ground :

φελλός cork : *φλοιός*. 24.

φέναξ cheat : Hesych. *φεννίς* ball-play.

φέρβω feed : Lat. *forbea* food *herba*, O Nor. *birgja* provide. 27. 20.

φέρτερος better : Lit. *géras* good. 27.

φέρω bear : Lat. *fero*, O Ir. *berim* I bear, Got. *bairan* bear Eng., O Slav. *berą* I take, Sk. *bhar* bear.

φεῦ Interj. : Lat. *fu*.

φεύγω flee : Lat. *fugio*, Lit. *bugti* be frightened : *πτύσσω*, 'bend'. 20.

φέψαλος spark : O Slav. *pepelŭ* ashes, *ψόλος*. 32. 5. 11.

φέως a plant : cf. *ἱππο-φαές* :

φή as : Lit. *bey* and, Zd. *bā* truly.

φηγός oak : Lat. *fāgus* beech, Ags. *bōc* Eng. : *φώγω*, 'good for fuel'. 8.

φήληξ wild fig, φηλόω cheat : Lat. *fallo*, Got. *balva-vesei* wickedness Eng. *baleful*.

φημί say : Lat. *fāri fāma*, O Ir. *ad-bo* I proclaim, O Slav. *bajati* converse, cf. *φάος*.

φήνη vulture : Sk. *bhāsas* a bird of prey : 35.

φήρ beast : Lat. *ferus*, Lit. *žwĕris* :

φήρεα mumps :

φθάνω am first : *σπεύδω*. 6. 11.

φθέγγομαι speak : Lit. *spengti* cry : *φέγγος* (cf. *φημί φάος*). 6.

φθείρω spoil : **φθέρ-jω*, cf. sq. So φθείρ louse (cf. Got. *lausjan* 'make of none effect' Eng. louse). 17.

φθίνω perish, φθόη decay : Sk. *kshi* destroy. 27. 6. 12.

I

φθόις cake : φωΐδες, 'soufflé'. 6. 30.

φθόνος envy : σπάνις, cf. ἄφθονος abundant. 6. 11.

φιάλη saucer :

φιαλῶ will undertake :

φῑλητής deceiver : φηλόω. 11.

φῑλος friendly : σ-φέ, 'one's own'.

(φιλύκη privet : al. φυλλική, foreign.)

φιλύρα linden : φλοιός. 2.

φῑμός nose-band, **φιτρός** log : 'compressing, compressed', Lat. *spissus*, Lit. *ap-spittu* I surround. 32. 17.

φῑτύω beget : σπεύδω. 32. 16.

φλαττόθρατ sound of lyre.

φλαῦρος = φαῦλος. 24.

φλάω crush, devour (cf. σποδέω) : OHG. *bliuwan* beat NHG. *bläuen* Eng. *a blow.*

φλέγω burn : Lat. *fulgeo flagro*, Got. *bairhts* bright Eng., Ags. *blīcan* shine, Lit. *blizgēti*, Sk. *bhrāj*, cf. φαλακρός. 25. Hence **φλέξις** a bird, 'flame-coloured'.

φλέω overflow : Lat. *flōs*, Ir. *bláth* flower, Got. *uf-bauljan* blow up Eng., *bloma* bloom Eng. Hence

    φλέδων babbler, **φλήναφος φλύαρος** babble, **φλύω** I babble : Eng. *blab blubber*, O Slav. *blędĭ* nugae.

    φλέως reed, **φλοιός** bark. 7.

    φλοῖσβος din : MHG. *blodern* rustle NHG. *plaudern* chatter.

    φλουδέω foam.

    φλυδάω grow soft. 31.

φλέψ vein : Hesych. φλέψ μώλωψ, φλίβω.

φλῑά doorpost :

φλίβω crush : Lat. *confligo*, Welsh *blif* catapult, Got. *bliggvan* beat, O Slav. *blizna* scar : cf. Lat. *flagellum*, cf. φλάω. 11. 27. 20.

(φλόμος πλόμος mullein : foreign.)

φλυζάκιον φλύκταινα blister : Lat. *confluges fluctus*, Sk. *bhuraj* to bubble, θύλακος πέλαγος, cf. φλέω. 19.

φνεί note of vulture.

φόβη hair : Lat. *fimbria fibra* : φέβομαι, 'shaking'. So **φόβος** flight. 7.

φοῖβος clear : Lit. *žibēti* shine. 27.

(φοῖνιξ red, palm, a bird, **φοινός** red : Heb. *puah.*)

φοῖτος wandering : Lett. *gaita* going, Zd. *gaēth* come. 27.

φολίς scale : φλοιός. So **φολλικώδης** scabby, **φόλλιξ** scab.

φολκός bandy-legged : Lat. *flecto falx*, βλάξ. 24.

φόλυς tawny :

φόνος slaughter : O Ir. *benim* I strike, Got. *banja* a wound Eng. *bane.*

φοξῖνος minnow, **φοξί-χειλος** tapering (χεῖλος), **φοξός** pointed :

ορτνη hide :

ορμιγξ lyre : βρέμω. 24.

ορμός basket, mat :

ορμύνιος a fig : local?

ορύνω φορύσσω knead, φορυτός rubbish : φύρω. 16.

ράζω indicate : Lit. *girdėti* hear. 27.

ράσσω fence : Lat. *farcio frequens*, O Ir. *bárc* multitude, Got. *bairgan* to guard, Lit. *brukti* press, βρέγμα πύργος. 24. 19.

ράτηρ clansman : Lat. *fräter*, Ir. *brathair* brother, Got. *brothar* Eng., Lit. *brotuszis* cousin, Sk. *bhrātar-* brother : φέρω, 'supporter'.

ρέαρ well : Got. *brunna* fountain Eng. *bourn* stream, φύρω. 34. 2.

ρέω see διαφρέω.

ρήν midriff : σπλήν. 32.

ρίγος strength : σφριγάω. 32.

ριμάσσομαι wanton : βρέμω. 11.

ρίσσω bristle : Lat. *hirtus hirsūtus fastīgium ferrum*, Ags. *byrst* bristle Eng., Sk. *bhrshtis* point. 19.

ρυάσσομαι wanton : φύρω. 24.

ρυγίλος (Lat. *fringilla*) = σπογίλος. 32. 24.

ρύγω roast : Lat. *frīgo*, Ir. *bruighim* I boil, Pruss. *birga-karkis* basting-ladle, Sk. *bharj* roast, φλέγω. So φρυκτός beacon, 'fiery.'

ρύνη toad : Lat. *furvus*, Ags. *brūn* brown Eng., Sk. *babhrus* : Lat. *ferveo*, Got. *brinnan* burn Eng., φύρω. 24.

ῦ Interj.

ύζα flight : φεύγω. 31. 19.

φῦκος seaweed : Heb. *pūk* paint.)

ύλαξ watchman : Got. *glaggvo* exactly, Lit. *żwelgti* see. 27. 2. 20.

ὑλή clan : φύω.

υλίη oleaster : φιλύρα.

ύλλον leaf : Lat. *folium*, Ags. *blåd* Eng. *blade*, φλέω. 19.

ύρω mix : Ags. *breóvan* brew Eng., *brod* broth Eng., Lit. *burzdėti* shake, Sk. *bhur* move quickly.

υσάω blow : *σπυσ-σάω, Lat. *pustula*, Lit. *pústi* blow, Sk. *phupphusas* lungs. 32. Hence φῦσιγξ garlic ('with hollow stalk'), φύσκη sausage, φυστή barley-cake.

ύω produce : Lat. *fui fīo fētus jēnus*, O Ir. *bíu* I am, Ags. *beon* be Eng., Lit. *buti*, Sk. *bhū*.

ώγω roast : Ags. *bacan* bake Eng.

ωΐδες blisters :

φώκη seal : foreign.)

ωλεός den, φωλίς a fish : O Nor. *baeli* den Eng. *build* : Got. *bauains* dwelling Eng. *booth bower*, Sk. *bhavanam*, φύω. 17.

ώνη voice : Ags. *ge-ban* proclamation Eng. *banns*, Sk. *bhan* sound, cf. φημί. 8.

φώρ thief : Lat. *fūr*, φήρ.

φωριαμός clothes-chest : φᾶρος.   8.

φώς man : φύω.   17.

φῶς light : φάος.

(φώσσων cloth : Egyptian.)

(φῶυξ heron : πῶυξ πῶυγξ, foreign.)

χάζομαι retire, χαίνω gape : χάσκω.

χάιος good (Laconian) : Hesych. χάσιος, *χάτιος ἀγαθός.

χαίρω rejoice : Oscan *herest* volet Lat. *horior hortor*, Got. *gairnjan* to desire Eng. *yearn*, Lit. *goróti*, Sk. *hary.*

χαίτη hair :

χάλαζα hail : Lat. *grando*, O Slav. *gradŭ*, Sk. *hrāduni* bad weather : Got. *gretan* to cry Scotch *greet*, Sk. *hrād* sound.   2. 25. 19.

χάλανδρος Epicharm. 41, epithet of κωβιοί :

χαλάω loosen, χαλί-φρων thoughtless : Lit. *gillus* deep, Sk. *jhar* fall down.

(χαλβάνη a gum (Lat. *galbanum*) : Heb. *chelb'nāh*.)

χαλεπός difficult :

χαλῖνός bridle (Sk. *khalīnas* bit) :

χάλιξ = κάχληξ.   2.

χάλις unmixt wine : O Ir. *gel* bright, χάρμη A.   25.

(χαλκός copper : Heb. *chālāk* smooth.)

(χάλυψ steel : Pontic.)

χαμαί on the ground : Lat. *humus*, Lit. *żéme* earth, Sk. *ksham, ksham* support, κάμαξ.   32.

χανδάνω contain : Lat. *prehendo praeda*, Welsh *genni contineri*, Got. *bi-gitan* find Eng. *get*, Sk. *gadhyas tenendus.*

χάος abyss : χάσκω.

χαράδρα torrent, gully : χάλαζα.   2.

χάραξ stake : σκάλλω.   32.

χάρμη A. battle, χαρ-οπός bright-eyed : 'burning', Sk. *ghar* shine.

χάρμη B. spear-head :

(χάρτης paper : Egyptian.)

χάσκω gape : Lit. *żoti* yawn, Sk. *hā* yield, cf. Ags. *gānian* yawn Eng.

χατέω want : Got. *gaidv* want, Lit. *geidu* I desire, ἀγαθός.   20.

χαυλι-όδους tusked : χωλός.   9.

χαῦνος spongy : O Ir. *gó* false, χάσκω.   17.

(χέδροπες pulse : Hesych. κέδροπα κέρδοπα, foreign.)

χέζω caco : Ags. *sceōtan* Eng., Sk. *had*.   32. 19.

χειά hole : Lat. *favissae fovea faux*, cf. χάσκω.   30.

χεῖλος lip : O Nor. *gjölnar* gills Eng.   17.

χεῖμα winter, χείμαρος plug in a ship's hold (to let out water after a
   storm) : Lat. *bīmus* (= *bi-himus), O Welsh *gaem* winter (Rhys), Lit.
   żéma, Sk. *himas*.

χείρ hand : O Lat. *hir*, O Ir. *gil* : Lat. *hirūdo*, Ags. *gelm* handful Eng.
   glean, Sk. *har* take off (cf. μάρη, Eng. hand Got. *us-hinthan* 'capture').

χείρων inferior : Sk. *hras* grow less.   17. 35.

χελῖδών swallow : Lat. *hirundo* : χείρ, 'seizing flies'.   25. 17.

χελισκον dish : χέλυς, 'concave'.

(χελλών a fish : χειλών χαλλών, foreign.)

χελύνη A. = χεῖλος.   2.

(χελύνη B. χέλυς tortoise : Hesych. κλεμμύς, O Sláv. *żelĭvĭ*, Sk. *harmutas*.)

χέραδος gravel, χερμάδιον stone : Lat. *glārea*.

χερνής poor : χείρων.   35.

χέρσος dry land, barren : χρίω, 'rubbed, worn'.   24.

χέω pour : Lat. *fundo*, Got. *giutan* Eng. *gush gust in-got*.   34.

χηλή hoof ('divided'), χηλός chest χηραμός hole ('hollow'), χῆρος
   widowed : χάσκω.   30.

χήν goose : Lat. *anser*, O Ir. *goss*, Ags. *gōs* Eng., *gandra* gander Eng.,
   ganod coot Eng. *gannet*, Lit. *żasis* goose, Sk. *hạsas :*

χηράμβη mussel, χηραμίς mussel-shell : χοιρίνη.   17.

χηρωσταί guardians : Lat. *hērēs* : χείρ, 'taking the estate'.

χῆτος want : χατέω.   30.

χθαμαλός low : Lat. *humilis*, χαμαί.   6.

χθές yesterday : Lat. *heri*, Got. *gistra-dagis* tomorrow Eng., Sk. *hyas*
   yesterday : 6.   Hence χθι-ζός hesternus : Lat. *dies*, δῖος.   13. 19.

χθών ground : χαμαί (see εἶς).   6.

(χἱ Ch : Heb. *he*.)

χῖδρα groats : χόνδρος.   17.

χίλιοι thousand : *χέσλιοι, Sk. *sa-hasra* : 17. 25.

χῖλός fodder : *χεσ-λός, Sk. *ghas* eat.   17.

χίμαρος goat : Ir. *gabhar*, O Nor. *gymbr* lamb : χεῖμα 'one winter old'
   (cf. Eng. twinter 'beast of two winters old', see ἔτος).   31.

χίμετλον chilblain : χεῖμα.

(χιτών tunic : Heb. *k'thōneth*.)

χιών snow : Lat. *hiems*, χεῖμα (see εἶς).

(χλαῖνα cloak (Lat. *laena*), χλαμύς mantle : Sk. *ghar* cover.)

χλαρός cheerful, χλεύη jest : Lat. *hilaris*, Ags. *gleó* play Eng. *glee*, Lit.
   glaudas.

χλῆδος rubbish : χέραδος.   25. 24.

χλιαίνω warm, χλιδή luxury, χλίω revel : Ir. *gris* fire, Got. *glitmun-
   jan* glitter Eng., Ags. *glōvan* glow Eng. *gläd* bright Eng. *glad*, *gläm*
   gleam Eng., Sk. *ghar* shine.

χλόη verdure : Lat. *helvus holus*, Ags. *grēne* green Eng., Lit. *żálas*,
   żĕrĕti glow.

χλούνης, epithet of a boar : χοῖρος.   25. 24. 17.   Hence χλοῦνις Aesch. Eum. 189 vigour.

χναύω nibble, χνόη nave of wheel ('eaten away' by the axle) χοῖνιξ a measure ('like a wheel-box'), χνόος down : Lit. *genéti* lop, Zd. *ghnij* gnaw.   9. 17. 24. 34.

χοιράς reef, χοιράδες glands, χοιρίνη mussel-shell : χέρσος χρίω.   17. So χοῖρος porker : O Nor. *griss*, Sk. *ghrshnis* boar.

χολάδες χόλικες guts : OHG. *gil* hernia, O Slav. *żelądŭkŭ* stomach.

χολέρα cholera : χολέρα χολέδρα gutter :

χόλος bile : Lat. *fel*, Ags. *gealla* Eng. *gall*, O Slav. *żlŭtĭ* : Ags. *geolo* yellow Eng., Lit. *geltas*, χλίω (cf. Hor. splendida bilis).

χόνδρος groats, gristle : Ags. *grút* groats *gristel* gristle Eng., Lit. *grúdas* corn.

(χόνδρυλλα endive : χονδρίλη κονδρίλλη, foreign.)

χορδή gut : Lit. *hira hillae haru-spex*, O Nor. *görn* Ags. *gearn* yarn Eng., Lit. *żarna* gut, Sk. *hirā* vein.

χόριον caul : Lat. *corium*, O Nor. *skrá* dry skin Eng. *scroll*, Lit. *skura* skin, Sk. *carman :* σκάλλω (see ξαίνω).   32.

χορός dancing-ground, χόρτος straw-yard, χορωνός crown : Lat. *hara hortus cohors*, Got. *bi-gairdan* gird Eng., Ags. *geard* yard Eng., Lit. *żardis* garden : χείρ, 'enclosure'.

χόω heap up : χέω.   7.

χραίνω touch, χραύω graze, χράω furnish, χράομαι use, χρηΐζω desire, χραι-σμέω ward off : χείρ.   24.

χρεμετίζω neigh, χρόμαδος crashing : Ags. *grimetan* roar Eng. *grumble*, O Slav. *gromŭ* thunder, Zd. *gram* angry.   7.

χρέμπτομαι clear the throat : O Nor. *skirpa* spit, Lit. *skréplei* phlegm. 32.

(χρέμυς χρέμψ χρόμις a fish : κρέμυς, foreign.)

χρίμπτομαι graze, approach : Got. *graban* dig Eng. *grave engrave*, Lett. *grebt* scrape.   11. 19.

χρίω anoint, sting : Welsh *gired* grease, Sk. *gharsh* rub, cf. Lat. *frio frico*, Ags. *grindan* grind Eng.   34.

χροΐζω = χραίνω.

χροιά χρῶμα ✳χρώς skin, colour : χόριον.   24.

χρόνος time, χῶρος place : 'space', χόρτος.   24.

(χρῡσός gold : Heb. *chárūts*.)

χύτρος pot : χέω.   31. So χώομαι am angry, 'burst forth'.   17.

χωλός lame : Lat. *vārus*, Got. *giltha* sickle, Sk. *hval hvar* go crookedly. 32.

χωρίς apart : χῆρος.   8.

(ψάγδαν an unguent : Egyptian.)

ψαθάλλω scratch, ψαιστός ground, ψαύω touch, ψάω. rub : Sk. *bhas* chew. 31. Hence **ψάμαθος ψάμμος** sand (Lat. *sabulum saburra*): Lat. *harēna*, Sk. *bhasman* ashes.

ψαθυρός (cf. *θήρ*) **ψαφαρός** loose : Lat. *scaber*, Lett. *skabrs* rough. 24. 27.

ψαίρω graze, palpitate, **ψαλ-άκανθα** 'sensitive' plant, **ψάλλω** pluck, **ψαλίς** scissors : *σπαίρω*. 24. 25.

ψακάς drop : Lit. *spakas*. 24. Hence **ψάκαλον** young, see *ἔρσαι*.

(**ψάλιον** curb-chain, **ψέλιον** armlet : Persian.)

ψάρ starling : Lat. *sturnus*, Ags. *stearn* Eng. 24. 19. Hence **ψᾱρός** grey.

ψέγω blame : Lit. *spikti* admonish. 24. 28.

ψεδνός thin : *ψάω*.

ψελλός faultering : *ψαίρω*.

ψευδής false : O Nor. *spott* mockery : Ags. *on-spaetan* spit on Eng., cf. *πτύω*. 24.

ψέφος = *ζόφος*. 24. 27. 7.

ψηλαφάω feel about : *σκαριφισμός*. 24. 27. 25. 2.

ψήν gall-insect : Sk. *bhasanas* bee, *ψάω*. So **ψηνός** bald, **ψῆφος** pebble.

ψῆττα plaice :

ψιάδες drops :

ψιάζω am merry : *στίον* = *πεσσός*, 'play at draughts'. 24. 19.

(**ψίαθος** mat : Egyptian.)

(**ψίθιος ψύθιος** a wine : foreign.)

ψιθυρός whispering : *ψύθος*. 16.

ψῑλός bare : *σκύλλω*. 24. 27. 11.

(**ψῑμύθιον** white lead : Egyptian.)

ψίνομαι shed fruit : *φθίνω*. 24.

ψίξ crumb : *ψάω*. 12.

(**ψιττάκη** parrot : Sk. *pitsant* bird, *πέτομαι*.)

ψό Interj.

ψόα muscle of loins :

ψόθοιος smoke :

ψόλος smoke : O Slav. *paliti* burn. 24.

ψόφος noise : *σκόμβρος*. 24. 27. 32.

ψύθος lie : *ψευδής* (see *αἰδώς*). 31.

ψύλλα flea : Lat. *pūlex*, Ags. *fleā* Eng., Lit. *blussa* : 24.

ψύττα Interj.

ψῡχή life (cf. Lat. *anima*), **ψύχω** blow, cool : **σπύσ-χω*, *φυσάω*. 24.

ψωθίον crumb, **ψωμός** morsel, **ψώρα** mange : *ψάω*. 8.

ψωλός circumcised : *ψιλός*.

ὦ ὤ Interj.

ὦα sheepskin, apron : *ὅις*.

ὠδίς anguish :

ὤεον ὤιον ὠόν egg : Lat. *ōvum*, Ir. *ogh*, Ags. *äg* Eng., O Slav. *aje*, οἰωνός.

ὠθέω push : Lat. *vībex*, Sk. *vadh* strike. 33.

(ὠκεανός ocean : Ὠγενος, foreign.)

(ὤκιμον basil : ἄκινος basil-thyme, foreign.)

ὠκύς swift : Lat. *ācer*, Sk. *āçus*, ἀκίς. 8.

ὠλέκρᾱνον = ὀλέκρανον (ω on analogy of sq.).

ὠλένη elbow : Lat. *ulna*, Ir. *uile*, Got. *aleina* cubit Eng. *ell elbow*, cf.
    Sk. *arālas* bent. 2.

ὦλκα sulcum : αὖλαξ. 17.

ὤμιλλα circle :

ὦμος shoulder : Lat. *umerus*, Got. *amsans* umeros, Sk. *ạsas* shoulder :
    17.

ὠμός raw : Lat. *amārus*, Ir. *omh*, Sk. *āmas*.

ὠνή buying : Lat. *vēnum vīlis*, O Ir. *uain* loan, O Slav. *vēniti* sell, Sk.
    vasnas price. 33. 17.

ὦπα face : ὄπωπα.

ὤρα care : Got. *vars* wary Eng., ὁράω. 33.

ωρα season : Got. *jer* year Eng., O Slav. *jarŭ* spring, Zd. *yāre* year :
    εἶμι, Sk. *yātus* time. 18. 8.

ὠρᾱκιάω swoon :

ὠρύομαι howl : Lat. *rūmor rāvis raucus*, Ags. *rūnian*, O Slav. *rjuti*,
    Sk. *ru*. 1.

ὡς as : Got. *sve*, ὅς.

ὥς thus : ὁ.

ὠτειλή wound : οὐτάω. 17.

ὠφελέω help :

ὠχρός pale : ἀχλύς. 8. 29.

PART II.

FORMS.

Vowels : open *o* ω, ε η, *a* ā.
    ,,   close ι ῑ, υ ῡ.
Mutes : tenues κ, τ, π, mediae γ, δ, β, aspiratae χ, θ, φ.
Liquids : lingual ρ, λ, nasal γ-, ν, μ.
Spirants : s, *F, j,* '.
Double letters : ζ = δj, ξ = κs, ψ = πs.

A. GROWTH.

  I. Vocalic :

1. **πρόσθεσις** : before

 (*a*) double consonant :

  o before

    φρ ὀφρύς.

    στ ὀσταφίς ὄστρακον : *στρ ὀρύσσω, *σλ ὀλισθάνω.

  ε (7) before

    σχ ἐσχάρα : *σρ εἴρω A. ἐρωή A., *σν ἐννέα.

    ***Fρ** ἐρρηνοβοσκός, ἐρείκη ἐρύκω : *Fλ ἐλλεδανοί, ειλαπίνη εἴλη εἰλύω,
      εὐλάκα εὐλή εὔληρα, ἐλεφαίρομαι.

  ι (13) before

    κτ ἰκτῖνος-ἰκτίς : **γν** ἰγνύη : **χθ** ἰχθύς.

  a (8) before

    γρ ἄγρυπνος, **γλ** ἀγλαός, ***γF** ἀγαθός : **χν** ἄχνη A.

    βλ ἀβληχρός : *φλ ἀφαυρός.

    σκ ἀσκαλαβώτης ἀσκαρίζω ἀσκαρίς, *σκ (32) ἀκαλήφη ἄκαρνα ἀκούω :
      στ ἀσταφίς ἄσταχυς ἀστεροπή ἀστήρ ἀστράγαλος ἄστριχος, *στ
      ἀθέλγω : **σπ** ἀσπαίρω ἀσπάλαθος ἀσπάλαξ ἀσπίς A., *σπ ἄσβολος
      ἀσφόδελος.—*σλ ἀσελγής, ἀλείφω ἀλιταίνω : *σν ἄνευ.

    ***Fλ** ἀλώπηξ, with compensation (17) ἠλύγη.

 (*b*) liquid :

  o before **λ** νωλεμές, **ν** ὄνειδος, **μ** ὀμιχέω ὀμίχλη ὀμόργνυμι.

  ε before **ρ** ἀπ-εράω ἐρείκω ἐρέσσω ἐρεύγομαι ἔρευνα ἐρῆμος ἔριθος ἐρυθρός
    ἐρωδιός ἐρωή A. B.: **λ** ἐλάτη ἐλαχύς-ἐλαφρός-ἐλέγχω ἐλελίζω
    ἐλεύθερος ἐλινύω : **ν** ἐνεγκεῖν ἔνερθε.

a before ρ ἄραβος ἀραιός ἀράσσω ἀρέσκω ἀρήγω ἀρι- ἀριθμός, lengthened (3) ἠρέμα : λ ἀλαπάζω ἀλέξω ἀλεύομαι, lengthened ἠλακάτη :
ν ἀνάγκη ἀνήρ : μ ἀμαλδύνω ἀμαλός-ἀμβλίσκω ἀμαρύσσω ἀμαυρός
ἀμείβω ἀμέλγω-ἀμέργω ἀμεύομαι-ἀμύνω ἀμολγῷ-ἀμοργή ἀμορβέω
ἀμυδρός ἀμύσσω, lengthened ἠμαλάψαι ἠμορίς ἠμύω.

(c) digamma (cf. 23, 34) :

a αὐάτα, ἀάζω-ἄημι-ἄισθω-ἀυτμή ἀείδω ἀέξω.

ε (Homeric) ἔεδνα ἐείκοσι ἐέλδομαι ἐέλσαι ἐέργω ἐέρση, εἴση εἴσκω,
lengthened (3) ἠίθεος.

---

2. **ἀνάπτυξις** : insertion of vowel between two consonants :

o

between two liquids : ὄνομα, lengthened (3) κολώνη κορώνη.

before ρ δόρυ βορβορυγμός κορκορυγή τονθορύζω, lengthened
ἄγουρος : before λ ἀποσκολύπτω-κόλυθροι-σκόλυθρος ὀβολός πομφόλυξ.

after ρ μέροψ νώροπι ὀρόγυια ὀρόδαμνος ὀροθύνω σκόροδον στεροπή, and
so ὀρούω (23) : after λ ἄλοξ κολοβός κολοκύνθη κολοσσός μολοβρός
ὀλοφύρομαι σκάλοψ σκόλοψ, ὀλο(F)οίτροχος ὀλο(F)όφρων : after ν
ἀνήνοθε, lengthened κεάνωθος.

ε (7)

between two liquids : τέρεμνα, πελεμίζω ὠλένη.

before λ δέλεαρ κέλυφος ὀβελός πέλεθρον : before ν ἄφενος κενέβρειον.

after ρ ὀρέγω, φρέ(F)αρ : after λ ἀλεγεινός-ἀλέγω ἐνδελεχής ὀλέκρανον
ὀλέκω πέλεκυς.

a ι υ (11) :

a

between two liquids : τέραμνα, κελαρύζω λάρυγξ παλάμη σχινδαλαμός
τελαμών ἐλαύνω (= *ἐλανύω), ὄναρ, ἀμαρύσσω.

before lingual : ρ βάραγχος κάρηνον σκαριφισμός τανθαρυστός ταράσσω
τάριχος φάραγξ φάρυγξ χαράδρα : λ ἀκαλήφη ἀπαλός γάλα θάλασσα
κάλαθος καλύπτω σταλάσσω φάλαγξ χάλαζα.

after lingual : ρ ἀράχνη θεράπων κόραξ σφαραγέομαι, lengthened
κυρηβάζω : λ εὐλάκα ἠμαλάψαι θύλακος-πέλαγος κέλαδος κολάπτω
μαλακός φύλαξ.

ι

between two liquids : κυλίνδω ὀνίνημι, with compensation (17) ὀρίνω.

before λ φιλύρα, ν ἐξαπίνης καρκίνος κινάβρα κινάθισμα-κίναιδος κινυρός.

after ρ ἀριστερός κυρίσσω σκηρίπτομαι, λ δολιχός σκελιφρός χάλιξ, ν
κίναδος.

υ before λ ἄκυλος : after ρ κόρυζα κορυφή μορύσσω ἐρύ(σ)ω, λ ἤλυθον
τολύπη, ν ὄνυξ.   Lengthened between two liquids χελύνη.

So sometimes between two consonants not liquid : a ἔγκατα θυγάτηρ,
ι πίτυλος πίτυρον.

3. Lengthening :

(*a*) *metri gratia :*

before two short syllables (Homeric) : **α** becomes **η** ἠγάθεος ἠερέθονται ἠίθεος ἠπεροπεύς, esp. before liquid ἀπηλεγέως ἠλάκατη ἠλίβατος ἠρέμα ἠνορέη, and so **ε** becomes **η** ἠνεκέως or **ει** θειλόπεδον.

between two short syllables : **ε** becomes **η** ἐτήτυμος ; before liquid **ο** becomes **ου** ἐριούνιος, after it **ω** κεδάνωθος ; **υ** becomes **ευ** ἐλεύθερος.

(*b*) on analogy of the above : all prob. originally poetic :

between two liquids **ο** becomes **ω** κολώνη κορώνη.

before a liquid **ο** becomes **ω** ὠρύομαι or **ου** οὐλαί οὐλαμός οὖλιος : **ε** becomes **ει** πεῖραρ πείρινθα σειρινός, εἰλύω : **α** becomes **η** ἠμαλάψαι ἠμορίς ἠμύω.

after a liquid : **ε** becomes **η** κυρηβάζω.

II. Consonantal.

4. Initial Aspiration :

(*a*) from false analogy :

ἅλιος ἕρμα **A.** ἥκω ἧμαι on analogy of ἅλς ἕρμα **B.** ἵημι ἕξομαι, where ʼ = *s.*

ἕρσαι on analogy of ἔρση, where ʼ = **F**.

ἁβρός ἁγής, ἡμεῖς, ὕδωρ ὑλάω ὑπέρ-ὑπό ὕστερος on analogy of ἥβη ἅγος ὑμεῖς ὑσμίνη, where ʼ = *j*.

(*b*) without reason : prob. dialectic, cf. Att. ἕως **A.** ἥλιος ἵστωρ ὅρος :

ἀδήν ἅλως ἅρμα-ἁρμός ἁρπάζω, ἡγέομαι.

εἱμαρμένη εὕδω εὕω ἑῶμεν.

ἱερός ἵμερος ἵππος.

---

5. Reduplication :

(*a*) repetition of the root :

simply : ἀκάκητα ἀραρίσκω γάργαρα γαργαρεών μάρμαρος ὀλολύζω, and so καρκαίρω.

with Dissimilation (20) of

(1) the reduplication :

vowel-change : of quantity ἀγωγός ἀκωκή μέρμηρα, ἄρουρα, of quality μορμύρω πορφύρα-πορφύρω, κωκύω.

avoidance of double aspirate : τήθη, ἀπαφίσκω.

repetition of the first syllable alone : ἐλελίζω, βορβορυγμός κορκορυγή.

truncation : μίν.

(2) the root :

vowel-change, to ι : ἀτιτάλλω ὀιστός ὀπιπτεύω.

vowel-lengthening (3) : ἐτήτυμος.

consonantal loss (35) : δαρδάπτω πέμπε.

(*b*) nasal reduplication : repetition of the initial consonant +

ον γόγγρος A. B. γογγύλος, τονθορύζω, πομφόλυξ.

εν (7) δενδίλλω δένδρον : ιν (11) κίγκλος πίμπλημι πίμπρημι : α (10) καχλάζω κάχληξ πασπάλη παφλάζω.

αν (11) γάγγαμον γάγγραινα, τανθαρυστός τανταλόομαι, παμφαίνω παμφαλάω.

Compensation (17) :

ον = οι δοῖδυξ ποιπνύω ποιφύσσω, ον βουβών.

εν = ει δειδίσκομαι, ευ τευθίς.

αν = αι λαῖλαψ μαιμάω παιπάλη παιφάσσω.

(*c*) vocalic reduplication : repetition of the initial consonant +

ι (cf. δίδωμι) : κίκιννος γίγαρτον, τιταίνω τιτρώσκω τιτύσκομαι, διδαχή τιθαιβώσσω-τιθασός-τίθημι τιθήνη-τίτθη σισύμβριον δίζημαι, πίπτω πιφαύσκω, λιλαίομαι.—With loss of spirant in the reduplication : ϛ ἱστός (18) ἴσκε, in the root σιωπή, in both ϛ ἵημι (18), j ἰάπτω, F ἰαύω ἴουλος A. B. ἰωγή ἰωή ὀπ-ίουρος.

ε (cf. δέδωκα) : κεκρύφαλος γέγειος, τέτανος τετραίνω τετρεμαίνω, πέπλος βέβαιος-βέβηλος φέψαλος.

(*d*) reduplication after the root : repetition of the initial consonant before the termination :

κ ἀπο-κίκω κερκίς A. B. κρίκος, γ γάργαλος γέλγη γοργός B., χ καλ-χαίνω.

β βαυβάω βολβός : μ μερμίς μῖμος : F (23) εἰλύω.

---

6. Affrication : doubling of consonant for emphasis :

(*a*) simple doubling of mute before the termination (cf. Appendix A.) : κάκκη λάκκος ποδοκάκκη, with Dissimilation (20) τίτθη τυτθός κέπφος.

(*b*) partial doubling : 'Excrescence,' addition of a consonant after the original consonant :

    (1) τ suffixt to κ or π after loss of initial ϛ (32) :

σκ becomes κτ κτάομαι κτείνω κτείς κτύπος, and so prob. ἰκτῖνος : so σκ = σχ (21) = χθ χθαμαλός-χθών.

σπ becomes πτ πτάρνυμαι πτερόν πτίλον πτόρθος πτύρομαι πτύω : so σπ = σφ (21) = φθ ἄφθαι διφθέρα φθάνω φθέγγομαι φθείρω φθόνος.

And on this analogy without loss of ϛ :

χ = χθ ἰχθύς μυχθίζω χθές.

π = πτ πταίω πτελέη πτέρνη πτήσσω πτίσσω πτοέω πτόλεμος πτόλις πτύσσω : φ = φθ ἴφθιμος ὀφθαλμός φθίς.

    (2) j suffixt to Media and assimilated (19) :

γ + j = ζ ζόφος ὄζος ῥοῖζος, and so δ + j = ζ ἄίζηλος ἀρίζηλος μέζεα.

β + j = βδ αὐτοκάβδαλος βδάλλω βδέω ἐπίβδα κολύβδαινα ῥάβδος ῥοῖβδος.

(3) Media suffixt to Nasal before Lingual: ἄνδρα, ἀμβλίσκω ἀμβλύς ἤμβλακον (cf. ἄμβροτος γαμβρός μεσημβρία, μέμβλεται μέμβλωκα).

B. CHANGE:

  I. Vocalic:

7. Interchange of *o* and *e*.

  (*a*) **ω = η**:

    ἄωρος ἄωτος ἰωή—ἄημι.
    γωλεός—βλῆμα.
    θωή θωμός—θημών.
    κωφός—κηφήν.
    μῶλυς—μήλις.
    ὀκτά-βλωμος—βλῆρ.
    πώγων—πηγός.
    πωρητύς—πηρός.
    ὠκύς—ἥκω.

  So **ω = ε** (30):

    αἰώρα—ἀείρω.
    ἐριωλή—εἰλέω.
    μώλωψ—μέλας.
    νώγαλα—νέκταρ.
    νῶκαρ—νέκυς.
    ὀρεσ-κῷος—κεῖμαι.

  And so **ου = ε**: νοῦσος—νέομαι, πλοῦτος—πλεῖος.

  (*b*) **o = ε**:

ἀολλής—ἀελλής.	δόμος—δέμω.
ἄορ—ἀείρω.	δονέω—δεννάζω.
ἁπλόος—πλεῖος.	δόρπον—δρέπω.
βαύλομαι—βέλτερος.	ἐξ-ούλη—εἰλέω.
βροντή—βρέμω.	ἠνορέη—ἀνέρος.
βρότος—βρέτας.	θοός θορός—θέω.
γαργός Β.—ἀγείρω.	κόλαξ—κέλλω.
δνόφος ζόφος—ἰο-δνεφής ζέφυρος	κοντός—κεντέω.
κνέφας ψέφος.	λοβός Α.—λέβης.
δοάν—δεύομαι.	λογγάζω—λέγος.
δοάσσατο—δέατο.	λοξός—λέχριος.
δοκεύω δοκέω—δέκομαι.	λόχος—λέχος.
δολιχός—ἐνδελεχής.	μόδιος—μέδιμνος.

μόρος—μέρος.

νόστος—νέομαι.

νότος—νέω.

ὁδός—ἔδαφος.

ὀδύνη—ἔδω.

ὀλοοίτροχος—εἰλύω.

ὀμόργνυμι—ἀμέργω.

ὀμός—ἕν.

ὄπα—ἔπος.

ὀπαδός ὅπλον ὀπτάω—ἕπομαι ἕπω
  ἕψω.

ὄπισθεν—ἐπί.

ὀργάζω—ἔργον.

ὅρκος—ἕρκος.

ὁρμή—ἕρμα B.

ὄρνυμι—ἔρνος.

ὄρρος—ἔρσαι.

ὄρχαμος—ἔρχομαι.

ὀρχάς—ἔργω.

ὀχεύς ὀχυρός—ἔχω ἐχυρός.

πολέω—πέλω.

πολιός—πελός.

πομφός—πέμφιξ.

πόνος—πένομαι.

πορεῖν πόρνη—περάω.

πόρπη—πείρω.

πόσθη—πέος.

πούς—πέδη.

ῥόχθος—ὀρεχθέω.

σιλη-πορδέω—πέρδομαι.

σκοπέω—σκέπτομαι.

στόμβος—στέφω.

στόρνυμι—στέρνον.

στρογγύλος—στρεύγομαι.

στρόμβος—στρέφω.

σφοδρός—σφεδανός.

τόξον τόπος B.—τέκμαρ.

τορός—τερετίζω.

τρόπις—τρέπω.

φλοιός—φλέω.

φόβος—φέβομαι.

χόω—χέω.

χρόμαδος—χρεμετίζω.

So οι = ει :

ἔοικα—εἰκών.

κλοιός—κλείω.

κοιμάω—κεῖμαι.

οἶκτος—ἐπείγω.

στοῖχος—στείχω.

τοῖχος—τεῖχος.

---

8. Interchange of o and a :

(a) ω = ᾱ (Ion. η) :

ἀπο-φώλιος—φηλόω.

βωμός—βῆμα.

διώκω ἰωκή—διάκονος.

διωλύγιος—ἠλύγη.

θῶκος—θᾶκος.

θῶμιγξ—στήμων.

θώραξ—θρᾶνος.

θωχθείς—θήγω.

θώψ—τέθηπα.

ἰωγή—ἄγνυμι.

κατα-σώχω ψωμός—ψάω.

κῶλον—κλάω.

κωλύω—κηλέω.

κώμη—κτάομαι.

λωίων λωτός—λήιον.

πτώσσω—πτήσσω.

ῥώξ A.—ῥήγνυμι.

ῥώξ B.—ῥάξ.

σκώπτω—σκήπτω.

σμῶδιξ—σμάω.

σῶμα—σῆμα.

ὑπερ-ῴη—ἠϊόεις.

φώγω—φηγός.   ὥρα—ἡμέρα.
φωριαμός—φᾶρος.   ὠχρός—ἀχλύς.
χωρίς—χῆρος.

So ου = ᾱ (Ion. η) : κρουνός—κρήνη, μοῦνος—μήν **B**.

So ω = α (30) :

δίδωμι—δάνος.   τωθάζω—ἀτάσθαλος.
κώπη—κάπτω.   ὠκύς—ἀκίς.
σωρός—σαίρω.

(*b*) ο = α before double consonant (cf. 1 ὀσταφίς—ἀσταφίς) :

ὄκρις—ἄκρος.   ὄστακος—ἀστακός.
ὀξύς—ἀξίνη.

---

9. α from ο or ε before a close vowel :

αι from οι, cf. Lat. *oitor*—αἴνυμαι :

κοικύλλω—καικίας.   οἶτος—αἶσα.

αι from ει, cf. *κείνω—καίνω, Lat. *venio*—βαίνω, *re-cens*—καινός, τ(ε)ίω—ἔμπαιος :

δέρω—δαίρω.   κείω—καιάδας.
εἰ—αἰ.   κρείων—κραίνω.
ἐκεῖ—καί.   κύπειρος—κύπαιρος.
εἰλέω—αἱρέω.   μένος—μαίνομαι.
εἶμι—αἰών.   σείω—σαικωνίζω σαίνω.
ἐπείγω—αἰγανέη.   σπείρω—σπαίρω.
κειρία—καῖρος.   τείνω—προταινί ταινία τιταίνω.

αυ from ου, cf. Lat. *ovo*—αὔω **B**. :

ἔνιοι—ἐνιαυτός.   οὐ οὖν—αὖ.
κάλως—καλαῦροψ.   οὖρος **A.**—αὔρα.

So γ(ο)υρός—γαυλός, τρε(υ)ω—τραυλός, χωλός (= *χουλός)—χαυλιόδους.
And so *αυ, *αϝ, from *ου, *οϝ :

ὄις—αἰγυπιός αἴπολος.   ποίη πτοέω—παίω.
ὀίω—ἀίω **B.**   χνόος—χναύω.
οἰωνός—αἰετός.

αυ from ευ :

εὐλάκα—αὖλαξ.   εὔχομαι—αὐχέω.
εὔληρα—αὔληρα.   λευρός—λαύρα.
εὑρίσκω—ἀπαυράω.   λ(ε)ύγξ **B.**—λαυκανίη.

10. α from Sonant Liquid before Consonant :

 (*a*) from Vowel + Liquid :

  (1) **ορ** μαπέειν σπατίλη, cf. ὕδατος.

   ομ before Labial : ἀλλοδαπός ἄπιος ἄραβος αὐτοκάβδαλος.

  (2) **ελ** ζάλη.

    εγ- before Guttural : ἀγα-νακτέω δάκτυλος κάκαλα-ποδοκάκκη κακός, ἀχηνία ἐλαχύς κάχρυς παχύς στάχυς. So before original Guttural μάσσω, στάζω σταλάσσω σφάζω τάσσω, διδάσκω.

    εν ἀ- neg. copul., ἀ-, before Dental ἄτερ αὐάτα ἑκατόν ἐλάτη κρατύς πατάσσω, σφαδάζω σχάζω A. βάθος πάθος, before Sibilant ἄσις γαστήρ δασύς κάσις.

    εμ before Labial : δάπτω λάπη, ἐλαφρός σταφυλή.

 (*b*) from Liquid + Vowel :

  (1) **ρο** ταχύς.

   νο ἀγαθίς ἄμμες ἔλαφος : **μο** ἀλέω.

  (2) **νε** ἀβρός ἀμνίον ἀρετή ἀριστερός ἀρνευτήρ.

   με ἄνθρωπος ἄρταμος ἀτύζομαι ἄχρι.

  (3) **λα** (11) ἀφύσσω γάνος A.

 Before a double Consonant the vowel sometimes appears as **ο** (8) : from **μο** ὄνθος ὄρφνη ὄσχος ὀχλίζω, **νε** ὄβρια.

---

11. α (ι, υ) through neighbouring Liquid :

 (*a*) **α**

  (1) from **ε** before

    ρ ἀργαλέος ἄρνα ἄρσην ἀτάρ ἀταρτηρός βάραθρον γίγαρτον ἐγκάρσιος κάρ κάρα καρχαλέος νάρκη δαρ δαρος φάρμακον, and so δαρδά(ρ)πτω, καρκαίρω.

    λ ἀλέη ἄλη ἀλής-ἕλις-ἀλίσκομαι-ἄλυσις ἀλίνδω ἄλοξ ἄναλτος βάλλω γαλήνη θάλπω παλάθη σάλος σκάλλω φαλλός.

    γ- ἄγγος ἀγκάλη ἀνάγκη γάγγλιον.

    ν ἄνεω ἀνύω τανείαι-τανύω φθάνω.

    μ ἀμάω θαμά τάμισος.

    from **ο** before

    ρ ἀρημένος ἄρκτος ἀρρωδέω ἀρχός βάραξ γάργαλος γάργαρα γαργαρεών δαρθάνω εἱμαρμένη καρδία πάρθενος πάρνοψ πεπαρεῖν σπαργάω ταρσός ταρφύς τέσσαρες φαρέτρα.

    λ ἀλθαίνω ἄλλομαι ἀλφάνω ἀνάλδω βάλε θάλαμος κάλως μάλα μαλακός σκαληνός σκάλοψ σταλίς φέψαλος.

    ν ἀνία καναχή ξανθός πᾶς σάννας σπάνις τέτανος.

    μ ἅμα ἄμβων γάγγαμον-γάμος γαμφηλαί δαμάζω ταμίας.

    from **υ** before **λ** καλινδέομαι.

  (2) from **ε** after

    ρ ἄτρακτος βραβεύς βραχύς δραμεῖν ῥαπίζω στράγξ τραπέω.

    λ ἔφλαδον λάγνος λάξ λάχεια.

    μ μαδάω μακρός ματεύω μάτιον.

~ from o after

 ρ ῥαθαπυγίζω στράβηλος.

 λ λάσκω.

 μ μασχάλη.

from υ after ρ ῥάζω ῥάμφος, λ γλάφω.

(3) between liquids from

 ε λάμπη λάμπω λάρκος μάνδαλος μανθάνω μάντις μάρμαρος μάρτυς τέραμνα.

 ο βράγχος μάλευρον—μαραίνω.

(*b*) ι

 (1) from α before

  ρ σκιρτάω.

  λ στίλβω φῑλητής.

  ν πλίνθος σκινθός.

  μ σκιμβάζω.

 from ε before

  λ δενδίλλω ἴλλω.

  γ- γίγγλυμος. κιγκλίδες κιγχάνω, and so κῖκυς.

  ν κίκιννος.

  μ ἱμάτιον.

 from η before ρ σκῖρος, γ- σφίγγω, μ σκίμπτω.

 from ο before λ ἵλαος—ἱλαρός.

 from υ before λ ψῑλός.

 (2) from α after ρ θρίζω κρίζω.

 from ε after ρ ἀκρῑβής βρῑθω, λ γλίχομαι ἐλελίζω φλίβω.

 from ο after μ μίσχος.

 from υ after λ λίπτομαι.

 (3) between liquids from

  ε βλῑμάζω θριγκός ὀστλιγξ ῥίμφα φριμάσσομαι, η ἐλῑνύω.

  ο μίλτος μίνθα μίνθος μινύθω μινυρός.

(*c*) υ

 (1) from α before ρ σπύραθος—σφυράδες—σφυρόν, λ κύλα κύλιξ, μ τύμβος.

 from ε before ρ δύρομαι πτύρομαι, ν γυνή.

 from ο before

  ρ κύρβις—κυρηβάζω κυρέω κυρίσσω κύρτη κυρτός πίσυρες σπυρθίζω στύραξ A.

  λ κυλλός πύλη σκύλλω.

  ν τυννοῦτος.

  μ αἰσυμνήτης κοδύμαλον πύματος.

 (2) from α after ρ βρῡχάομαι, μ ἀμύσσω μυδάω μύσταξ μυστίλη.

 from ε after ρ δρύπτω.

K

from o after ρ βρύχιος–ὑπόβρυχα πρύλεες–πρύτανις τρυφάλεια, ν νύξ, μ μυστίλη–μυττωτός.

from ι after ρ στρυφνός τρύζω.

(3) between liquids from o μύλη φάρυγξ.

---

12. Radical open vowel becomes close :

(*a*) ι from

ᾱ ἀίσσω κίνδυνος κτίζω, α ξίφος σπιδής.

η ἀίω B.–ίον θίς, ε διαίνω σχίζω φθίνω.

ω πίνω, ο κίς.

So ει (31) from ε πείθω στείβω.

(*b*) υ from α πυγμή–πύκα.

So ευ (31) from ε τεύχω–τυγχάνω–τύκος, ο ἀδευκής–ἐνδυκέως, ι πευκάλιμος.

---

13. ι before double consonant from

α ἴκρια–ὑπερικταίνομαι ῥιπτάζω ἰπνός.

ε ἴκτερος λικριφίς τίκτω, ἱδρύω–ίζω σκίδναμαι χθιζός, διφθέρα ἵππος, ἀίσθω δειδίσκομαι ἱστίη κισσός νίσσομαι, and so originally ἴδιος πίσυρες.

---

14. υ (ᾰ) between two consonants :

(*a*) υ from α βυθός δύπτω κύπειρος–κύπελλον σκύφος συχνός σφύζω, ο δοῖδυξ κτύπος κύκλος τυτθός.

(*b*) α from ε πατάνη, ο πρόβατον ταπεινός φάσγανον–φάτνη.

---

15. Assimilation of Vowel :

(*a*) final α in Prepositions assimilates preceding ε or ο : ἐνί—ἀνά περί—παρά ποτί—κατά.

(*b*) initial *F changes a following vowel to υ : from α ὑβός ὑγρός ὕδωρ, ε ὕβρις–ὑγιής ὑφαίνω, ο ὕπαρ ὑπήνη ὕπνος. So following *F changes the vowel to υ : α δύη κυέω, ο βύας, ι μῦελός.

---

16. Dissimilation of Vowel : to avoid concurrence or juxtaposition of similar vowels : change of

(*a*) the former :

ε + ε become α + ε ἄεσα.

υ + υ become ι + υ *ἰλύς λιγνύς μιστύλλω φῖτῦω ψιθυρός*, or ο + υ *ὀλο-λύζω τορύνη φορύνω.*

(*b*) the latter :

α + α become α + ι *ἀτιτάλλω.*

ο + ο become ο + ι *ὀιστός ὀπιπτεύω.*

υ + υ become υ + ε *ὀξυρεγμία.*

. Compensatory Lengthening :

(*a*) a diphthong ending in υ becomes a long vowel :

αυ = ᾱ (Ion. η) *ἀήρ ἀκροάομαι ἆσαι γηθέω ἐπηετανός ἐπητής ἦια ἠλύγη ἠώς κηώδης ναός.*

ου = ω *νέωτα ὠτειλή*, and so from original ευ (7) *ζωμός μῶμος ὀλοφώιος ῥώομαι τρώω φωλεός φώς χώομαι ὦλκα.*

So ευ = η = ῑ (11) *ἱνέω.*

(*b*) one of two consonants is dropt and the preceding vowel length-ened or diphthongised :

(1) the first consonant is dropt and the vowel

lengthened : before original

χν *σπλήν*, δμ *βλῑμάζω* (11), θς *κνίση μῖσος.*

νλ *νεογῑλός* (11), νν *ἑᾱνος ἐλῑνύω.*

σβ *ἀκρῑβής*, σρ *λᾱρός*, σλ *σπήλαιον χῑλιοι χῑλός*, σν *ἡνία ἐπίξηνον γωνία ὠνή*, σμ *ἡμεῖς ἦμος κῶμος ἱμάτιον ἵμερος φῑμός ζύμη ὑμεῖς.*

diphthongised : with ending

ι before original νς *εἰς εἶς*, μμ *λαῖμα εἱμαρμένη*, σδ *κίναιδος λοίδορος*, σρ *εἴρω* A., σν *καίνυμαι ῥαίνω εἵνεκα*, σμ *εἷμα εἰμί*, Fλ *εἰλαπίνη εἴλη.*

υ before original σν *γουνός χλούνης.*

(2) the second consonant is dropt and the vowel

lengthened before original

ν after λ *μῖλαξ.*

ς after ρ *χηράμβη*, μ *ῶμος.*

F after λ *πήληξ πηλός ὕλη*, ν *μᾱνός*, ς *ἷσος κονίσαλος.*

j after λ *καλός.*

diphthongised : with ending

ι before original

ν after ρ *μεῖραξ*, λ *εἰλέω μειλιχος χεῖλος.*

ς after ρ *δειρή εἰρήν χοῖρος.*

F after δ *δείδω εἶδαρ*, ρ *καιρός εἴρη*, λ *εἴλαρ εἴλη*, ν *εἰνοσίφυλλος στεινός κοινός χοῖνιξ*, μ *λαιμός.*

j after ρ *εἴρω* B. *πεῖρα τείρω φθείρω χείρων*, ν *βαίνω πεῖνα τείνω.*

υ before original

ν after λ *βούλομαι οὖλα οὐλή οὖλος* B.

ς after ρ κοῦρος οὖρος–τό.

Ϝ after δ θεουδής οὖδας, ρ νεῦρον θοῦρος οὖρος **B. C.**, λ σαῦλος φαῦλος ἐξούλη οὖλε–οὖλος **A.**, ν ἐλαύνω κροινός, ς προυσελέω.

(c) the nasal before another consonant is dropt and the preceding vowel lengthened or diphthongised :

lengthened before original nasal +

κ κῖκυς σμῑκρός, γ σῑγαλόεις, χ ἰχώρ.

τ ἦτορ, δ ἀηδών χελῑδών χῖδρα, θ βῆσσα βρίθω ἰθύς Adj.

π λῑπαρής σκῑπων, φ σκῑφη στῖφος.

diphthongised : with ending

ι before original nasal +

κ αἰκάλλω δεικανάομαι εἰκῆ ἐρείκω πείκω ῥοικός, γ αἴγλη αἴξ, χ μοιχός.

τ καταῖτυξ κρείσσων κρειττόομαι, δ ἀείδω, θ πλαίσιον εἶθαρ πεῖσμα.

π αἰπύς κραιπάλη κραιπνός λαιψηρός δεῖπνον ἐρείπω, β ῥαιβός ῥοῖβδος, φ ἀκραιφνής ἀλείφω.

υ before original nasal +

γ αὐγή κραυγή στρεύγομαι στροῦθος, χ αὐχήν καύχη.

τ οὐτάω, θ εὐθύς ξουθός.

π γαυσός δοῦπος, β βουβών, φ κοῦφος.

(d) a root ending in a nasal loses the nasal and lengthens the vowel :

εν = ᾱ (Ion. η) ἀάω βηλός ἐπιτηδές–τῇ μαιμάω–μάομαι–μῆτις πῆμα.

ομ = ω δῶμα.

II. Consonantal.

18. Initial Spirant appearing as Rough Breathing.

   (a) **s** :

αἷμα αἴνω ἅλλομαι ἅλς ἅμα ἅρπη **B.**

ἕδος εἷς ἕλίκη ἕνος ἑξῆς ἑπτά ἕπω ἑρμηνεύς ἕρπω, αὐθέντης.

ἡμι- ἥρως.

ἵημι ἵλαος ἱμάς ἵστημι.

ὁ ὁδός ὁλκός ὅλος ὁρμή ὅρμος **A.**

ὕει υἱός–ὗς ὕλη ὑμήν.

ῥάπτω ῥέω ῥῖγος ῥίνη ῥύγχος ῥῶπες.

   (b) **Ϝ** :

αἱρέω–ἀλής ἁπτοεπής.

ἑανός–ἕννυμι ἑάφθη ἕδνα εἵλη εἵνεκα ἑκών ἑλεῖν ἑλίσσω ἕλκω ἕλμινς ἕλος ἕρκος ἕρση ἕσπερος ἑστία εὑρίσκω.

ἵεμαι ἵκω.

ὅλμος ὁράω ὅρμος **B.**

ὑβός ὕβρις–ὑγιής ὑγρός ὕδωρ ὕπαρ ὑπήνη ὑφαίνω.

ῥάβδος ῥαδινός ῥάδιος ῥαιβός ῥαίνω ῥάκος ῥέπω–ῥίπτω ῥήγνυμι ῥῆμα
  ῥῆνιξ ῥίζα ῥίον ῥοικός ῥύζω ῥῦμα–ῥυσός ῥύομαι.

(c) *j* :

  ἅγος.

  ἑτοῖμος ἐψιά.

  ἥβη ἡνία ἧπαρ.

  ὑμεῖς ὑσμίνη.

  ὥρα.

---

19. Assimilation :

(a) of the former consonant :

Guttural

  weakened : κ before δ ἴγδις, χ before δ λίγδην or μ βρέγμα.

  sharpened before τ : γ ἀκτίς νέκταρ οἶκτος φλύκταινα, χ λέκτρον.

  dentalised : γ before τ σάττω, before ν δνοπαλίζω δνόφος.

Dental

  weakened : with anaptyctic vowel ἕβδομος.

  assibilated : before Guttural ἀσκός φάσγανον γλίσχρος, Labial
    λίσπος μέσφα ὀσφραίνομαι, μ ἄσμενος κέκασμαι θεσμός πεῖσμα
    ὑσμίνη, s λισσός.

  gutturalised : δ γλυκύς.

Labial

  weakened : π ἀβδης ἤμβλακον, φ before Lingual βράσσω βράχε
    βρέγμα βρέμω βρίθω βρύω βλάβη βλαστάνω.

  sharpened : β before ν στιλπνός, φ before τ ἀποσκολύπτω ἅπτω
    λίπτομαι σκάπτω σκηρίπτομαι χρίμπτομαι.

  nasalised : π ὄμμα, β before ν ἀμνός γυμνός σεμνός τέρεμνα, φ be-
    fore ν ῥαμνός.

μ

  before Dentals becomes ν βροντή γέντο τένδω τύντλος, and so
    before original *j* βαίνω.

  before Linguals becomes γ γλάγος γλήχων or β βραχύς βρέτας–
    βρότος ἐμβραμένα βλήχων βλίτον βλίττω βλώσκω.

s completely assimilated before Liquids : ρ ἐπίρροθος (and so
  ζάλη = *ζέλλη, *ζέσλη), ν ἐννέα ἔννυμι ζώννυμι κίκιννος κοννέω,
  μ ἄμμες κομμόω.

F completely assimilated before Linguals : ἀναρρύω ἐρρηνοβοσκός–
  πολύρρηνος περιρρηδής ἐλλεδανοί.

So with a vowel intervening : ν is assimilated to following original
γ γυμνός, μ to following ν νίν.

(*b*) of the latter consonant :

Tenues :

after ς : τ is labialised σπιλάς σπολάς, with Metathesis (24) ψάρ ψιάζω; π is weakened ἄσβολος, dentalised στάδιον στροῦθος. So after original ς : κ is weakened before ρ γράφω γρῖφος γρομφάς γρύτη, λ γλάφω γλύφω, ν γνόφος; κτ is weakened ἐρίγδουπος.

after μ a Labial is weakened : π ἴαμβος, φ ἀτέμβω θάμβος κίμβιξ κόρυμβος κράμβη–κρομβόω ὄμβριμος ὄμβρος στέμβω στόμβος στρόμβος τύμβος.

ν is labdacised after λ ἐλλός Subst. ὄλλυμι, and after original ς λάρκος.

ζ after ρ becomes δ ἔρδω.

Spirants are completely assimilated :

ς after ρ ἄψορρος ἔρρω ὄρρος ὀρρός, μ κρόμμυον.

Ϝ after κ ἴκκος μικκός, ν ἐννέπω ἐννοσίγαιος, ς ἐπίσσωτρον.

j after λ ἅλλομαι ἄλλος φύλλον, ν ἔννηφιν, ς νίσσομαι πτίσσω.

So with a consonant intervening : κ after original γς is weakened μίσγω, after original θς is aspirated πάσχω.

(*c*) of both consonants, the first a Guttural or Dental, the second Ϝ or *j* :

(1) τϜ become σσ τέσσαρες, = initial ς σάκος σαργάνη σεῦτλον σήμερον or Dor. Att. τ τηλία τῆτες τύντλος τυρίσδω.

(2) Tenuis or Aspirate + *j* become σσ :

κj ἀίσσω ἀοσσητήρ δράσσομαι ἐνίσσω κολοσσός λεύσσω λύσσα νύσσω ὄσσα ὄσσε παιφάσσω πάσσαλος πέσσω πίσσα πτήσσω τάσσω φράσσω φρίσσω.

χj ἀμαρύσσω γλῶσσα θάλασσα-θράσσω πτύσσω ταράσσω.

τj ἐρέσσω κρόσσαι πρόσσω τόσσος, = initial ς σά.

θj βῆσσα βυσσός κίσσα κισσός μέσσος πάσσω πλάσσω.   So κνίση = *κνίθjη.

Media + *j* become ζ :

γj γλάζω γρύζω A. ἐμπάζομαι ζάω λάζομαι μᾶζα ὄζος πλάζω ῥέζω A. στάζω σφάζω φύζα.

δj δοζος ζα- μαζός πέζα πιέζω πρώιζα–χθιζός ῥέζω B. ῥίζα σχάζω A. B. χάλαζα χέζω.

---

20. Dissimilation : to avoid

(*a*) concurrence of similar Dentals : assibilation of

τ before τ ἀριστερός κύστις μυστίλη or θ ἀίσθω ἄσθμα.

δ before τ ἵστωρ μαστός μεστός ὀνοστός ὕστερος or θ ἐσθίω.

θ before τ βλαστάνω οἶστρος or θ ἰσθμός ὀλισθάνω.

(*b*) juxtaposition of Liquids : λλ become νλ ἀμάνδαλος, νν become λν λίκνον.

(c) juxtaposition of Aspirates :

  (1) the first is sharpened :

    χχ καλχαίνω, χθ κόθορνος λέκιθος–ἡ σκεθρός (and so originally κίττα κνίση), χφ κέπφος κεφαλή κοῦφος.

    θχ τεῖχος, θθ τεθμός τῆθος (and so τηλεθάων), θφ τάφος A. τάφρος τέφρα τύφω (and so originally ἀτέμβω).

    φχ παχύς πῆχυς πτυχή, φθ πάρθενος πειθω πένθος πίθος πόθος πυθμήν πυνθάνομαι, φφ ἀπαφίσκω.

    So with final weakening (28) after sharpening of the first aspirate : χφ κόβαλος, θχ τρύγη τρύξ, φχ πέλαγος πυγή πύργος, φθ πύνδαξ.

    More rarely the first aspirate is weakened : χθ ἀγαθός, θχ δολιχός, φθ βόθρος.

  (2) the second is sharpened :

    χθ χατέω, θχ θύλακος (and so after final aspiration, 29, θριγκός), θφ θάπτω, φχ φύλακα, φθ φάτνη.

    More rarely the second aspirate is weakened : θχ θέλγω θιγγάνω, φχ φεύγω, φφ φέρβω φλίβω.

---

21. Aspiration of Tenuis through neighbouring Sibilant or Liquid :

  (a) preceding s aspirates

    κ ἔσχατος ἰσχάς ἰσχίον σχαδών σχάζω A. B. σχεδία σχελίς (cf. 32 χαμαί etc.).

    τ σθένος.

    π σφαδάζω–σφονδύλη σφαῖρα–σφῦρα σφάλλω σφαραγέομαι–σφριγάω σφήξ σφίγγω.

  (b) following ρ aspirates

    κ βληχρός λέχριος μέχρι (cf. 29).

    τ θρῖδαξ–θρῖναξ–θρῖον ἐρίψ θρύπτω νάθραξ.

  (c) following ν aspirates (cf. 29).

    κ ἀράχνη ἄχνη B. λάχνη λύχνος πάχνη πρόχνυ συχνός τέχνη.

    π αἰφνίδιος–ἀκραιφνής–ἄφνω.

    So before μ : κ αἰχμή ἰωχμός λαχμός.

---

22. Assibilation of Dental before a close vowel :

  (a) before ι : τ ἀνεψιός διαπρύσιος εἴκοσι ἐψιά κάσις λάσιος πέρυσι πόσις τηύσιος, θ διπλάσιος–πλαίσιον ἐρυσίβη–ἐρυσίπελας.

  (b) before υ : τ ἀήσυρος πίσυρες σύ συρβηνεύς σύρω.

---

23. Vocalisation of F :

  (a) υ from Fε (cf. 31) before consonant : ἀυτμή πέρυσι τηύσιος, and combining with preceding vowel ἐνιαυτός εὐλάκα εὐλή εὔληρα οὗτος.

(*b*) υ from *F* before

    vowel : εἰλύω, ἀπολαύω αὐάτα αὐερύω, ἀκούω λούω.

    consonant : γαῦρος θαῦμα καλαῦροψ πιφαύσκω ταλαύρινος χαῦνος, πλεύμων.

---

24. Metathesis :

  (*a*) of vowel + liquid :

    (1) simple Metathesis : from original

      αρ ἀραιὸς ἀτραπός βραδύς κραίνω κραιπνός κράμβη κραταίλεως κράτος ῥαιβός ῥάπτω τράμις τρασιά φράσσω.

      ερ ἀρέσκω βρέφος ἐρέσσω κρέκω ῥέζω **A. B.** ῥέθος ῥέπω τρέπω τρέφω.

      ορ ἀβροτάζω βρόμος **B.** βροτός γόγγρος θρόνος κρομβόω κρόταφοι κρότος κρότων πρόξ πρός ῥοφέω στροῦθος χροιά χρόνος.

      υρ ἀντικρύ ὀρύσσω ὀφρύς τρύβλιον φρυάσσομαι φρύνη.

      αλ ἤμβλακον κλαίω λαπαρός λαπίζω λάφυρα πλάδη πλάζω πλάνη πλατύς **B.** φλαῦρος, ᾱλ λᾶας.

      ελ ἐλεφαίρομαι ἐλλεδανοί φλέω.

      ολ ἐπίπλοον κλόνος χλούνης.

      υλ γλυκύς λύκος.

      αν κνάπτω, ᾱν μνήμη.

      εν κνέφας.

      ον ὀνοπαλίζω νόθος.

      υν κνυζάομαι.

    (2) with vowel modified by the liquid (11) to

      α : from original

        ερ ἀχράς βραχύς κράνος ὀρθόκραιρος ὄστρακον ῥάβδος στράπτω τετραίνω, **ορ** δράκων ἐμβραμένα κράνον ῥάκος στρατός.

        ελ γλάγος εἰλαπίνη λάσιος πλάθω, **ολ** λάμπη.

        εν γνάθος.

      ι : from original

        αρ ἀρι- σφριγάω, **ερ** κρίνω στριφνός τρίβω, **ορ** ῥίζα, **υρ** κρίκος.

        αλ κλισίη χλίω, **ελ** βλίτον.

      υ : from original

        ερ διαπρύσιος πρυμνός, **ορ** ἀμαρύσσω φρύγιλος.

        ελ ἀναβλύω.

    (3) with vowel lengthened by the liquid (3) : from original

      αρ ῥηίδιος χράω, **ερ** ἐρῆμος ἐρρηνοβοσκός–ῥῆνιξ κρηπίς πρήθω ῥῆμα, **ορ** βιβρώσκω δρώπτω ἐρωή **B.** κρωβύλος κρωπίον κρωσσός ῥωδιός στρώννυμι, **υρ** τρυτάνη.

      αλ κάχληξ λήμη τλῆναι, **ελ** λῆνος πλησίος σκληρός χλῆδος, **ολ** βλώσκω κλώθω.

      αν θνήσκω, **εν** γνήσιος, **ιν** νίκη πνίγω.

      εμ τμήγω.

(4) with vowel both modified and lengthened by the liquid : to
ᾱ (Ion. η): from original ε γρηῦς πράσσω, ο τρανής.
ῑ : from original α ἔριθος τάριχος φρίκη σκνίψ, ε δριμύς κριθή κριός
πρῖνος πρίω ῥίνη ῥιπή χρίω ἄγλιθες ῥινός σκνιπός.
υ from original ε γρῦ ἐρύκω, ο γρῦλος δρῦς.

(b) of liquid + vowel : from original
ρα ἄρδις ἁρπάζω, ρε ἕρμα A., ρο ὄργυια πόρκης φόρμιγξ, ρι κίρκος, ρυ
φύρω.
λα ἄλπνιστος ἀλφάνω ἀλφός βαλβίς, λε ἀθέλγω ἀσελγής, λο πόλις–
πολύς φολκός.   So from λε with modification (11) ἄλγος.
να ἄνθραξ, νο ὀμφαλός χοῖνιξ (= *χόν-Ϝιξ).

(c) complex Metathesis involving a liquid :
of 2 letters νάρθηξ, of 3 δίφρος κάμινος μέλος πνύξ τάφρος, of 4 ἀμιθρός
ἐπηγκενίδες.

(d) Metathesis of non-liquids :
(1) of s + Mute :
σκ become ξ : ἰξός ξαίνω ξανθός ξεῖνος ξερός ξέω ξίφος ξύλον ξύν
ξυρόν.
σπ become ψ : δέψω ψαθυρός ψαίρω ψακάς ψάρ ψέγω ψευδής ψέφος
ψηλαφάω ψιάζω ψιλός ψίνομαι ψόα ψόλος ψόφος ψύλλα ψυχή.
Conversely. of Mute + s : ἔσχατος.
(2) of Ϝε into ευ (23) εὔδω εὔκηλος εὐνή εὖνις εὐρύς εὔχομαι εὔω, = αυ (9)
αὐδή αὐλή–αὐλός–αὔσιος αὔξω.
(3) of consonants with vowel between ἀπέσκης σκοπέω, and with
consonant also between σπάλαξ.
(4) of aspiration :
χδ become κθ κριθή, and so κισσός.
τχ become θκ θράσσω.
τφ become θπ θάλπω θεράπων θρύπτω τέθηπα, or θβ θύμβρα.

5. Labdacism : change of ρ to λ :
(a) initial : λαιψηρός λακίς λάσιος λέγω B. λέκιθος–ὁ λέπω λῆνος λύπη
λύσσα.
(b) between vowels : ἀγέλη ἀκαλήφη ἄλη γογγύλος δέλεαρ δηλέομαι
δολιχός ἐθέλω εἰλέω ἐλαφρός ἑλεῖν ἠμαλάψαι θάλασσα θειλόπεδον
θολός καλύπτω κελαινός κελαρύζω κῆλον κολάπτω κολοιός κολοφών–
κολυμβάω μέλαθρον μέλω μῆλον B. μῖλαξ–ὁ μολοβρός μολύνω μύλη–
μῶλος–μῶλυς ὀβελός οὖλα οὐλή πόλεμος πτίλον σάλος σέλινον σκάλοψ
σκολοπένδρα σκόλοψ σμῖλαξ σταλάσσω συλάω τηλύγετος τολύπη ὑλάω
χάλαζα χάλις χελιδών χίλιοι ψηλαφάω.
(c) before consonant : ἀθέλγω ἀλδαίνω ἀλκή ἄλπνιστος ἀμαλδύνω ἀμέλγω
ἀμολγῷ γέλγη δενδίλλω ἔλδομαι ἐλθεῖν θάλπω θέλγω κέλλω κυλλός
ὁλκός ὄλλυμι πάλλω σέλμα.

(*d*) after consonant : ἀμπλακεῖν ἀφλοισμός βλαστάνω κάχληξ κλαδάσσομαι κλάω κλέπτω κλίβανος κλώζω ναύκληρος πλάδη πλέκω στλεγγίς φλέγω χλῆδος χλούνης.

---

26. Dentalism : velar guttural palatilised :

(*a*) κ*j* (for κϝ) becomes τ*j* (19) = τ (32) before

     α πάντα ποταίνιος, ε πέντε τὲ τέλλω τέλσον τέσσαρες τευμάομαι, η τῆλε τηλύγετος, ι τινάσσω τίς–τίς τίω, υ ἄντυξ.

     liquid ἄντλος τέτμον.

(*b*) γ*j* (for γϝ) becomes δ*j* (19) = ζ (19, dialectic) before α ἐπιζαρέω ζάψ, or δ (32) before

     ε δᾶ (= *δέα) δέλεαρ δελφύς δεσπότης δεῦρο ὀδελός, η δήλομαι, ο δόχμιος, υ δύπτω.

     liquid ἰδνόομαι.

(*c*) χ*j* (for χϝ) becomes θ*j* (19) = θ (32) before

     α θάλλω, ε ἐθέλω θερμός–θέρος.

---

27. Labialism : κϝ = πϝ (19) = ππ ἵππος ὅππως = π (35).—In ἵππος ἀλλοδαπός θεοπρόπος ἐπιζάφελος the ϝ belongs to the termination.

(*a*) κϝ = π before

     α ἀσπάλαθος ἔμπαιος ἧπαρ πάλαι–πάλιν πάρνοψ πατάσσω σπατίλη, ᾶ ἐνοπή πάομαι.

     ε δυσπέμφελος ἕσπερος θεσπέσιος πέλω πέμπε πέσσω πέτορες σπένδω.

     ο (ω) αἴπολος ἀλλοδαπός δρέπω ἐννέπω ἕπομαι ἔπος ἐρείπω θεοπρόπος ἶπος λάμπω λείπω πέπων A. B. ποινή πότμος ποῦ σποδός τόπος B. τρέπω.

     ι ἀσπίς A. νώροπι πινυτός πίσυρες σπινθήρ.

     υ ἄμπυξ πύανος σπυρθίζω.

     τ λάπτω μάρπτω πτήσσω ῥάπτω.

     ρ ἐξαμπρεύω πραπίδες πρίαμαι πρῖνος, ν ἰπνός.

     With metathesis σκϝ = σπ = ψ ἐψιά ῖψ ἰψός κομψός ψαφαρός ψέφος ψηλαφάω ψιλός ψόφος.

(*b*) γϝ = β before

     α βαίνω βαιός βάλλω–βάλανος βάπτω βάραθρον βάραξ βαρύς βαστάζω βάτος κρέμβαλα λαμβάνω σκιμβάζω, ᾶ ἀμφισβητέω ἥβη.

     ε ἀμορβέω βείομαι βένθος ὀβελός σβέννυμι σοβέω, η ἀκριβής.

     ο (ω) ἀμείβω βοή βολβός βορά βόσκω βουβῶν βούλομαι βουνός βῶλος ἐγκομβόομαι θόρυβος κολοβός ῥαιβός σέβω στείβω στίλβω τρίβω ὑβός φέβομαι φέρβω φλίβω.

     ι βαλβίς βία βιός.

ν βύρσα βύω πρέσβυς.

τ νίπτω (19), δ βδέω ῥοῖβδος-ῥύβδην.

ρ βραβεύς βραδύς βρέφος βρέχω βρόχος βρύχω ὄβρια ὕβρις, λ βλέπω βλῆρ στρεβλός, ν (19) ἀμνός γυμνός πρέμνον.

(c) χϜ = φ before

α ἀλφάνω νίφα φαίδιμος φαιός, ᾱ λωφάω.

ε ἐπιζάφελος φέρτερος, and so originally (6) φθείρω.

ο (ω) κάρφω νήφω ῥάμφος στρέφω φοῖβος φοῖτος.

ι ὄφις, υ φύλαξ.

ρ ἐλαφρός τέφρα φράζω, ν ἀφνειός λοφνία μόρφνος and so originally ῥάμνος.

---

8. Weakening of final consonant of root : of

κ θυγάτηρ κραυγή-κρίζω μάγειρος-μᾶζα μίγνυμι ὄρτυγα ψέγω, χ σιγαλόεις σιγή σίζω.

τ διάζομαι (19).

π καλύβη κρίβανος, φ ἄραβος κρωβύλος-κύρβις λάβρος.

---

9. Aspiration of final consonant of root : of

κ ἀδαχέω ἄχυρα δέχομαι ἰχώρ καγχάζω κιχάνω μάχαιρα-μάχη μόρυχος νύχιος νωχελής ῥέγχω ῥύγχος τεύχω-τυγχάνω ὠχρός, γ ἐρχατάομαι-ὀρχάς ῥαχία.

τ ἀμιχθαλόεις, δ ἀγαθίς.

π ἄφαρ βλέφαρον δυσπέμφελος κεκαφηότα μορφή πέμφιξ σαφής τρέφω-τροφαλίς.

Ⅰ. Loss :

I. Vocalic :

0. Vowel-shortening :

(a) shortening of vowel before vowel :

ᾱ (Ion. η) becomes ε before

ᾱ θέα, ω ἕως A. λέως νέω B. προπρεών and so ἑώρα.

ι γέγειος-γείτων κλείς λεία παρειά, υ λεύω πρευμενής.

η becomes ε before υ εύς εὖτε.

ω becomes ο before ᾱ δα, ι φθόις.

(b) shortening of root-vowel :

ᾱ ἄγος ἄγω ἄδος ἀκᾱ ἀκίς ἀλαός ἄνεμος ἐπιζάφελος ζάκορος μακρός πάγος πάλαι πλάξ πτάξ σκάλλω χάσκω χατέω.

η ἀεσίφρων ἄπλετος γέρων ἔθος ἑκών μέδω μέρμερα μέτρον ξερός ῥέγος στερεός.

ω βλοσυρός βολβός λοβός **B.** μόλις μοχλός ὀφείλω πολύς.

ῑ δίψα ἱκανός ἴτυς πίτυς.

ϑ ἐγκυτί σύ.

---

31. **Compression of root: loss of radical ε before a close vowel or a consonant :**

(*a*) **simplification of radical diphthong :**

ει δίω εὐδιεινός ᾖα ἰθύς Adj. ἴλη ἴλιγγος λιάζομαι λιτός σκιά τίω, **ει**κ δίκη ἴ(κ)σκω, **ει**θ πίθηκος and so κίττα, **ει**μ δύσχιμος-χίμαρος, **ει**Ϝ βίος.

ευ ἀλύσκω-λύω ἀμύνω-μύνη δύω νυστάζω περιφλύω-φλυδάω πλύνω ποιπνύω στύω φύω, **ευ**κ γλυκύς ἐνδυκέως λυκάβας-λύχνος, **ευ**γ ζυγόν λυγρός and so φύζα, **ευ**χ τιτύ(χ)σκομαι, **ευ**νθ πυνθάνομαι, and so **ευ**λ = **αυ**λ (9) γύλιος.

So **o** (7) is lost in

οι ἴα, **οι**κ πικρός, **οι**χ ἴχνος στίχος, **οι**β λίψ στίβη.

ου λύθρον ῥύμη χύτρος.

(*b*) **loss of ε before a consonant ; in**

εκ θέσκελος and ⁚ so ἐγγύς, **ε**χ ἀσχαλάω-ἰσχύς, **ε**τ αὐτμή πίπτω-πτηνός-πτῶμα, **ε**β ἀμφισβητέω.

ερ ἀπουράς εἴρω **A.**, **ε**λ ἀμβλίσκω ἀμβλύς βλίττω ἔπιπλα, **ε**ν γίγνομαι πέφνον, **ε**μ ὄγμος.

ες ψάω and so (σ)ετάζω.

II. Consonantal :

32. **Loss of one of two consonants :**

(*a*) **of the former (cf. 35) :**

κ before μ *init.* μέλαθρον, ς *init.* (dialectic) σύν, σς *med.* τόσσαις : γ before δ *init.* δοῦπος, θ *med.* στροῦθος, μ *med.* σιμός.

θ before ρ *med.* ὄναρ (2), μ *med.* ἀμφίσμαινα.

π before ς *init.* κατα-σώχω (σ)άμαθος : β before ς *med.* γαυσός.

ν before ς *med.* εὔχομαι (= *εὔν-σκομαι).

ς before

κ *init.* ἐγ-κάρσιος ἐγ-κυτί κάμαξ κάπετος καρπός **A.** κάρφω κεδάννυμι-κίδναμαι κείω **B.** κέλαρύζω κέλυφος κέρτομος κεύθω κηκίς κηλίς κῆτος κίμβιξ κοέω κολάπτω κόλυθροι κόνυζα κόπτω κόρδαξ κορδύλος κόρυζα κυκάω κύλλαρος κυλλός κυρίσσω κῶας κώψ, κλῆτς κνάπτω κνέφας κνίψ κνώδαλον κρέμβαλα κρηπίς κρίνω ; *med.* ἀκαλήφη ἄκαρνα ἀκούω προΐκτης. So before **γ** (original **κ**) *init.* **19 b**, **X**

(original κ, 21) *init.* χαμαί χάραξ χέζω χόριον χρέμπτομαι, *med.*
γλίχομαι εὔχομαι ἀρχός, ἀμυχνός αὐχμός κάχληξ.

τ *init.* ταγγή ταγυρί ταῦρος τέγος τελαμών–τέλμα τενμάομαι τοπεῖον
τύπτω τύρβη, τρίζω τρύζω τρύχνος ; *med.* ἔγκατα (2). So before θ
(original τ, 21) *init.* θάμβος θάομαι θέλυμνα θόλος θύρσος θῶμιγξ,
θριγκός θρύον ; *med.* ἀθέλγω. Before δ *med.* αἰδώς ; θ (original δ)
med. κριθή.

π *init.* ἀπο-πυτίζω ἐμ-πάζομαι πάλλω πέλεθος πέρθω περκνός πηδάω
πῖλος πῖνος πυρός, πνίγω πρέσβυς πρήθω (cf. 6) ; *med.* πέπλος. So
before β *med.* τρίβω, φ (original π, 21) *init.* φανός φέγγος
φέψαλος φιμός φιτύω φυσάω, φρήν φρίγος φρυγίλος ; *med.* δέφω
ποιφύσσω (cf. 6).

λ *init.* λαγγάζω λαιός λάμπη λαπίζω λάρυγξ λοβός B. λύγξ B.

ν *init.* νέος νεῦρον νέω A. B. νίφα νόος νόσφι νυός νώγαλα νώροπι.

μ *init.* ἀπο-μύττω μάραγνα μάστιξ μειδάω μέλδομαι μέριμνα μετά
μῆλον A. μήρινθος–μηρύομαι μία μικρός μῖλαξ–ἤ μόγος μοῦνος
μύραινα μύρον μῦς μυχός.

F *init.* ἔ ἔξ ἡδύς ἱδρώς ὕπνος (cf. 33) ; *med.* ἀείρω σιωπή, ἐννέπω.

F before λ *init.* λάσιος λάχνη λέκιθος–ὁ λῆνος λιγαῖος λύκος, ν *init.*
νίκη.

(*b*) of nasal before mute (cf. 10) : of

γ- before κ διηνεκής λέκιθος–ἡ ὄκνος B., γ ἀστράγαλος, χ ἄχος ἔχις
καχάζω κιχάνω τύχη.

ν before δ σφεδανός σχάζω B., θ ἀθήρ πεύθομαι πυθμήν.

μ before π δέπας ἐνοπή κόπτω κυδοιδοπάω λάπη τύπτω, β κολύβδαινα
κυβιστάω ὄβριμος, φ ἀμφιλαφής κορυφή στέφω στρέφω στυφελίζω
τάφος B. ψόφος.

(*c*) of the latter consonant : loss of spirant after consonant : of

F after

κ (cf. 27) ἀποκαπύω ἀρτοκόπος καναχή κατά-κοῦ κηλίς κῆτος and so
αἴσσω ἀοσσητήρ, γ ἀγαθός γαστήρ γυρός and so ζάω (19), χ ὀμίχλη
σχαδών χωλός.

τ (cf. 26) τετίημαι, δ διά–δίζω–δίκελλα, θ θαιρός θάνατος.

ς σαγηνεύω σαίνω σάλος σάλπιγξ σάννας σάττω σαυρωτήρ σέβω σειρινός
σηκός σίαλος σιγαλόεις σιγή σίδηρος σίζω σίνομαι σομφός σῦριγξ
σύρφαξ σῦς σωπάω, = Dor. τ τύντλος.

ρ δριός.

j after

δ δα- δαύω.

ς κασσύω σάω.

---

33. Loss of initial spirant before a vowel :

(*a*) s, Gk. ʼ (18) :

ἀ- copul.–ἄμαξα–ἀμόθεν–ἄμυδις ἄεσα ἄμμος ἀνύω ἄσις ἄτερ.
ἐάω ἔναρα ἔνος ἐτάζω.

ἡμί.

ἰκμάς.

ὁ- ὀλοόφρων ὄλπις ὀρός ὄρπηξ ὀπαδός οὖδας οὖλος A.

(b) F:

(1) otherwise represented by ' (18) : ἀλέη ἄλοξ εἰλύω ἤλιθα ἦμος ὠνή
ὥρα and so ἄμπελος, and after loss of preceding ς (32) ἄσμενος-
ἦδος ἔτης-ἐτός-ἴδιος ἴδος.

(2) otherwise unrepresented :

ἄγνυμι ἀπ-αυράω ἄστυ.

ξάρ εἶδον εἴκοσι εἴκω εἰκών εἶλαρ-εἰλέω εἴργω-ἔργον εἶρος εἴρω B.
εἴση ἔλδομαι ἐλπίς ἐμέω ἔπος ἐρι- ἔρρω-ἐρύω ἔτος.

ἠπίολος ἦρα ἠχή.

ἰά-ἰαχή-ἰωή ἰνέω ἰξός ἴον ἰός B. ἴς ἴσος ἰτέα ἰύ ἰωγή, and after loss
of preceding ς (32) ἴνις.

ὄκνος A. ὄνησις ὀργάω ὀρθός ὄρτυξ ὄσσα οὐρανός οὖρος B. οὖρος-τό, and
so from original ε (15) οἴγω οἶκος οἶσος οἴσω οὐτάω.

(c) j, Gk. ' (18) :

ἀβδης-αἰπύς-ἄφνω-ἰάπτω ἀγής ἄκος.

εἰνάτερες ἔτνος.

ἦ ἦμαρ.

ἴκτερος.

---

34. Loss of spirant between vowels :

(a) of s between

α and ε ἄεσα, ο (ω) ἀοσσητήρ ἀπεράω γράω κνάω λάω B., ι μαίομαι
ναίω A.

ε and α ἐανός ἔαρ κεάζω κεάνωθος, ο (ω) βδέω ζέω θεός νέομαι ξέω πέος
σπέος τρέω, ι θέειον.

η and ι ἠία ἠιόεις ἤιος.

ο and ι ὀιστός.—ω and ι ὑπερώιον.

ι and η ἴημι, ο ἰός B. ἰότης ῥίον.—αι and ο βαιός ἐρυσίχαιος φαιός, ει
and α εἰαμένη.

υ and α μύα, ο (ω) ἐρύω κρύος μυῶν νυός ξύω, ι μυῖα.—ευ and ω γεύω
εὕω ; ου and ω κρούω.

(b) F between

α and α ἄανθα ἀάω cf. αὐάτα-ἄτη, ο (ω) ἀγλαός θάομαι λάω A. ναός
φάος, ι ἀίω B. πάις τριχάικες γαίω παίω, υ βαῦζω, see I.-ā
(Ion. η) and ι κληίς ληίη-λήιον παρήιον.

ε and α ἐάω ἐννέα κρέας φρέαρ, ε θέειον and so δεῖ, ο (ω) ἐόλει θέω
κλέος νέος πλέω πνέω ῥέω συφεός χέω, ι δέελος ζειά σείω χειά.

η and ε ἠέ.

ο and α ἀκροάομαι δοάν, ε κοέω, ο θυοσκόος μνόος σόος χνόος, ι δις
κοῖλος λοιμός ποιέω στοιά.

ι and α μαίνω, ο βίος δῖος κρῖϐς, ω after loss of ς (32) σιωπή.—αι and
ε αἰεί, ο σκαιός ; ει and ο βείομαι λεῖος.

(c) *j* between
  α and α δαπτος, η ἄητος, ι ἀίσσω.
  ε and α δέατο, ε δέελος, ο περίνεος, ω ἕως B.
  ο and ᾱ στοά.
  ι and α ἰάπτω and so δείδω (= *δείδοια).
  υ and ο ἀμφίγυος, ω μύωψ.

5. **Loss through Dissimilation (cf. 20) : of**
(a) the first of two similar consonants :
  (1) the first of two gutturals separated by ς : κσκ δειδίσκομαι διδάσκω
    δίσκος ἔίσκω ἴσκω λάσκω, γσγ μίσγω, χσκ τιτύσκομαι.
  (2) a liquid after or before a consonant, through a liquid in the
    following syllable : λρ ἀφ(λ)αυρός, λλ γ(λ)άγγλιον ἔκπ(λ)αγλος
    π(λ)ύελος, νν ὀ(ν)θνεῖος.
  (3) initial aspiration through an aspirate following, ' representing
    ϐ ἔχω ἰσχάς, εὐθύς ἠθέω, ἀφρός ὄφρα, and so ἀπαφίσκω ὀλοφυκτίς.
    F ὄχος, ἔθος ἐσθής ἰθύς Subst. ἰσθμός ὠθέω.
(b) the first of two similar syllables : the final syllable of the first
  half of a compound lost before a consonant similar to that in the
  final syllable :
    ἐλί(κο)-χρυσος πο(τι)-ταίνιος σκίμ(πο)-πους κοδύ(μο)-μαλον.
  So with compensatory lengthening of the vowel (17) :
    μῶνυξ = *μον-ὀνυξ, τριβωλετήρ = *τριβολ-ολετήρ.
  So (τε)τάρες (τε)τράπεζα (τε)τρυφάλεια.
(c) the second of two adjoining linguals : δαρδά(ρ)πτω δρύφα(ρ)κτος,
  ὀλοφ(λ)υκτίς, and so a third λελι(λ)ημένος.
(d) one of two consonants produced by Assimilation (19) : in
  ρρ from σρ κραῦρος δρύσσω, ρF ὄρομαι ὄρος ὅρος, ρς χείρων.
  λλ from σλ ἀλείφω ἀλιταίνω μάλη ὀλισθάνω, Fλ ἀλώπηξ ἐλεφαίρομαι.
  γγ from γκ ἐγγύς.
  νν from γν σπλήν σφήν, σν ἄνευ ἐνενήκοντα κυνέω φήνη χερνής, νF
    ἔνοσις.
  μμ from σμ ἀμυδρός ἧμαι κόμη οἶμα ὄνομαι πύματος τῆμος, μς κρόμυον.
  σς from τς κόρση, δς μασάομαι μύσος, θς βλοσυρός ἐξαμβρόσαι ἔνοσις
    πάσχω and so originally γλίχομαι.
  So σς become ς δύστηνος θέσκελος- θεσπέσιος.

APPENDIX A.

ONOMATOPOEIC WORDS: IMITATIONS OF SOUND

A. human :

  (1) Interjections :

    (a) vocalic ἆ ἒ ἤ ὃ ὤ ὒ.—ἆ ὅ ὒ.—ἰή ἰύ ἰώ.

    diphthongal αἲ οἴ. — εἶα εὐαί εὐοῖ.—ἰαί ἰαῦ ἰεῦ ἰοῦ.

    nasalised ἔνη ἤν εἶεν εὐάν.

    (β) consonantal :

    Guttural κόκκυ.

    Dental ἀτταταῖ ἰατταταῖ τότοι.

    Labial ὄπ παπαί ἀππαπαί πόποι.—βᾶ βαβαί βοῖ.—φεῦ φῦ, ἰόφ.—
    μῦ, ὅμ.

    Lingual ῥυππαπαί, ἀλαλαί ἐλελεῦ.

    Sibilant σεῖν σοῦ ἴσσα, ψό ψύττα.

    with ending αξ ἰατταταιάξ πάξ πόπαξ πύππαξ, βαβαιάξ βομβάξ.

  (2) Nouns : names of

    relations ἄττα τέττα, ἀπφάριον πάππος, μᾶ μαῖα μάμμη.

    persons βάβαξ λάλος μωκός.

    sound βόμβος.

  (3) Verbs : βαμβαίνω μακκοάω ποππύζω.

B. animal :

  (1) interjectional :

    dog αὖ, sheep βῆ, porker κοΐ, frog βρεκεκεκέξ κοάξ.

    vulture φνεί, screech-owl κικκαβαῦ, hoopoe ἐποποῖ ποποποῖ ἰτώ τιό
    τορο-λιλίξ τορο-τίξ τοτοβρίξ τριοτό.

  (2) Noun κόκκυξ.

  (3) Verbs :

    sheep μηκάομαι.

    blackbird πιππίζω, partridge κακκαβίζω τιττυβίζω.

C. inanimate : cithara τήνελλα θρεττανελό φλαττόθρατ.

Of these the following combine Reduplication (5) with Affrication (6) :
κακκαβίζω μάμμη πάππος, τέττα, κόκκυ κόκκυξ ποππύζω, κικκαβαῦ πιππίζω·
τιττυβίζω.

160

APPENDIX B.

LOAN-WORDS.

A. Indoceltic : 157 root-words, 37 by-forms : from

(1) Asia : 89 root-words, 20 by-forms :

(α) Indian :

ἀβρότονον Sk. *mrātanam.*
ἄρακος ἀράχιδνα Sk. *arakas.*
ἄρωμα ?
βέρβερι.
βίττακος ψιττάκη Sk. *pitsant.*
βούβαλις Sk. *gavalas.*
γάρος Sk. *garas.*
γήθυον γήτειον Sk. *gandholī.*
δίκαιρος.
θρόνα Sk. *trna.*
κανθήλια Sk. *kandolas.*
κάνναβις Sk. *çanam.*
κάππαρις Sk. *çaparī.*
κάρδαμον Sk. *kardamas.*
κέδρος Sk. *kadaras.*
κνῆκος Sk. *kāncan.*
κόνδυ Sk. *kundas.*
κόστος Sk. *kushtam.*
κουράλιον Sk. *kuruvilvas.*
κροκόττας.

κυπρῖνος Sk. *çapharas.*
κώμακον.
λάβυζος.
μανδραγόρας Sk. *madanas.*
μαργαρίτης Sk. *manjarī.*
ναῖρον νάρτη.
ὀρίνδης ὄρυζον Sk. *vrīhis.*
παλλακή Sk. *pallavas.*
πάνθηρ Sk. *pundarīkas.*
πάρδαλις Sk. *prdākus.*
πέπερι Sk. *pippalā.*
ῥοιά ῥοιάς ῥοῦς Sk. *sravā.*
ῥυνδάκη.
σανδαράκη Sk. *sindūram.*
σιπταχόρας.
σμάραγδος Sk. *marakatam.*
τετράδων τέτραξ τέτριξ Sk. *tittiris.*
χέλυς Sk. *harmutas.*
χλαῖνα χλαμώς.

(β) Persian :

ἀβυρτάκη.
ἄγγαρος ἄγγελος Sk. *angiras.*
ἄδδιξ ?
ἀκινάκης κινάκη.
ἀκταία.
ἀναξυρίδες Pers. *chāhchūr.*
ἀρτάβη.
ἀσπάραγος Pers. *ispargām.*
ἄσφαλτος ?
ἀχάνη.
βελένιον.
βόμβυξ B. Pers. *pamba.*

γάζα.
γύψος Pers. *jabs.*
δάπις τάπης.
δαρεικός Pers. *dār.*
εὔμαρις ?
κάνδυς κανδύταλις μανδύη.
καπίθη Sk. *kapatī.*
κάσας.
κάστωρ Pers. *khaz.*
καυνάκη.
κίνδος μίνδαξ.
κιννάβαρις τιγγάβαρι Pers. *zinjafr.*

L

κίταρις Heb. *kether.*
κράσπεδον μάρσιπος.
κύπασσις.
κυρβασία.
λαβρώνιον?
λείριον Pers. *lāla.*
μάγος.
μυρσίνη μύρτος Pers. *mŭrd.*
ὀά.
ὅλυρα Zd. *urvara.*
παρασάγγης Pers. *farsang.*
σάγαρις.

σαλαμάνδρα Pers. *samandar.*
σάνδαλον Pers. *sandal.*
σαννάκιον.
σάραπις.
σατράπης O Pers. *khshatrapāvā.*
σίδη Pers. *sĭb.*
ταβαῖτας.
ταῶς Pers. *tāwŭs.*
τέρμινθος.
τίγρις Zd. *tighri.*
τιήρης.
ψάλιον ψέλιον.

(γ) Armenian:
ῥόδον *vart.*   σῦκον *thwouz.*

(2) Asia Minor: 36 root-words, 9 by-forms:
Carian γεῖσον.
Cyzicene ἀμάρακον.
Lydian:

ἀτταγᾶς?	καρύκη	πίσυγγος?
βάκκαρις	μάγαδις	σεῖστρος.
βάσανος	μαυλιστήριον	
κάνδυλος	πάλμυς	

Mariandynian βάρβιτος–βάρωμος.
Mysian σκαμμωνία.
Pamphylian δάφνη ἑορτή–ἔροτις.
Phrygian:

ἀμυγδάλη.	βεκός.	μίτρα.
ἄναξ.	γλάνος γάνος B.	νηνίατον.
βάκηλος.	ἔλεγος?	πικέριον.
βαλήν.	ἔλυμος A. ἰάλεμος.	σίκιννις.
βέδυ.	κίβισις κιβωτός.	

of doubtful nationality:

ἀνθρήνη τενθρηδών.	ἴφυον τίφυον.
ἄτταγον ἤγανον τήγανον.	πύξος.
γέφυρα.	τύραννος.

(3) Europe: 32 root-words, 8 by-forms:
Celtic:

δαῦκος?	λόγχη.
ἤλεκτρον Scyth. *sualiternicum.*	μόρμυρος.
ἠρύγγιον Gall. *arinca.*	πάδος Gall. *padus.*
κόκκος ὕσγη.	ὕρχα.
κόφινος Gall. *covĭnus.*	φάκελος φάσκωλος Gall. *bascauda.*

Italian :

ἄργιλα ῥόγος Lat. *rogus.*
ἀσχέδωρος.
βαλλίζω.

κολοιτέα (Liparaean).
σωδάριον Lat. *sūdārium.*

Macedonian :

γλῖνος κλινότροχος.
κάμμαρος.
καυσία.
ματτύη.

σάρισσα.
σιβύνη σίγυνον συβήνη.
σκοῖδος.

Thracian :

βόνασος μόναπος (Paeonian).
βορέας,
βρῦτον.
ζειρά.
ζέλα.

λέμβος (Illyrian).
παραβίας πράμνειος (Paeonian).
περιστερά.
σῖτος.
σκαλμή.

B. Semitic : 92 root-words, 25 by-forms :

Hebrew (through the Phoeniçians) :

ἄβρα ἄββρα *chabrāh.*
αἴλινος λίνος *hēlil-nā.*
ἄλφα *aleph.*
ἄμωμον.
ἀρραβών *ºerābōn.*
βάλσαμον *besem.*
βῖκος *baqbūq.*
βύσσος *buts.*
γάμμα *gimel.*
γίγγρας *kinnour.*
γλάνις.
δάκτυλος B.
δέλτα δέλτος *daleth.*
ἔβενος *hobnīm.*
ἔρεβος *erebh.*
θῆτα *teth.*
ἴασπις *yash'pheh.*
ἰῶτα *yod.*
κάδος *kad.*
καδύτας.
κακκάβη.
κάμηλος *gāmāl.*
κάναβος κάναθρον κάναστρον κάνειον

κάνεον κάνης κάνναι κανών κινάβευμα *qāneh.*
κασία *q'tsiºāh.*
κίβδηλος ?
κιθάρα.
κιννάμωμον *qinnāmōn.*
κιξάλλης *shālāl.*
κίων *kiyūn.*
κοκκύ-μηλον.
κόλλαβος.
κόππα *koph.*
κρόκος *karkōm.*
κύμινον *kammōn.*
κυπάρισσος κύπρος A. *kōpher.*
λάμβδα *lamed.*
λειμόδωρον.
λέσχη *lishkhah.*
λέων λῖς *layish.*
λήδανον λῖνδος *lōt.*
λίβανος *l'bhōnāh.*
λύρα ?
μάλθα *melet.*
μάννα *man.*

μαστροπός ματρυλεῖον *misht°ārib.*
μέσαβον °*asab.*
μέταλλον?
μνᾶ *mānēh.*
μόρον.
μῦ *mem.*
μύρρα σμύρνα *mōr.*
νάβλα *nebhel.*
νάρδος *nerd.*
νέτωπον *nātāph.*
νίτρον λίτρον *nether.*
ὀθόνη 'ētūn.*
οἴνη οἶνος *yāyin.*
ὄνος 'āthōn.*
σάκκος σάκος-ὁ *saq.*
σάν *shin.*
σάπφειρος *sappīr.*

σαράβαρα *sar'bol.*
σηπία σήψ *tsabh.*
σής *sūs.*
σίγλος *sheqel.*
σούσινος *shūshan.*
στήραξ B. *tsorē.*
συκάμινον *sheqmāh.*
ταῦ *tav.*
φάσσα φάψ.
φοῖνιξ φοινός *puah.*
φῦκος *pūk.*
χαλβάνη *chelb'nāh.*
χαλκός *chālāk.*
χῖ *he.*
χιτών *k'thōneth.*
χρυσός *chārūts.*

Aramaic :
πεσσός *pīsā.*
πράσον *karrat.*

σαμβύκη *sabb'kā.*

Assyrian κασσίτερος *qizasaddir.*

Babylonian :
παράδεισος Pers. *firdos.*

σινδών Babyl. *sindhu.*

Cappadocian :
μῶλυ.

σιρός—σόρος—σωρακός.

Cilician :
γωρυτός—κώρυκος.

τράγος *tarkus.*

Cyprian κέρκουρος.

Pontic :
κάστανα.
μόσσυν.

σαπέρδης.
χάλυψ.

C. Hamitic : 46 root-words, 7 by-forms :

Egyptian :
ἄβαξ?
ἀθάρη.
αἴλουρος?
ἄμαλα?
βᾶρις Copt. *bāri.*
βασσάρα Copt. *bashar.*
βίβλος βύβλος.

γύψ.
ἕρπις Copt. *ērp.*
ζῦθος.
ἡμιτύβιον.
ἶβις Copt. *hippen.*
ἴτον οὔιτον οὔιγγον.
καλάσιρις Egypt. *kelashir.*

κάνθαρος A. ?
κῆβος Egypt. *kaf.*
κίκι.
κόιξ κοῦκι.
κολοκάσιον.
κόμμι Copt. *komē.*
κύλλαστις.
κυρβαίη ?
μαλινα-θάλλη.
μίσυ.
μνάσιον.
πάπυρος.
πέλτης.
περσέα.

σαργῖνος σαργός.
σάρι.
σέσελις.
σιλλι-κύπριον.
σίναπι νᾶπυ.
σίσαρον.
στίμμις Copt. *stēm.*
ὕαλος.
φάσηλος.
φώσσων.
χάρτης.
ψάγδαν σάγδας.
ψίαθος.
ψιμύθιον.

Cyrenaic ὕκης.
Libyan ἀττέλαβος ? ὄρυς ὕστριξ.

D. of unknown nationality : 185 root-words, 92 by-forms :

ἄγχουσα.
ἀδράχνη ἀνδράχνη ἀθραγένη.
αἰγίθαλλος αἴγιθος.
αἰγώλιος αἰτώλιος.
ἀλάβαστος.
ἀλλᾶς ὀροῦα.
ἀνάγυρος.
ἀναρίτης νηρείτης.
ἀνδράφαξις ἀτράφαξις.
ἄνηθον ἄνισον.
ἄνθρυσκον.
ἀνιακκάς.
ἀνόπαια.
ἀντακαῖος.
ἀπάπη.
ἀπήνη λαμπήνη λέπαδνον.
ἄρριχος ῥίσκος σύριχος ὑρισός.
ἀσκαλώπας σκολόπαξ.
ἄσπρις ὀστρύα.
ἀφάκη φακός.
ἀψίνθιον.
βαλλάντιον.
βάλλις.
βαμβραδών βεμβράς μεμβράς.

βασκάς.
βατιακή.
βάτραχος.
βερβέριον.
βεῦδος.
βόλινθος.
βόστρυχος βότρυς.
βρένθος.
βρίγκος βρύσσος βλιτάχεα.
βροῦκος βροῦχος.
γάδος.
γαλάδες γάλακες.
γέργυρα γόργυρα κάρκαρον.
γίννος γύννις.
γράσος.
δενδαλίς.
διθύραμβος θρίαμβος.
ἐλασᾶς ἐλέα ἐλεᾶς ἐλεός ἐλειός
    ἐλειός B.
ἐλεδώνη ἐλεδώνη.
ἐλειός ἐλειός A.
ἐλλέβορος ἐλλέβορος.
ἔλλοψ B. ἔλοψ.
ἐμύς ἐμύς.

ἐπίσειον.
ἔποψ.
ἐρέβινθος ὄροβος.
ἐρινεὸς ὄλυνθος.
ἔτελις.
ζιγνίς.
θραύπαλος θραυπίς.
ἰλλάς Β.
ἰξαλῇ ἴξαλος.
ἴπνον ὕπνον.
ἰσάτις.
κάλαρις.
κάλλαιον.
καλλαρίας.
κάλχη κόχλος.
κάμμαρον κόμαρος.
κάνθαρος Β. κήθιον κύαθος κώθων.
κάραβος κράβυζος γραψαῖος.
κάρβανος.
καρβάτιναι κρούπαλα κρούπεζαι.
κάρδοπος χέδροπες.
καρὶς κωρὶς κράγγη.
κασαλβάς κασώριον.
καύηξ κῆυξ.
καυκαλίς.
κελεὸς κολιός.
κεμάς.
κέρασος.
κερχνής κεγχρηΐς.
κηκίβαλος.
κίκκαβος.
κίσθος.
κιχόρεια.
κοκκάλια.
κόλλαβος κόλλιξ κολλύρα.
κολλυρίων κορυλλίων.
κορίαννον.
κόρκορος.
κότινος κύτινος κύτισος.
κοττίς.
κόττυφος κόψιχος.
κράστις.

κράταιγος.
κρῆθμον.
κριός Β.
κύβηλις.
κύδαρος.
κύχραμος.
κωβιὸς κώδεια.
λαβύρινθος.
λάγυνος.
λαῖφος λῆδος.
λακάρη.
λίνον λῖτα.
λόκαλος.
μαγγανεύω.
μαγύδαρις.
μάνης.
μαρῖνος σμάρις.
μάσπετον μεσπίλη.
μιμαίκυλον.
μίμαρκυς.
μίτυς μύτις.
μόλυβδος.
μύλλος.
μυρίκη.
νίγλαρος.
ξιρίς.
δα Α.
ὄγχνη.
οἶδνον ὕδνον.
οἴσπη οἰσύπη οἰσπώτη.
ὄνωνις.
ὄρθαπτον.
ὀρίγανον.
ὄρκυς.
ὀροβάγχη.
ὄσπριον.
ὄχθοιβος.
πάγουρος φάγρος.
παρείας παρώας.
πίννα σπίνα.
πῖνον.
πίφιγξ.

πόλτος πολφός.

πρημάς πρμαδίας.

πρίστις.

προύμνη.

πτύγξ φῶυξ.

πυκτίς.

ῥάπυς ῥάφανος.

ῥητίνη.

σαβαρίχη.

σαθέριον σαπείριον.

σαλάμβη.

σαλητὸν σαρητόν.

σάλπη σάρπη.

σανίς.

σάρβιτος.

σαύνιον.

σέλαχος.

σεμίδαλις.

σέρφος σίλφη τίφη.

σέσιλος.

σημύδα.

σήσαμον.

σίλφιον.

σιπύη.

σισύρα.

σισυρίγχιον.

σίττυβος.

σκάλιδρις κάλιδρις.

σκίλλα σχῖνος B.

σκινδαψός.

σόγχος.

σόλοικος.

σπατάγγης.

σπλεκόω.

σπόγγος.

στελίς.

σφάκος φάσκον.

σφραγίς.

τάκων.

τάρανδος.

τίτανος.

τρίγλη τριγόλας.

τρύγγας.

ὕσσακος.

φάλλαινα.

φιλύκη.

φλόμος πλόμος.

φώκη.

χελλών.

χόνδρυλλα.

χρέμυς χρέμψ χρόμις.

ψίθιος.

ὠκεανός.

ὤκιμον.

𝔈𝔡𝔦𝔫𝔟𝔲𝔯𝔤𝔥 𝔘𝔫𝔦𝔳𝔢𝔯𝔰𝔦𝔱𝔶 𝔓𝔯𝔢𝔰𝔰:

THOMAS AND ARCHIBALD CONSTABLE, PRINTERS TO HER MAJESTY.

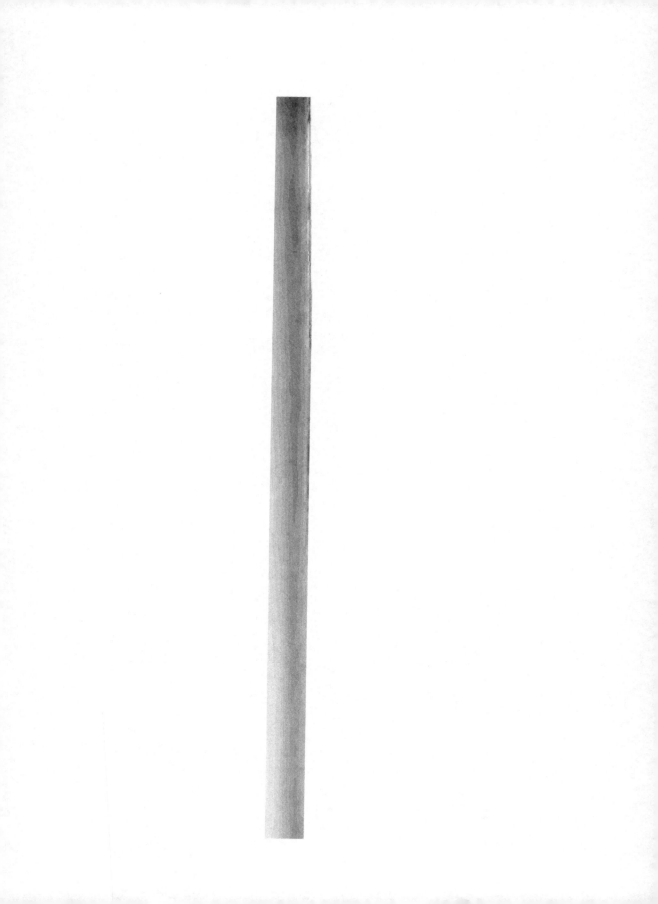

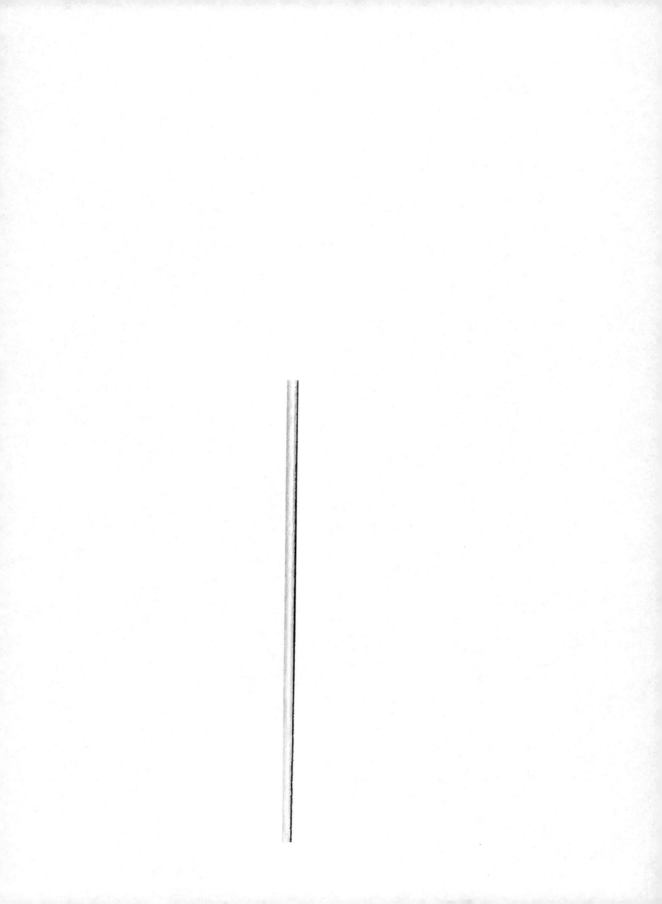

Lightning Source UK Ltd.
Milton Keynes UK
UKOW021814050413

208762UK00006B/82/P